Teaching Reading Vocabulary

SECOND EDITION

DALE D. JOHNSON
University of Wisconsin, Madison

P. DAVID PEARSON
University of Illinois, Urbana

HOLT, RINEHART AND WINSTON

New York • Chicago • San Francisco • Philadelphia • Montreal • Toronto
London • Sydney • Tokyo • Mexico City • Rio de Janeiro • Madrid

Library of Congress Cataloging in Publication Data

Johnson, Dale D.
  Teaching reading vocabulary.

  Includes index.
  1. Reading comprehension.   2. Vocabulary.
I. Pearson, P. David.   II. Title.
LB1050.45.J64   1984   372.6'1   83-12751

ISBN 0-03-062778-8

Copyright © 1984 by CBS College Publishing
Address correspondence to:
383 Madison Avenue
New York, N.Y. 10017

CBS COLLEGE PUBLISHING
Holt, Rinehart and Winston
The Dryden Press
Saunders College Publishing

Preface

Teaching Reading Vocabulary, Second Edition is intended for student use in undergraduate and graduate reading classes as well as by teachers in the field. We think of the book as something more than a "cookbook" of teaching recipes despite its heavy instructional emphasis. Our goal has been to prepare a book that is practical as a teaching tool but that at the same time provides a solid rationale for each of its major topics.

The essential style of the second edition has been unchanged, but the major emphasis on the importance of vocabulary for reading comprehension has been strengthened. There is a much greater emphasis on the development of meaning vocabulary, with three chapters replacing the one found in the first edition. New chapters on vocabulary instruction in the basal reading program and in the content areas have been added. Word identification skills have been deemphasized, and one chapter on word identification replaces the three chapters on phonic, structural, and contextual analysis in the first edition. Thus the second edition of *Teaching Reading Vocabulary* is, we think, a book rich in the theory and practice of direct vocabulary instruction.

We are grateful to our students and colleagues with whom many of these ideas have been formed, discussed, and molded. We wish especially to acknowledge our indebtedness to Sandra Dahl, Susan Pittelman, Susan Toms-Bronowski, Kathy Levin, Bonnie Wilson, and Lavonne Berkvam, who have provided invaluable support, advice, and assistance in the development of the second edition. Finally we would like to thank David Boynton, just retired as Education Editor of Holt, Rinehart and Winston, for his patience, confidence, and helpfulness in this project. Obviously, though, the responsibility for the final manuscript and any misinterpretations it may contain, are ours.

Madison, Wisconsin
Urbana, Illinois
December 1983

D.D.J.
P.D.P.

Table of Contents

1
The Importance of Vocabulary Development

Knowledge of vocabulary, along with basic comprehension strategies, is the key to understanding both spoken and written language. A language user who recognizes and produces a diverse number of words orally has a much greater chance of becoming a successful reader. The young child who opens a book and finds it filled with known words and familiar meanings is free to concentrate on combining unique strings of words in order to arrive at the meaning intended by an author.

The importance of understanding word meanings cannot be overestimated (McKee 1937; Dale 1969; Duffelmeyer 1980). Consider a reading interaction for a moment. A writer carefully codes ideas into word sequences with the expectation that readers will retrieve the message. Comprehension of the written selection cannot occur until the reader identifies the author's chosen words, recognizes interrelationships between those words, and attaches meaning to the unique word combinations used by the author. The communication process is successful only if the reader can approximate the same ideas the author had in mind. A basic function of language is communication of ideas; efficient, effective communication cannot occur, however, unless the word meanings used to transmit information hold similar values in the minds of both the author and the reader.

Reading educators have long accepted the notion that reading comprehension is based on a number of component factors (Barrett 1968; Davis 1942, 1944, 1968, 1972; Otto and Askov 1974; Rosenshine 1980). Among identified factors, knowledge of word meanings has been selected by authorities as one of the most critical factors related to success in reading (Hunt 1957; Davis 1972; Spearritt 1972–73; Becker 1977; Barrett and Graves 1981; Johnson et al., 1983). It is not the words themselves that are so critical. Rather it is the rich reservoir of meaning—the conceptual base—underlying words that matters. The words become a summary symbol for all those concepts, a set of abbreviations that allow us to communicate a lot of meaning in a brief amount of space or time.

One of the major tasks facing you as a teacher is the expansion of children's knowledge of words and their meanings. Reading instruction will be easier for children to grasp if they are familiar with the words an author uses; learning to read will be difficult if the words encountered in print are confusing or

1

unknown. In our opinion, teachers of reading have three basic tasks related to vocabulary development. They are:

1. to offer teacher-directed vocabulary lessons regularly, using effective strategies and quality resource tools
2. to teach language generalizations that children may use themselves to increase their reading vocabularies and comprehend printed text
3. to expose children to a word-rich environment so that they may learn words indirectly through reading, conversation, and listening

One very strong bias underlies our view of vocabulary instruction. Lessons designed to improve the language abilities of children must be meaning-based. That is, we do not advocate isolated word drills or segmented vocabulary-skill lessons as ends in themselves. Rather, we hope that each lesson you plan will include a total language experience. For example, let us suppose that you plan a flash-card drill based on troublesome words from a child's reading book. The list of vocabulary words includes *orange, will, cannot,* and *away.* Following the drill, children could be asked to create oral sentences using the difficult words. Next, as a follow-up activity, children could independently develop written sentences using the hard words along with known vocabulary items. Perhaps one child would create:

I *cannot* see the *orange* ball. *Will* you find it for me? I think Eric took the *orange* ball *away.*

In this lesson sequence, drill was not offered as an end in itself but as a prerequisite to completing a meaningful reading/writing experience. Lessons such as the one described help children understand why basic drills are useful — the result is directly related to a real language task.

DEVELOPMENT OF A BASIC VOCABULARY

In our view of vocabulary development, we identify three broad categories of basic words children must acquire as they learn to read: 1) high-frequency sight words, 2) selection-critical words, and 3) old words/new meanings. Knowledge of these basic words is essential to a successful reading experience. A child who rapidly identifies and calls to mind correct meanings of the basic vocabulary found within a passage is free to concentrate on meaning.

High-frequency Sight Words

The category of *high-frequency sight words* refers to a relatively small corpus of words that occur in such high frequency in printed matter they are deemed essential to fluent reading, especially at the beginning stages. Many basic sight words are neither particularly meaningful in and of themselves nor picturable *(but, to, for)*; thus, they are not often very interesting to children. Yet they are the glue words of language that cement meaningful communication.

Fluent reading obviously requires high-speed recognition of words and their syntactic arrangements. Some words are clearly important to learn to read because they appear in printed material so frequently that having to identify each new occurrence of them would (and does) make reading a laborious task.

The importance of direct instruction of high-frequency sight words for reading development will be explained in Chapter Six, which presents a basic sight vocabulary of 306 high-frequency words, discusses the origin of the vocabulary list, and provides instructional strategies for sight-word development.

Selection-Critical Words

Selection-critical words are those vocabulary items absolutely necessary to the understanding of a particular selection. An author chooses certain words to represent specific concepts. A child reading a story about dogs may be required to read and understand vocabulary items such as *tail, fur,* and *paw* (parts of a dog); *bark, howl,* and *whine* (sounds of a dog); and *leash, collar,* and *harness* (items a dog uses). Passage comprehension is difficult, if not impossible, for children who do not know the exact meanings of these words. Let us illustrate what we mean by asking you to read the following sentence.

> Scuffy's fretful *fluges* turned to impatient *cefts* as his front *galp* became impossibly tangled in the *frax* that confined him to the sturdy wall of his *knilp.*

You may be able to guess at the approximate meanings of the words in the above sentence; however, it is not possible to understand Scruffy's dilemma without identifying and attaching meaning to the synthetic words. Each synthetic word (a word that is not real) in the sentence stands for a word we would classify as critical to total reading comprehension.

The next sentence, complete with the actual selection-critical vocabulary items, will not pose any problems to you as a mature reader.

> Scruffy's fretful *whines* turned to impatient *howls* as his front *paw* became impossibly tangled in the *leash* that confined him to the sturdy wall of his *kennel.*

Think of all the selections children read in their basal textbooks, library books, news articles, and magazines. There will always be a core of vocabulary items relating specifically to the selection.

FARM STORY	CAMEL STORY	BASEBALL STORY
silo	desert	pitcher
elevator	hump	mound
milking parlor	oasis	umpire
grain bin	dromedary	breaking ball
bulk tank	caravan	cleats

As teachers, we must pay careful attention to this specific category of words (Herber 1978; Estes and Vaughan 1978; Stieglitz and Stieglitz 1981). We cannot assume that children will understand these words even though they may be quite able to decode them (sound them out).

Our suggestion is that as you prepare to teach any reading selection, pull out words that may cause comprehension problems. Preteaching of these potentially difficult items (in meaningful contexts) will pay dividends when children read the selection independently.

Old Words/New Meanings

As language users, we increase our total vocabulary bank vertically by adding new words regularly. At the same time, we expand our personal banks horizontally by learning new meanings for old words. Our English language is expanding rapidly; technology adds new meanings to old words constantly.

Acquiring new meanings for known words is yet another challenge facing readers of all ages, a challenge you as a teacher must help children meet. Reading comprehension will be extremely difficult for the child who is not encouraged to develop vocabulary on a horizontal basis. Suppose a child has the word *brown* registered in the word bank we refer to as high-frequency sight words. To the child, *brown* refers to the crayon in a crayola box or the color of paint on Uncle Tim's car. In reading group, the child is asked to join peers and the teacher as they work to create a recipe for vegetable-beef soup as a motivating activity for an upcoming story in the reading textbook. Someone in the group offers the suggestion that "Mom usually starts to *brown* the meat before she makes soup at home." The teacher then makes a notation on the board:

RECIPE FOR VEGETABLE-BEEF SOUP
By Group 3
Step 1: Brown the meat

To the child who can only relate to the word *brown* as a color, a comprehension problem has developed. The teacher must take time out to explain, demonstrate, or in some other way help the youngster understand this new-meaning-for-an-old-word.

The list of words with multiple meanings is endless. Even among the very basic high-frequency sight words, *multimeaning words* are common *(run, back, head, can, light)*. Children need direct, continuous instruction in order to 1) become aware of the fact that words do indeed have multiple meanings and 2) expand their vocabularies to encompass diverse meanings for known vocabulary words.

Growth in each category of the three types of basic vocabulary — high-frequency sight words, selection-critical words, and old words/new meanings — must be initiated during the early primary years and continue, essentially, forever. Continuous, steady vocabulary growth is a key ingredient in developing reading comprehension.

TECHNIQUES FOR VOCABULARY DEVELOPMENT

The three kinds of activities cited so far represent ways teachers can help students learn specific words to help them understand specific selections. But students need to learn some vocabulary development strategies they can use on their own. Since the task of vocabulary development is so important to reading success, we have designed and refined a set of the major components of vocabulary instruction to help in the planning of vocabulary development lessons for children. Though initially teacher-directed, the components are conceived to encourage students to become independent learners. Our ultimate goal is for students to assume responsibility for personal vocabulary growth.

COMPONENTS OF VOCABULARY DEVELOPMENT

1. CLASSIFICATION
   A. Synonyms
   B. Antonyms
   C. Denotation/Connotation
   D. Semantic Maps
   E. Semantic Feature Analysis
   F. Analogies
   G. Homophones
2. MULTIMEANING WORDS
   A. Polysemous words
   B. Homographs
3. RESOURCES
   A. Dictionary
   B. Thesaurus
   C. Etymology

Classification

The process of classifying objects is not new to youngsters; in fact, it is a common intellectual activity even in early childhood. For example, consider the category *dogs*. A child learns to recognize attributes of the family poodle—four legs, curly, short fur, barks, does tricks, chews on bones, etc. As the child meets the neighbor's hunting dog, a trained circus dog, a set of frisky puppies at the pet store, and a seeing-eye dog at the park, each new stimulus is identified as belonging to the class of things the child has previously labeled *dogs*. The new, slightly different attributes (length of fur, size of animal, etc.) are assimilated and classified.

As soon as we can identify the class of things to which a new stimulus belongs, we are able to assign all the attributes of that class to the new stimulus. We assimilate the new information. As a consequence, we are able to call up from our memory a whole range of experiences for comprehending and dealing with the new information. We pet the new thing instead of running away from it. We expect it to bark; we are surprised if it moos. Classification is not only convenient, it is absolutely essential for dealing with one's world; if we had to treat each new stimulus as a unique entity, our memory stores would be overloaded very soon.

We believe that instruction in vocabulary can take advantage of youngsters' built-in, well-practiced habit of classifying new objects or ideas into previously established groups. In Chapters Two, Three, and Four, we will carefully describe activities based on the following categories: *synonyms, antonyms, denotation/connotation, semantic maps, semantic feature analysis, analogies*, and *homophones*. These exercises represent ways of encouraging children to use classification as a means of increasing and retaining words in personal vocabulary banks.

Multimeaning Words

Polysemous words are commonplace in our language. Labov adeptly stated that "Words have often been called slippery customers and many scholars have been distressed by their tendency to shift their meanings and slide out from under any simple definition" (1973, p. 76). Many words in our language exhibit a variable quality; the variation in meaning poses yet another problem to readers.

Homographs are a subset of multimeaning words. They are words that are spelled the same but have different pronunciations and carry different meanings *(read, reject, wind, bow)*. They rely on the context of a sentence or passage for accurate interpretation and pronunciation.

We know that in oral language development, very young language users have begun to deal with multimeaning words (Kessel 1970; Anderson et al. 1978). A two-year-old may use sentences such as:

1. Rub my *back*, Mommy.
2. Come *back* here, kitty.
3. I can't sit in the *back* seat.

Because multimeaning words are used by children at a very young age, instruction can begin orally during the very early school years and progress to reading/writing instruction as the child matures. In Chapters Two and Three, we will discuss multimeaning vocabulary more extensively and suggest a variety of activities you may wish to use with children in your classroom.

Resources

Resources for vocabulary building include the dictionary and thesaurus along with activities designed to help children explore the etymology or background and evolution of words in our language. We have found that many exercises purported to build skills with these three tools are dull and uninspiring. In developing this book, we have attempted to include teaching hints and activities that will motivate children to turn to the dictionary and thesaurus as valuable learning aides. We hope that our treatment of the history and evolution of words will inspire a lifelong curiosity for word origins.

A FINAL WORD

Direct vocabulary instruction takes many forms and fulfills a number of specific purposes. The work of Davis (1944) and of many others since has shown that the knowledge of word meanings makes a potent contribution to reading comprehension. This book is devoted almost entirely to assisting children in developing and enlarging meaningful vocabulary within three categories of basic words: 1) high-frequency sight words, 2) selection-critical words, and 3) old words/new meanings.

Teachers are well aware of the importance of a strong, expanding reading vocabulary and of their role in helping children develop this vocabulary through direct instruction. We are confident that the processes and strategies included under the headings *Classification, Multimeaning Words,* and *Resources* will help you as you encourage the essential language skill of vocabulary growth.

Bloomfield has called learning to read "the greatest intellectual feat of anyone's lifetime" (1961, p. 16), and Huey has said:

> And so to completely analyze what we do when we read would almost be the acme of a psychologist's achievements, for it would be to describe very many of the most intricate workings of the human mind as well as to unravel the tangled story of the most remarkable specific performance that civilization has learned in all its history. (Huey 1908, p. 324)

In this book our aim is in no way so grand as to presume to "unravel the tangled story." Our modest hope is to help provide teachers with some understanding of and suggestions for vocabulary development so that they may better help their pupils achieve that "greatest intellectual feat," the ability to read.

REFERENCES

Anderson, R.; Stevens, K.; Shifrin, Z.; and Osborn, J. "Instantiation of Word Meanings in Children." *Journal of Reading Behavior* 10 (1978): 149–57.

Barrett, M. T., and Graves, M. F. "A Vocabulary Program for Junior High School Remedial Readers." *Journal of Reading* 25 (1981): 146–50.

Barrett, T. C. "Taxonomy of Cognitive and Affective Dimensions of Reading Comprehension." In *What Is "Reading?": Some Current Concepts,* edited by T. Clymer. Chicago: University of Chicago Press, 1968.

Becker, Wesley C. "Teaching Reading and Language to the Disadvantaged — What We Have Learned from Field Research." *Harvard Educational Review* 47 (1977): 518–43.

Bloomfield, L., and Barnhart, C. *Let's Read: A Linguistic Approach.* Detroit: Wayne State University Press, 1961.

Dale, Edgar. *Audiovisual Methods in Teaching*. New York: Holt, Rinehart and Winston, 1969.

Davis, F. B. "Two New Measures of Reading Ability." *Journal of Educational Psychology* 33 (1942): 365–72.

——— "Fundamental Factors of Comprehension in Reading." *Psychometrika* 9 (1944): 185–97.

——— "Research in Comprehension in Reading." *Reading Research Quarterly* 3 (1968): 499–544.

——— "Psychometric Research on Comprehension in Reading." Reading Research Quarterly 7 (1972): 628–78.

Duffelmeyer, Frederick A. "The Influence of Experience-Based Vocabulary Instruction on Learning Word Meanings," *Journal of Reading* 24 (1980): 35–40.

Estes, T. H., and Vaughan, J. L. *Reading and Learning in the Content Classroom: Diagnostic and Instructional Strategies*. Boston: Allyn and Bacon, 1978.

Herber, H. L. *Teaching Reading in Content Areas*, 2nd ed. Englewood Cliffs, N.J.: Prentice-Hall, 1978.

Huey, E. B. *The Psychology and Pedagogy of Reading*. New York: Macmillan, 1908.

Hunt, C. L., Jr. "Can We Measure Specific Factors Associated with Reading Comprehension?" *Journal of Educational Research* 51 (1957): 161–71.

Johnson, D. D.; Toms-Bronowski, S.; and Buss, R. R. "Fundamental Factors in Reading Comprehension Revisited. In *Reading Research Revisited*, edited by L. Gentile and M. Kamil. Columbus, Ohio: Charles Merrill, 1983.

Kessel, F. "The Role of Syntax in Children's Comprehension from Ages Six to Twelve." *Monographs of the Society for Research in Child Development* 35 (1970): 13–27.

Labov, W. "The Boundaries of Words and Their Meanings." In *New Ways of Analyzing Variation in English*, edited by C. Bailey and R. Shuy. Washington, D.C.: Georgetown University Press, 1973.

McKee, Paul. "Vocabulary Development." In *The Teaching of Reading: A Second Report*, edited by Guy M. Whipple, pp. 277–302. The Thirty-sixth Yearbook of the National Society for the Study of Education, Part I. Bloomington, Ill.: Public School Publishing Company, 1937.

Otto, W., and Askov, E. *Rationale and Guidelines: The Wisconsin Design for Reading Skill Development*. Minneapolis: National Computer Systems, 1974.

Rosenshine, B. "Skill Hierarchies in Reading Comprehension." In *Theoretical Issues in Reading Comprehension*, edited by R. J. Spiro, B. C. Bruce, and W. F. Brewer. Hillsdale, N.J.: Lawrence Erlbaum Associates, 1980.

Spearritt, D. "Identification of Subskills of Reading Comprehension by Maximum Likelihood Factor Analysis. *Reading Research Quarterly* 8 (1972–73): 92–111.

Stieglitz, E. L., and Stieglitz, V. S. "SAVOR the Word to Reinforce Vocabulary in the Content Areas." *Journal of Reading* 25 (1981): 46–51.

2
Components of Vocabulary Instruction

Vocabulary development occurs spontaneously during early childhood. Language is learned in the context of expressing and comprehending meaning (Mass 1982). Children discover that they must use specific words in order to make requests, issue commands, or engage in any type of conversation. The basis for language growth during the preschool years is oral/aural in nature. The child's verbal environment (conversations with adults and peers, books read, radio, television, and records) introduces vocabulary in meaningful settings. Words and their meanings are stored and later retrieved for use in language interactions. Young children resemble miniscientists; they are constantly making attempts to discover how their world works. A rich linguistic environment is all that is required by a normal child to make significant gains during early stages of language acquisition. No direct instruction is offered or required.

Youngsters bring an enormous amount of self-motivated learning to the reading classroom (Shuy 1982); but due to the nature of school learning, their ability to acquire word meanings spontaneously must be supplemented with direct instruction. In fact, it is often necessary to isolate and teach specific words that might otherwise result in reading comprehension problems (Lapp et al. 1982). We believe that any responsible reading program will provide for a systematic plan of vocabulary development.

A sound program of vocabulary development must expose students to many new words but must also help them learn techniques for independent vocabulary acquisition. Vocabulary development can lead students forward; as new concepts and related words are acquired, the child is equipped with rudimentary tools that allow the generation of new experiences. Learning to use new words and using them in a variety of ways form a dynamic process.

We are not alone in assigning a high priority to vocabulary growth. Durkin (1981) has admitted that the evidence in favor of vocabulary instruction is indisputable. Educators and researchers agree that students who lack background knowledge have difficulty understanding what they read (Farr and Roser 1979; Allington and Strange 1980; Gipe 1980; Hayes and Tierney 1982). Teachers must do a better job of helping students acquire "the most important building blocks for intellectual functioning—a knowledge of words and what they refer to" (Becker et al. 1981, p. 146). Unfamiliar concepts coded into unknown words in a reading selection represent a chasm students cannot cross without assistance.

9

Teachers who take time to preteach and review vocabulary in reading lessons provide a bridge between ideas that are unfamiliar to students and knowledge they have already acquired. This bridging process allows students to make use of cognitive skills and the vast storehouse of information they have brought to the reading assignment. Interaction between the text and the reader becomes possible, and the reader is better able to reconstruct the meaning of a written passage (Rumelhart and Ortony 1977; Rumelhart 1980).

We have designed an activity-based framework we believe you will find useful as you design lessons to help students develop and sharpen their vocabularies. The following outline presents three basic categories within the framework and a series of twelve components teachers can use when planning programs of vocabulary development.

COMPONENTS OF VOCABULARY INSTRUCTION

1. CLASSIFICATION
   A. Synonyms
   B. Antonyms
   C. Denotation/Connotation
   D. Semantic Maps
   E. Semantic Feature Analysis
   F. Analogies
   G. Homophones
2. MULTIMEANING WORDS
   A. Polysemous words
   B. Homographs
3. RESOURCES
   A. Dictionary
   B. Thesaurus
   C. Etymology

The remainder of this chapter will define each of the twelve components. We believe that activities based on these components will help students bring almost-known words into focus, sharpen their reading skills, and lead them to appreciate and enjoy their language.

In Chapter One we suggested three broad categories of basic words children must acquire as they learn to read: 1) high-frequency sight words; 2) selection-critical words; and 3) old words/new meanings. All words falling into these three broad categories lend themselves to instruction in one or more of the eleven vocabulary components we have designated.

THE VOCABULARY COMPONENTS

Classification

Classification exercises involve the systematic arrangement of ideas, objects, pictures, or words into groups or categories formed by predetermined criteria. Sample relationships are illustrated in the following schema:

CATEGORY	WORDS
Class/Example	*Toys:* bear, truck, blocks
	Food: eggs, meat, cake
Word/Feature	*Plant:* flower, stem, leaves
	House: floor, roof, windows

According to Kurth (1980) the categorical assignment of words is an effective means of vocabulary growth. The ability to classify is an important mental activity practiced from early childhood on. As students work on classification tasks, they are gaining skill in conceptualizing information.

Young children categorize perceptions even before they accurately discriminate between them. Once a label such as *kitty* has been associated with Taffy (the family cat), all small-sized, furry, long-tailed animals are held in the *kitty* category until life's experiences allow the child to form more precise categories with mature language labels.

School-age children have had years of experience in the classification of concepts and words. Most children will have little difficulty when a teacher introduces classification activities in the classroom. The key is to offer initial lessons based on words already registered in children's meaningful vocabulary banks. Given sets of familiar words, most children are quite able to use their power of recall and join the teacher in developing meaningful groupings of words.

We have selected seven diverse, but complementary, classification categories we feel will help your students improve their natural ability to organize ideas into specific categories. These seven categories—synonyms, antonyms, denotation/connotation, semantic maps, semantic feature analysis, analogies, and homophones—will now be defined. Chapters Three and Four will be devoted to practical classroom activities based on each of them.

Synonyms *Synonyms* are words that have similar, though not identical, meanings. For example, *eerie* is something like, but not the same as, *weird*. *Live* is something like, but not the same as, *exist*. In our language we can identify numerous groups of words *(plump, chubby, portly; spry, nimble, blithe)* that bring to mind nearly the same feelings, ideas, or concepts; however, no two words are exactly synonymous. Rather, synonymous words reflect slight differences or shades of meaning that seem to be based on our own personal experiences.

Lessons designed to encourage students to compare synonyms will help them see the relationship between words grouped together by meaning. It helps them realize that when a hungry man *devours* or *gobbles* a juicy steak, he is demonstrating ways of *eating* steak. Fine discriminations are made between words quite close in meaning. For example, if we say we have had a *quarrel* with a friend, we may imply a shorter *argument* than if we had used the term *feud*. Comparing synonyms helps students learn that we can express the same idea in several ways, depending on the context or situation that is present. Study of synonyms increases and sharpens students' vocabularies, helping them to perceive the similarity, not identity, of two or more words.

Antonyms *Antonyms* are words that are opposite or nearly opposite in meaning: *hot—cold, gather—separate, dull—witty*. Antonyms can be used effectively to promote vocabulary development, beginning with primary-age children. Simple antonym combinations such as *night—day* can be introduced to very young children; older children will be challenged by more difficult pairs such as *fraudulent—authentic*. Through learning the concept of opposites, students practice an important mode of thinking that will prove useful as they deal with contrasting concepts and statements in all areas of academic curriculum.

Denotation/Connotation   *Denotation* refers to the literal meaning of a word. As shown in the following sentences, one word may carry several denotative meanings.

1. Grandpa built a shoe *tree* for my bedroom closet.
2. Little Ann can *tree* a coon faster than Old Dan.
3. The *tree* in our back yard was struck by lightning.

Most words in our language have more than one denotation. Words in the various academic areas take on very specific meanings essential for children to learn. The word *culture* refers to "a group of people" in social studies but denotes "a growing organism" in the science curriculum. Restricted, specific denotative word meanings must be mastered if students are to read with total comprehension.

Connotation refers to the circle of ideas and feelings that encompass a word. The interpretive or emotional qualities of a word can be noted in these sentences:

1. John felt *sheepish* whenever he thought about the lie he had told.
2. We were all *green* with envy when Sarah won the award.
3. Sally made a *scene* when she lost her temper at the meeting.

Words used in a connotative sense are often intended to sway our feelings.

Children in the early grades begin to master basic word definitions. Primary-age children may be able to tell us that *jail* and *prison* both refer to places people must go if they break the law. As children gain more experiences through such linguistic activities as conversations and reading, they begin to realize that a *jail stay* connotes a different (perhaps less serious) shade of meaning than does a *prison term*. We believe that children will benefit from direct instruction in discriminating subtle shades of meaning, especially as they proceed to the middle, upper-elementary, and secondary school years.

Semantic Maps   *Semantic maps* are diagrams that help children see how words are related to one another. Semantic mapping, an excellent format for vocabulary expansion, is enjoyed by most students. As maps are developed, "old" words are seen in a new light. Building a semantic map could encompass the following steps (variation may be necessary in some lesson settings):

1. Choose a key word from a story the class will be asked to read, or from any other source related to classroom work.
2. List the word on a large chart tablet or on the chalkboard.
3. Encourage the class to brainstorm for as many words as they can that are related to the selected key word and to list them by categories on paper.

4. Students then share the prepared lists orally and all words are placed on the "map" in categories.
5. The joint effort of the class might resemble Figure 2.1.
6. Students can gain further practice in classification by labeling the categories on the semantic map:
   a. Words to describe our feelings about school
   b. People who work in the school
   c. Subjects studied in school
7. Discussion of the semantic map is, perhaps, the most important part of the lesson. The purpose of the exercise is to encourage students to become aware of new words, to gather new meanings from old words, and to see the relationships among words.

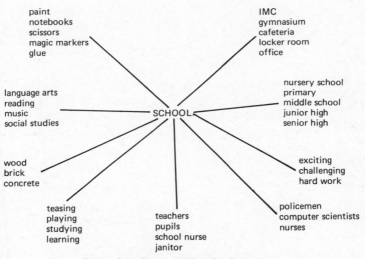

Figure 2.1. Semantic Map for School

Semantic Feature Analysis *Semantic feature analysis* is another vocabulary-building technique students of all ages will find challenging and enjoyable. Readers bring a memory bank full of attitudes, background experiences, ideas, and knowledge of words to every reading selection. Reading comprehension involves an interaction between what the reader has stored in that memory bank and the textual material. Comprehending is really a process of building bridges from the new to the known. Information stored in each person's memory bank is organized into semantic categories. As we gain proficiency in language, specific rules for membership in these categories evolve; at the same time we record procedures for interlinking the categories. In other words, as we grow intellectually, we gather a great deal of knowledge that our brain classifies into categories.

Semantic feature analysis is an instructional practice that builds on and expands the categories of concepts tucked away in our memory banks. The technique helps children understand that no two words in our language have the exact same meaning.

The object of this vocabulary-building activity is to complete a matrix that identifies both common and unique traits of words classified into the same category. A lesson on semantic feature analysis might be developed in the following manner.

1. Organize a list of words that share some common features. You may select the category *vehicles* and include words such as *bicycle, motorcycle, car,* and *skateboard.* These words are listed in a vertical column on the chalkboard or chart paper.
2. Assisted by the children, begin to list some features commonly associated with at least one of the vehicles. Place these words in a row across the top of the board or paper.
3. Children complete the vocabulary matrix by supplying pluses or minuses beside each word under each feature (see Fig. 2.2).
4. Once the original activity has been completed, you may wish to add additional words and features as a means of expanding the matrix. Pluses or minuses are then entered to complete the matrix.
5. Group discussion of the completed matrix is essential. Examine the patterns of pluses and minuses as they appear on the chart. Lead the children to an understanding that no two words have exactly the same pattern of pluses and minuses and therefore have slightly different meanings.

	two wheels	four wheels	motor	passengers	enclosed
bicycle	+	−	−	+	−
motorcycle	+	−	+	+	−
car	−	+	+	+	+
skateboard	−	+	−	−	−

Figure 2.2. Semantic Feature Analysis: *Vehicles*

Analogies   *Analogies* are problem-solving activities requiring that the learner create mental sentences summarizing comparisons between four words that are usually drawn from the same part of speech. To complete the analogy *box : cereal :: bottle* _____, the learner must first create a mental sentence something like "a box holds cereal and a bottle holds _____ (milk, juice, soda pop, etc.). Very precise reasoning is required as the learner solves the analogy. Very similar to the *cloze procedure,* or sentence completion exercises, analogies are very effective vocabulary builders.

There are several classes of analogies that can be used to build instructional lessons, and, of course, the difficulty level within any class can be altered by increasing or decreasing the difficulty level of selected vocabulary items. The specific class is determined by the relationship that exists between the first two words of the analogy. If the first two words in the analogy are verb synonyms, the second two words must also be verb synonyms (*touch* is to *feel* as *hear* is to *listen*). In Chapter Four we will present several analogy classes and lesson examples useful in planning instructional lessons for students.

Homophones   *Homophones* are words that are pronounced alike but have different spellings and meanings. *Bear* (the animal) and *bare* (uncovered) are examples of homophones, as are *reed — read* and *strait — straight.*

Without direct instruction in the difference in spelling and meaning for homophonic pairs of words, they can become a source of ambiguity and confusion for children.

Multimeaning Words

Polysemous words (*polysemous* is derived from the Greek "many meanings") are abundant in our language. Jot down any twenty random words, then look them up in a dictionary. Chances are, more than half the words on your list will have more than one meaning. In a recent study (Johnson et al. 1983) it was demonstrated that on a list of 9000 words of great importance to elementary school children, more than 70 percent are multimeaning words.

Children are going to encounter many words like *run, fly, check, back, chair, green,* and *house* in their daily reading. The teacher's task is more than simply to teach children the various meanings of certain specific multimeaning words. We must help children develop an expectation that many words will have more than one meaning and help them form the habit of using context to determine the appropriate meaning — if sufficient context is available.

Homographs   *Homographs*, a subset of multimeaning words, are words that are spelled alike but are pronounced differently and have different meanings. In this word category we find terms like *bow* (a social grace) and *bow* (a ribbon tied fancily) or *lead* (rhymes with *reed*) and *lead* (rhymes with *bread*). These multimeaning words are demons that can be a barrier to comprehension for some readers. Fortunately, there are not too many homographs recorded in the English language. Direct instruction in homographs might well begin in the primary grades just as soon as the words begin to appear in written materials. Homograph exploration can also be fun at more advanced levels with words like *console, forte, contract,* and *invalid.*

Resources

Two excellent resource books that encourage vocabulary development are the dictionary and the thesaurus. Many companies have developed excellent dictionaries and thesauruses for use with elementary students. Etymology, the study of word origins, is another resource we think you will find beneficial as you offer direct instruction in vocabulary development.

Dictionary   The use of a dictionary is viewed solely as a reference skill by most teachers. Dictionary entries, however, provide useful information about word pronunciation, origin, and spelling. More importantly, a good dictionary can help a reader verify a meaning tentatively assigned to an unfamiliar word. Chapter Five will provide activities designed to help your students use this valuable reference as a means of vocabulary expansion.

Thesaurus   The thesaurus is another invaluable reference book that offers an excellent opportunity for vocabulary expansion. Competent use of the thesaurus will be an asset to students as they work in all areas of the language arts. A thesaurus contains synonyms and antonyms grouped by ideas. Students begin with an idea they want to write or talk about and can turn to the thesaurus in order to find just the right words or phrases to express the idea. Several modern, up-to-date thesauruses are available for elementary school children. We have devoted part of Chapter Five to this handy reference book.

Etymology   *Etymology*, our final resource for vocabulary development activities, is the study of the history and evolution of words. Our language is a living language that is constantly changing. One very apparent change is the addition of new words *(astronaut, hamburger, motel)*; a less obvious change is that of the pronunciation of some words. In some regional dialects we commonly drop the middle vowel sound in three-syllable words (*interest, restaurant,* etc.). Study of language change is pleasurable to most students. A certain fascination exists over the coining of new words.

Study of the history of a word, while intriguing, helps to fix the word's meaning firmly into students' minds so that recall is much easier. Learning a word's origin helps place it into a specific category — another mode of assisting with memory and recall.

A FINAL WORD

Using these twelve components of vocabulary instruction will enable you to provide your students with numerous opportunities to develop and expand their vocabularies. Reading is a process of gaining meaning from print, and meaning comes when students can interact with the specific words they meet on the page of print. The more words and word meanings that students acquire, the better readers they will become.

REFERENCES

Allington, R., and Strange, M. *Learning Through Reading in the Content Areas.* Lexington, Mass.: D. C. Heath, 1980.
Becker, W. C.; Engelmann, S.; Carnine, D. W.; and Rhine, W. R. "Direct Instruction Model." In *Making Schools More Effective,* edited by W. R. Rhine. New York: Academic Press, 1981.

Durkin, D. "Reading Comprehension Instruction in Five Basal Series." *Reading Research Quarterly* 16 (1981): 519–44.

Farr, R., and Roser, N. *Teaching a Child to Read.* New York: Harcourt, Brace, Jovanovich, 1979.

Gipe, J. P. "Use of a Relevant Context Helps Kids Learn New Word Meanings." *The Reading Teacher* 33 (1980): 398–402.

Hayes, D. A., and Tierney, R. J. "Developing Readers' Knowledge Through Analogy." *Reading Research Quarterly* 17 (1982): 256–80.

Johnson, D. D.; Moe, A.; and Baumann, J. *The Ginn Workbook for Teachers: A Basic Lexicon.* Lexington, Mass.: Ginn and Co., 1983.

Kurth, R. J. "Building A Conceptual Base for Vocabulary." *Reading Psychology* 1 (1980): 115–20.

Lapp, D.; Flood, J.; and Gleckman, G. "Classroom Practices Can Make Use of What Researchers Learn." *The Reading Teacher* 35 (1982): 572–85.

Mass, L. N. "Developing Concepts of Literacy in Young Children." *The Reading Teacher* 35 (1982): 670–75.

Rumelhart, D. E. "Schemata: The Building Blocks of Cognition." In *Theoretical Issues in Reading Comprehension,* edited by R. J. Spiro, B. C. Bruce, and W. F. Brewer. Hillsdale, N.J.: Lawrence Erlbaum Associates, 1980.

Rumelhart, D. E., and Ortony, A. "The Representation of Knowledge in Memory." In *Schooling and the Acquisition of Knowledge,* edited by R. C. Anderson and R. J. Spiro. Hillsdale, N.J.: Lawrence Erlbaum Associates, 1977.

Shuy, R. W. "What Should the Language Strand in a Reading Program Contain?" *The Reading Teacher* 35 (1982): 806–12.

3
Developing a Meaning Vocabulary: Part I

The next three chapters have been designed to offer many suggestions to assist you in making plans for direct instruction in meaningful vocabulary development. Since there are so many ideas we want to share with you, we decided to divide the material into three separate but related parts. The present chapter will deal with five components of vocabulary development: synonyms, denotation/connotation, antonyms, homophones, and multimeaning words. Chapter Four will present classroom activities based on semantic mapping, semantic feature analysis, and analogies. In Chapter Five we will demonstrate how the dictionary, thesaurus, and activities on etymology can be used to promote the development of meaningful vocabulary. All three chapters have one common goal: to encourage you to plan daily exercises aimed at helping students broaden and expand their meaning vocabularies.

Reading comprehension problems occur when children do not recognize or understand the words in a passage. As a teacher you will want to do the best job possible of helping students learn new, difficult words. Learning a word is not simply a matter of word calling (recognizing and pronouncing); it is a task involving identification of a word's meaning as well. We believe that a total language experience must surround any lesson on vocabulary development. Students must hear new words in meaningful context, discuss the words so that expressive vocabulary develops, and then read or write the new words, again in a meaning-based lesson. The four communication processes of listening, speaking, reading, and writing reinforce one another. Lessons designed to include attention to each of the four processes will help students better understand and retain new vocabulary.

In the following sections on vocabulary development you will find we often emphasize total language experiences. Skills taught in isolation just do not make sense to us. We want children to understand that they are learning new words *not* as ends in themselves but as a means of becoming more capable in the communication skills. The best way we have found to reach our goal is to insist that by the end of any lesson a total language experience has been offered. That is, any vocabulary lesson must encourage students to really experience new words — to hear them used, to discuss and define meanings, to read or write them in meaningful context. We want to make certain that words we present make sense to students.

Naturally a good deal of vocabulary growth takes place in the natural environments of listening, conversing, reading, and participating. These, too, constitute total language experiences. Thus we learn many words "naturally" — without direct instruction. We are certainly unopposed to the notion of natural learning but feel obligated in this book to describe and exemplify a variety of approaches and techniques for vocabulary instruction.

The remainder of this chapter is devoted to an explanation of five vocabulary categories (synonyms, denotation/connotation, antonyms, homophones, and multimeaning words) you can draw on as you offer direct instruction in vocabulary development. Table 1 outlines, defines, and offers examples of each of them. A discussion of the five will be followed by a series of stimulating and challenging classroom activities. These suggested activities should stimulate you to think of variations and additional tasks that will meet the needs of the students you teach.

Table 1 Five Categories of Vocabulary Development		
Category	Example	Student's Goal
Synonyms	gentle — docile	Recognize that two words represent similar meanings
Denotation/Connotation	a *green* tree *green* with envy	Recognize literal and interpretive meaning of words
Antonyms	squander — hoard	Recognize that two words represent nearly opposite meanings
Homophones	blue — blew	Recognize that two words with the same pronunciation differ in spelling and meaning
Multimeaning words	light, plant	Recognize that many words carry several distinct meanings

SYNONYMS

Synonyms are words that have similar, though not identical, meanings. Two words never represent exactly the same ideas. For example, suppose a relative you are very fond of has been bothered for years by a debilitating injury. Each time family members speak of the situation the word *illness* (as opposed to *ailment*, *chronic disorder*, or *disease*) is used: Aunt Betsy's *illness* kept her from attending

Suzanne's wedding. As time passes, you may register the term *illness* as a more negative term than other synonyms that could have been used in reference to Aunt Betsy's condition. If asked to rank the following words in terms of intensity, you may on a scale of 1 to 4 (1 = most intense) assign the following ranking:

4 ailment
1 illness
2 disease
3 sickness

The word *illness*, with its number-one ranking, registers the most intensity in light of your personal experiences. However, another person, whose life experiences differ from your own, may elect a very different hierarchy, such as:

3 ailment
4 illness
1 disease
2 sickness

Our point is that no two words mean exactly the same thing in all situations and may, in fact, represent quite different meanings. Each term in any synonymous word grouping carries just a shade of difference in meaning.

Synonym exercises are excellent defining devices. The best lessons are initiated with key words whose meanings are already known by children. Difficulty of the synonymous pairs should, of course, increase with grade level. For instance, primary-age children can learn that to run *fast* could mean to run _____ (*quickly*, *swiftly*, or *rapidly*). Middle-school-age children can learn that a *piece* may be a _____ (*segment*, *portion*, or *fragment*). Older children may learn that a *shy* girl is _____ (*modest*, *reserved*, or *diffident*). Lessons on synonyms can be powerful devices for bridging the gap in students' minds between what they know and what is new.

As you design lessons on synonyms, give students numerous opportunities to note the relationships between synonymous terms that can be grouped into broad categories. For example:

BROAD CATEGORY: Books/Periodicals

Types of Books	Storehouses for Books	Writers
paperback	library	journalist
booklet	bookroom	newsman
leaflet	bookery	pressman
pamphlet	bookmobile	gazetteer
brochure	bookwagon	reporter
tract		correspondent
circular		columnist

Synonym Activities

Children must learn that the term *synonym* refers to "something like" rather than "the same as." A fine line of distinction often lies between several synonyms in a group. Direct instruction should include discussions, visual demonstrations, or perhaps even personal dramatizations to help children develop a feel for the uniqueness of synonymous terms. Semantic precision can be developed through lessons modeled after the following exercises.

1. Ranking Synonyms on One Feature. Children are asked to rank lists of words on the basis of intensity, strength, approval, seriousness, or any other shared feature. Lists such as the following are representative of words amenable to this activity:

Lower-elementary

Look	run	big	cool
stare	romp	huge	frosty
gave	race	monstrous	icy
glare	log	gigantic	chilly
glance	jog	large	cold

Upper-elementary

ailment	astound	loathe	afraid	love
poor health	astonish	abhor	panicky	like
illness	flabbergast	dislike	terrified	adore
sickness	surprise	hate	scared	admire
disease	amaze	despise	frightened	tolerate

2. A creative writing session could be initiated by group discussion using a children's thesaurus as a resource. Hold a class discussion in which students, using the thesaurus, contribute a synonomous word to be used in writing a paragraph about an animal or person. A few starter terms and accompanying lists may include *tall*, *fat*, and *smart*:

tall	fat	smart
lofty	fleshy	clever
towering	beefy	keen
high	brawny	bright
elevated	portly	quick-witted
soaring	unwieldy	shrewd

Ask the boys and girls to select a strip of paper from a hat on which is written the name of a well-known person or famous animal or the name of a relative (*father*, *aunt*, *grandmother*, etc.). Then ask the students to think of several words to use in place of the name: *he* or *him*, *she* or *her*, *that fragile creature*, *large fluffy-tailed animals, three-year old imp, sassy tomboy, fantastic girl*, and so on. Ask the children to construct a paragraph using many of the chosen words. Upper-elementary students will especially enjoy this activity.

3. Art activities and reading/language skill-building exercises can be paired to add a unique change of pace to the usual paper and pencil tasks. In the activity that follows, the reading skill involves skimming a list of words in order to select an appropriate synonym for given target words.

Smile	Fast	Boy
grin	porch	phone
swing	glow	lad
sit	rapid	orange

Once the synonyms are selected and discussed by the group, ask the children to draw or paint a picture that includes, for example, at least two people, two animated characters, or two vehicles that demonstrate one pair of the synonymous terms from the exercise. Also request that children write two sentences about the picture that incorporate the synonyms. As a follow-up, children's sentences and pictures can be displayed, mounted into a book, and read orally in a group meeting.

DENOTATION/CONNOTATION

A discussion of synonymous terms leads naturally to the category of denotation/connotation. As discussed in Chapter Two, *denotation* refers to the literal meaning of a word, whereas *connotation* refers to the "excess baggage" or emotional tone a word carries with it. To say that John *walked* down the hall is denotatively similar to saying that he *strutted* down the hall, but the word *strutted* carries with it some additional emotional meaning that is lacking in *walked*. Direct instruction in denotative/connotative word meanings is especially important as children enter the middle, upper-elementary, and secondary school years. As they progress through school, children are exposed to more and more printed material. The ability to direct subtle shades of meaning will be extremely important to total reading comprehension.

A curious feature of language is that two words that are synonymous at one level of meaning (denotative level) may be quite different at another level (connotative level). Teaching strategies must be designed to help students acquire the distinction between denotative and connotative word meanings. The primary or literal meanings of words are important, but so are the slight differences in meanings conveyed by words that denote the same object, action, or feeling. For instance, the words *wander, stroll, stray, range, rove, ramble, drift*, and *prowl* can all be used to denote walking, but the connotative difference between each of these words is evident. Most of us are quite sensitive to the way words are used in conversation. Wouldn't you rather be thrifty than cheap? Uninformed rather than ignorant? Sweet rather than cloying?

Denotative/Connotative Activities

1. Middle, junior-high, and secondary school students will benefit from work on synonyms as they build discriminative vocabularies. In the next activity, students are asked to place a checkmark next to the word in each pair that usually has a more negative connotation.

___ stubborn	___ blemish	___ thrifty ___ convince
___ bull-headed	___ zit	___ stingy ___ induce
___ thin	___ pacify	___ arrogant ___ haven
___ skinny	___ please	___ proud ___ asylum

A group discussion and sharing of responses will help students retain the terms. It might be interesting to have groups of students select any topic and prepare two nearly identical descriptive passages. In passage one, positive synonyms would be used; in passage two, negative synonyms are substituted. Oral reading of the paragraphs by a group member will demonstrate the powerful effect of vocabulary in creating mood or feeling.

2. Group activities can be used effectively as you initiate direct instruction on denotative/connotative word meanings. An efficient way to begin work in this area is to develop a cloze, or sentence completion, exercise on the chalkboard or transparency sheet. Insert a variety of words having the same denotative meaning. For example:

> Lavonne _____ down the country road.
> (walked, skipped, trudged, strolled,
> ambled, sneaked, strode)
> The Sabers _____ the Kickers in the championship game.
> (beat, walloped, edged, trounced,
> clobbered, sneaked by, defeated)

You might wish to modify the activity by inserting two cloze blanks in the sentence frame.

> The _____ rabbit _____ through the garden.
> sly   sneaked
> bold   strode
> happy   skipped
> shamed   slithered

Following exposure of each sentence frame, ask students to write their sentence completion choices on a piece of paper. Select several students to read their choices. Young children might enjoy dramatizing or pantomiming their sentences while others in the class guess which words were selected. Older students should be encouraged to discuss how the selected words alter the meaning of a sentence.

3. The following activity requires that students examine groups of words

that share denotative meanings. The learning task is to identify the appropriate meaning from a list of descriptions:

> *ingest, consume, shovel in* are all
> _____ ways of talking
> _____ ways of walking
> _____ animal names
> _____ ways of eating

> *wail, sob, whimper* are all
> _____ ways of talking
> _____ sea animals
> _____ ways of crying
> _____ kinds of cars

Again, follow-up instruction is an important component of the lesson. Request that students prepare sentences that make use of the terms given in the lists. You may assign one set to each student in the group. Oral sharing and discussion of prepared sentences completes the lesson cycle.

4. Older students could be asked to search through periodicals such as the magazines in the school library or newspapers and record all the different words used to denote *seeing*, for example. Individual word lists are likely to include words such as *perceive, recognize, examine, watch*, and *look*. Perhaps the comic section or editorial page would offer some distinctive terms. Differences between words, unique words, and commonly used words could all form the basis of class or group discussions evolving from this individual activity.

ANTONYMS

Words that have opposite or nearly opposite meanings *(whole—part; trite—fresh; frivolous—serious)* fall into a category labeled *antonyms*. Antonyms often represent mutually exclusive concepts that completely *contradict* one another. An answer to a mathematical problem is either right or wrong. A fish in the aquarium is either dead or it is living. In each of these sentences, the choice is simple—there is no chance of being caught "in between." Other antonyms may be thought of as having a *contrary* relationship. Terms such as *happy—sad, dry—wet*, or *hot—cold* represent opposite concepts, but many words could fall into a range between the two extremes, for example: HAPPY-merry-gay-content-melancholy-gloomy-remorseful-SAD.

Some antonyms appear to reflect a complete reversal of meaning. Examples include terms such as *stop—go, arrive—depart*, and *accept—reject*. Antonym pairs classified as *relative* pairs, or *counterparts*, are also common in the English language. In word pairs such as *mother—father, upstairs—downstairs*, and *aunt—uncle*, one term implies the other, its counterpart.

Still other pairs of words seem to exhibit a reciprocal nature. In these *complementary* antonym pairs the existence of one term leads one to anticipate the other. Complementary pairs would include examples such as *question—answer*, *attack—defend*, and *give—take*. Finally, there is a group of antonyms we refer to simply as *contrasted* terms. These word pairs do not seem to represent extreme or absolute opposites of any continuum of meaning. Examples falling into this final category might include *open—close*, *cloudy—sunny*, or *awake—asleep*. These terms do not connote the same degree of opposition as words falling in the first three categories we have discussed.

Study of antonyms represents a powerful learning device. Teachers might design lessons that fall into the five categories of antonyms (contradictory, contrary, relative-pair, complementary, contrasted). Activities based on antonyms offer students practice in the type of thinking that will be valuable when they must sort out contrasting concepts and statements from reading assignments in all areas of study.

Antonym Activities

1. Simple items within children's sight-reading vocabulary should be used during the early primary years to initiate the study of antonyms. Develop a group of sentences containing words children can read and understand. Ask children to change the underlined word in each selection so that the sentence has an opposite meaning.

> a. Eric Jon *likes* cornflakes.
> b. I like to play *inside*.
> c. The rain makes me feel *sad*.
> d. Our cat is *pretty*.
> e. My father is a *good* ball player.

Oral sentence re-creation will yield more interesting, diverse terms. If children are limited to words they can spell and write, the lesson will not be as effective.

2. A chalkboard or worksheet exercise can form a springboard for a creative writing exercise based on antonyms. Ask children, in pairs, to define each word on a list by writing other words that carry an opposite meaning.

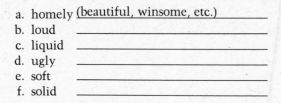

> a. homely (beautiful, winsome, etc.) _____
> b. loud _____
> c. liquid _____
> d. ugly _____
> e. soft _____
> f. solid _____

The total language task is to then assign children to select the most unique word from their list of opposites and to create a sentence. For example:

Sentence 1: The *winsome* young girl wore a lacy dress to the party.

Other children in the class listen to the reading of the sentence and try to decide if *winsome* means the opposite of *homely*, *loud*, *liquid*, *ugly*, *soft*, or *solid*. Continue until all sentences are shared. Save the lists of antonyms for additional lessons.

3. Recognizing antonyms takes a unique turn in this exercise. Here students must examine each sentence and underline the word in parentheses that *cannot* be used to complete the sentence correctly.

    a. A *powerful* lion is a (firm, strong, <u>feeble</u>) animal.
    b. *Heat* is related to (flame, <u>frost</u>, warmth).
    c. The joggers watched the mountain climbers' (<u>descent</u>, rise, ascent) *to the top.*

4. Many antonyms are created when prefixes and suffixes are added to base words. The contrastive nature of antonyms can be used to motivate attention to the structure of words. Pairs of words can be introduced and discussed in a direct teaching lesson.

    *in*flate — *de*flate
    use*ful* — use*less*
    *under*fed — *over*fed

Students can be asked to locate at least five additional pairs, using their reading books or reference books as a resource.

5. Rhyming words offer yet another mode of antonym study. Logical thinking is practiced as students complete sentences such as these:

    a. *New* is to *old* as *meek* is to _____. *(bold)*
    b. *Come* is to *go* as *yes* is to _____. *(no)*
    c. *Earth* is to *sky* as *laugh* is to _____. *(cry)*

The real challenge comes when children attempt to create their own rhyming activities. Add a few simple illustrations, and the children's contributions could be bound into a simple book for class sharing.

6. Creative, analytical thinking skills are practiced in the next activity. Children are challenged and quite intrigued by the result of this exercise in which they can change only one letter at a time to form the antonym of the beginning word. Examples you may use in creating a lesson include:

Give	**Work**	**Heat**	**Walk**
gave	**p**ork	hea**d**	————
cave	por**t**	hel**d**	————
ca**k**e	pos**t**	hol**d**	————
take	p**e**st	**cold**	————
	rest		**stop**

HOMOPHONES

The term *homophone* is used to refer to words that are pronounced the same but have different meanings and different spellings. Examples of homophones include *blew—blue, in—inn, rode—road,* and *main—mane.* Words in this category must be written in order for meaning to be determined. Children need to see the homophones in order to truly understand any lesson in this category. Vocabulary lessons on homophones should be built on meaningful sentences since context clues usually indicate a word's meaning.

Homophones are certainly a part of a young child's oral vocabulary. Words like *no—know*, *be—bee*, and *ate—eight* are used well before a child begins learning to read and write. Since primary-age children already have many homophonous words in their vocabulary bank, it is quite appropriate to call attention to the different spelling patterns as soon as they appear in reading selections. As children mature, direct instruction using more difficult, teacher-selected pairs of homophones *(cannon—canon, horse—hoarse, steal—steel)* is beneficial. Search for pairs of very challenging words like *cue—queue, fold—foaled, liken—lichen* to spark the interest of very capable learners. The key to the success of any lesson on homophones is twofold: 1) to call attention to the word's spelling and 2) to build individual word meaning.

Homophone Activities

1. Primary-age children will benefit from lessons in which words are presented visually in simple formats. An activity may use words such as:

hall — haul	blew — blue
mail — male	bare — bear
fir — fur	son — sun

Word cards can be developed for each pair of homophones. The child's task is to read a given homophone, select its homophonous mate, and use both terms in a sentence. We suggest that games of the type just mentioned be used as reinforcement or review only. Direct instruction in distinctive word meanings must precede any activity designed to test children's understanding or recall.

2. An awareness of words that sound alike but carry distinct meanings is created in lessons such as the one below. The students' task is to come up with a homophone for the underlined word in each sentence. Children may know the correct homophone but may need to consult a dictionary for accurate spelling.

   a. People go up and down on these.
      It sounds like *stares.* (stairs)
   b. It is done to presents with bright and cheerful paper.
      It sounds like *rap.* (wrap)
   c. You pay it on the bus.
      It sounds like *fair.* (fare)

As a follow-up activity students could be asked to construct sentences using both members of an homophonous pair.

   a. rode — road
      Timothy *rode* his bicycle down the country *road.*

  b. allowed — aloud
     The children were not *allowed* to shout *aloud* in school.
  c. straight — strait
     We never thought the ship would pass *straight* through the narrow *strait*.

3. "Hink-Hinks" presents an enjoyable challenge to children fourth grade and above. This vocabulary activity is similar to the Hink-Pink rhyming word game children have played for years. To create a *hink-hink*, one person creates a definition and another supplies a two-word answer (using the same word twice). Answers can be homophones, for example, *coarse-course* (a rough class) or *hoarse-horse* (a circus animal with a sore throat). Multimeaning words can also be used in creating hink-hinks, for instance, *novel-novel* (a unique work of fiction) or *brief-brief* (an attorney's short portfolio). Introduce a few hink-hinks in your classroom and encourage children to create original riddles of this nature. You might want to have a hink-hink box or small chart on display all year long. Children could volunteer hink-hink definitions daily and others in the class attempt to answer the riddle as the school day progresses. The children view the activity as a game, but as a vocabulary exercise, it is a terrific learning device.

MULTIMEANING WORDS

If you enjoy *lemon* pie but have just recently purchased a car that turned out to be a *lemon*, you know just what we mean by multimeaning words. Numerous words in our language have more than one meaning. In fact, if you examine the Ginn lexicon (1983) of 9000 words, you will find that 72 percent have multiple meanings. Due to the high frequency of multimeaning words in children's materials, direct instruction is necessary, beginning at the primary-grade level. Teachers need to help children develop a mind set for diversity when it comes to word meaning.

Multimeaning words reveal the richness of our language. Words in this category can be used to serve a variety of functions:

  1. Verb function: *Plant* these bulbs early in the fall.
  2. Noun function: The *plant* you sent is lovely.

Clearly, the meaning of our key word *(plant)* is determined by the context of each sentence. Instructional activities designed to teach variant word meanings should always be based on meaningful sentences or passages.

Multimeaning Activities

1. The *narf* game provides enjoyment as well as a good learning experience for children. In this activity, any nonsense word (*narf*, *falg*, etc.) is substituted for an actual word in a series of sentences. In each consecutive sentence, a nonsense word represents a variation of meaning.

a. A stuffed *narf* is the kind of animal you would like for a pet.
b. That pear tree should *narf* fruit this year.
c. I can't *narf* to stay alone.   (narf = bear)

Children begin with sentence one and try to solve the narf puzzle. When they think they know the word, they must turn to the page in the dictionary where the word is located. Dictionary reference skills are practiced in a meaningful way. Once children are familiar with the *narf* game they will enjoy creating narf puzzles to share with classmates.

2. Drawings or paintings can be used to complement multimeaning lessons. Youngsters can be asked to draw pictures representing variant word meanings. As a motivator you may wish to read two humorous selections from children's literature: *A Chocolate Moose for Dinner* (Gwynne 1976) and *The King Who Rained* (Gwynne 1970). Following the reading and discussion of unfamiliar figurative language (on the *lamb*, in the *pen*, etc.), children can be asked to create their own pages for a class book. Upon completion, the children's pictures and accompanying sentences can be shared and discussed. As an additional motivator you might ask the class to develop a list of words and word meanings to use in the activity.

> *School:* picture of school building and picture of a school of fish
> *Bat:* picture of baseball bat and picture of flying animal
> *Fly:* picture of object in air, a plane, and picture of black insect

A variation would be to use pictures from magazines or a picture file. The students could hunt through resources to find pictures that illustrate alternate meanings for the same word. Word posters of the word, bulletin board displays, or simply pictures to share with the class could be made.

3. A series of sentences can be used to expand knowledge of multimeaning words. Several sentences using different definitions for a key word should be provided in a group situation. The students' task is to match each sentence with the proper definition.

a. Money is kept in the bank.   Slope near water
   Jack likes to fish from the bank   Place to keep money
   of the river.
b. Mom wore a wedding ring.   Sound of a bell
   The tired boxer left the ring.   A number of objects in a circle
   The animal hid inside that ring   Circular band worn on finger
   of bushes.
   I heard a loud ring.   Site of a boxing match
c. John arose feeling fine.   Very thin in texture
   My hair is long and fine.   Very well
   He will pay a fine for overtime   Money to be paid for an offense
   parking.

To build a total language experience, follow this activity with an assignment that requires the students to create their own sentences and definitions. The individual products will provide input for an additional group discussion on vocabulary.

4. The dictionary will prove to be a valuable resource as you teach lessons on multimeaning words. In the following activity students may consult the dictionary if necessary to select a contextually appropriate word meaning.

    a. The *bank* closes at 4:30 P.M. _____.
       See that pilot *bank* his plane. _____
       The inner tubes are on the *bank*. _____
    b. Baked beans are in the gaudy *can*. _____
       Can Marilyn go swimming with me? _____
       Can that racket! _____

Let your imagination and your students' creative minds develop some additional activities. The possibilities are limitless.

5. *Homographs* represent one subset of multimeaning words. You will recall that homographs are words that are spelled alike but have unique pronunciations and different meanings. Examples include:

    a. We *read* three books last night.
    b. Do you *read* something every day?
    c. I *object* to your very inaccurate statements.
    d. The third *object* on the left belongs to Kathy.

A matching activity can be used to promote a recognition and understanding of homographs. In this exercise children match each homograph-bearing sentence to the appropriate definition.

    a. Charlie will *lead* us into the zoo.   1. guide
       That *lead* pipe was so heavy it fell.   2. a metal
    b. She wore a pink *bow* in her hair.   1. ribbon
       The *bow* was pointed seaward.   2. front of boat
    c. The salty *tear* fell down her cheek.   1. rip
       My book had a *tear* on the cover.   2. fluid secreted from the eye

Returning to our suggestion that most vocabulary lessons be total language experiences, we suggest that students use these examples to create new sentences employing both members of the homographic pair. Sentences should be shared orally.

    a. Charlie will *lead* us into the *lead* mine.
    b. The garbage man better not *refuse* to take our *refuse*.
    c. The warden will not *permit* us to enter the prison without a *permit*.
    d. Bonnie will *record* your new *record* on her tape recorder.

6. Oral exercises help students master the pronunciation of homographic pairs while they offer reinforcement of word meaning. Given a set of sentences such as the following, pairs of students can practice reading with appropriate stress and intonation.

    a. We *object* to chewing gum in school.
       Is that flying *object* from this planet?
    b. The club will *present* you with a *present* the first time you are
       present.
    c. Are you *content* to just sit before the TV?
       Tell her the *content* of that newspaper article.

The pairs of students could develop additional sentences to trade with classmates for more practice. A short humorous speech could be developed from a list of common homographs. Pictures might be used to add a little more interest.

A FINAL WORD

The five vocabulary processes presented in Chapter Three should be helpful as you teach and reinforce vocabulary. We hope that you will not limit your instruction to our activities but will use them as springboards for developing your own vocabulary exercises. The more words you help students acquire the better chance they will have for success in reading. Don't forget our warning: the key to success will be lessons taught from the perspective of a total language experience. Discuss word meanings, provide concrete and vicarious examples to clarify meaning, encourage students to use new words orally, and provide reinforcement and practice through the avenues of writing and reading.

REFERENCES

Gwynne, Fred. *The King Who Rained*. New York: Windmill Books, E. P. Dutton, 1970.
———— *A Chocolate Moose for Dinner*. New York: Windmill Books, E. P. Dutton, 1976.
Johnson, D. D., Moe, A., and Baumann, J. *The Ginn Workbook for Teachers: A Basic Lexicon*. Lexington, Mass.: Ginn and Co., 1983.

4
Developing a Meaning Vocabulary: Part II

Germane to the development of meaning vocabulary is the organization of reality into *concepts*. Most symbols do not represent a unique object or event but rather a general class linked by a common element or relationship. These generalized classes of meaning are called concepts. *Holidays*, *vegetables*, *blue objects*, *females*, and *books* are examples of concepts based on relationships. Language is both the storehouse and the vehicle of concepts at various levels of generality — for example, *Jonathan*, *apple*, *fruit*, and *food* are all interrelated at a certain level.

In a recent position paper on vocabulary development, Block (1976) cited Carroll's definition of concepts: "Concepts are properties of organismic experience — more particularly, they are abstracted and often cognitively structured classes of 'mental' experiences learned by organisms in the course of their life histories" (1976, p. 180). Block continued:

> Many concepts (classes of experience) will acquire names, i.e., the words or phrases in a particular language. Concepts get learned through experiences that are in one or more respects similar. The "respects" in which they are similar constitutes the concept that underlies them. Experiences that embody this concept are positive instances of it; experiences that do not embody it are negative instances. The situation graphically represented is this:

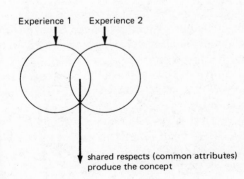

Experience 1   Experience 2

shared respects (common attributes)
produce the concept

Words often correspond to, or come to stand for, concepts. A word can be thought of as a physical symbol; the meaning of the word corresponds to those aspects of the concept that are shared by members of the same speech community; hence, a meaning of a word is a societally standardized concept. When we say that a word stands for or names a concept, it is implied that we are referring to the set of attributes that are commonly understood to be contained in the concept. Stated another way, the distinction is often made between a concept as a personal mental construct (*my* personal concept of the attributes of democracy; *your* personal concept of the attributes of democracy) and as a public entity (those attributes of democracy that are common to both of our concepts of democracy, and shared with other members of our speech community). (Block 1976, pp. 43–44)

So, what are words? Words may be referred to as morphemes, free morphemes, physical symbols for concepts, word-length units of meaning, graphic configurations bordered by space, or simply words. But, however labeled, they are inescapably important components of language, which *in their written forms*, must be dealt with by readers.

In this chapter we will use the terms *concept* and *word* interchangeably, recognizing that concepts are the meanings associated with the surface forms of words as they occur in speech or print. The following describes distinctions we make between class, example, and property relationships among concepts.

CLASS RELATIONS

Dogs, for example, are related to pets and animals in that dogs belong to the *class* of things called animals and are likely to belong to the *class* of things called pets. Such relations are called *class relations*, implying that the stimulus concept belongs to the class of things denoted by the associative response. (See Fig. 4.1, p. 36.)

EXAMPLE RELATIONS

Fido and *collie* are related to *dog* in that *collie*, as a category, and *Fido*, as a particular individual, represent *examples* of dogs. Such relations are designated *example relations*. Notice that class and example relations are reciprocal, at least up to a point. If a dog is a member of the class *animal*, then a dog is an *example*, or an instance, of an animal. Likewise, if a collie is an example of a dog, then any collie is a member of the class of dogs. However, particular individuals may not have reciprocal relationships.

For example, let's stipulate that Fido is a collie, in which case Fido is a member of the class *collie*. But can anything be a member of the class *Fido?* Assuming that by Fido we mean a particular individual dog — not all dogs with that name — the answer is no.

PROPERTY RELATIONS

In addition to the reciprocal class and example relationships, there is also an important *property* relation: concepts have properties or attributes. Animals ingest food and oxygen; pets are domesticated; dogs bark, have hair, and often exhibit loyalty; collies have long shaggy hair; and Fido may have a spot of red hair under his chin. Notice that the *property* relationship interacts with the class relationship. If Fido is a member of the classes *collie, dog, pet,* and *animal,* then he inherits all the properties of collie, dog, pet, and animal by virtue of his various class memberships.

SEMANTIC NETWORKS

This whole set of relationships has been graphically portrayed in what is referred to as a *semantic network* by Collins and Quillian (1969) and Lindsay and Norman (1972), among others. Such a network consists of nodes and links between nodes (see Fig. 4.1). Nodes represent concepts, and links represent relations between concepts. In Figure 4.1 the various concepts related to our discussion of dogs are presented. The network can be thought of as an incomplete semantic map for the concept *dog* (Pearson and Johnson 1978).

To summarize the foregoing, we view words as rather arbitrary labels within a language for concepts that are symbols for general classes of objects or events sharing common elements or relationships. Concepts are derived from repeatable, segmentable reality, which is the composite of one's internal and external experience. Thus the relation between vocabulary expansion and experiential growth is parallel and inseparable. Fortunately, one need not physically "experience" something to grow. Through books, pictures, tapes, films, diskettes, and other objects of communication we can and do gain vast amounts and kinds of experience and concurrently learn many new words and many new uses for old words.

Most children enter school with extensive listening and speaking vocabularies. These words represent the many experiences they have had in their short lives, and thus no two children's vocabularies are identical. Beginning reading instruction, then, sensibly utilizes printed words that are already in the listening vocabularies (the experience) of the children. But as children mature and develop skill in reading they very quickly begin to use reading as a way to add to their meaning vocabularies. From the point of initial reading development there begins to be a shift from learning to read to reading to learn.

Since words represent concepts, which reflect experience, common sense tells us that the principal contributor to reading comprehension is vocabulary knowledge. Certainly the processes and generalizations of word identification, as well as the many subskills of comprehension are crucial to continued reading development. Though it is fashionable — and indeed important — to be concerned with syntactic structures and phonological relationships as important planks in bridging the gap from printed surface structure to the writer's or reader's own

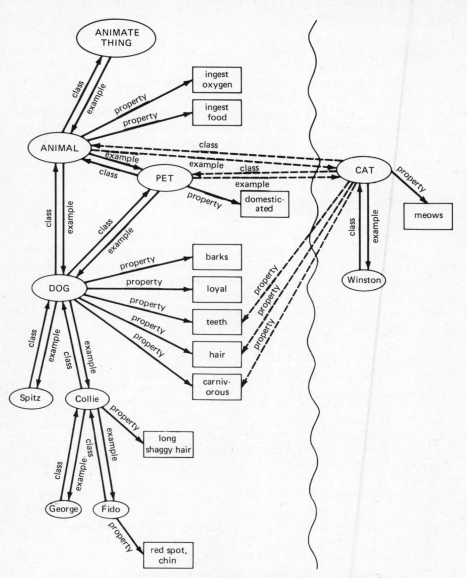

Figure 4.1. An incomplete semantic network representation of the concept dog and some of its related concepts*

---

*The network is neither complete nor totally accurate. For example, if mammals were included as well as some of the subsets of types of mammals, then properties like teeth and hair would appear as properties of these concepts and would be inherited by dogs and cats because of their common class memberships.

36

deep structures, we still hold that without *words* these are meaningless. Many words have more than one meaning and many "meanings" are represented by more than one word. We believe that the more words a child knows the meaning of and the greater the child's vocabulary flexibility and precision, the greater that child's ability to comprehend what is read. Davis's research (1944) clearly demonstrated the importance of the knowledge of word meanings in reading comprehension, as has the research reported by many others (Hunt 1957; Spearritt 1972–73; Becker 1977; Barrett and Graves 1981; Hayes and Tierney 1982; and Johnson et al. 1983).

In this chapter we will continue to emphasize the importance of developing and expanding children's meaning vocabulary. Three teaching processes based on classification will be described in detail. In classification activities, new knowledge is related to that which is already known. Conceptual frameworks are built as children learn new words and relate them to concepts they have previously acquired.

We think that classification activities are vitally important to any developmental vocabulary program. Our experiences in the classroon and discussions with other teachers have convinced us that students have expanded their meaning vocabularies through classification activities, which include semantic mapping, semantic feature analysis, and analogical thinking. All three activities have the potential to improve reading comprehension by building bridges between the new and the known in the minds of learners.

SEMANTIC MAPPING

Semantic mapping is an excellent device for encouraging vocabulary development. As shown in Chapter Two, semantic maps display concepts in categories and indicate how words are related to one another or how they "go together." Children learn new words, view "old" words in a new light, and see the relationships among words on the map.

Creating a semantic map has the added advantage of total student involvement. Children are active participants throughout the entire development of the vocabulary lesson. We have found that the following steps lead to a successful lesson on semantic mapping, but do not hesitate to alter the procedure in order to fit your individual purposes.

1. Choose a word from a reading selection that represents the main subject of a story, chapter, or book students will be required to read (science, mathematics, etc.).
2. Write the chosen word on the chalkboard or on a large sheet of chart paper.
3. Assign groups of students the task of jotting down on paper, in categories, as many words as they can that are related to the theme word you have selected.

4. Next, students share words from their lists while you write them on the chalkboard or chart in broad categories. You may wish to add additional words to categories that arise—especially those words you know will be critical to understanding the reading selection. For example, if the children were beginning a unit on the farm, the key word selected could be *farm* and the resulting semantic map might look something like that in Figure 4.2.

5. Next, you might want to have students identify and name the categories of words that appear on the map:
   a. Farm buildings
   b. Field chores
   c. Animal feeds
   d. Farm machinery
   e. Types of crops, etc.

6. The most important aspect of the activity is the discussion that goes on as categorical items are entered on the map and as the entire map is discussed upon completion: "How does a *feed nutritionist* assist a farmer?" "What does *silage* refer to?" (or *combining, veterinarian, poultry,* etc.) "When do farmers *disc* a field?" "What is a *silo* used for?"

   No matter what topic you select to form the basis of the semantic map you will find that students differ in their background and knowledge of the topic. Expect some disagreement; be flexible enough to change a word or eliminate the term if necessary. You may be surprised to find that some words fit into several

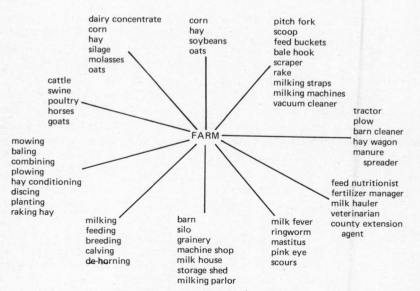

Figure 4.2. Semantic Map for *Farm*

categories. Also, maps tend to grow as discussions develop and new ideas emerge.

7. Using the semantic map as a basis for teaching requires some thought and leadership on the part of the teacher. Once a map has been constructed, you will want to focus attention on one or two categories. For example, in reference to our *farm* map, you could say something like this:

> We have created an excellent map about *farming* and have listed some terrific words. The chapter we are going to read in our social studies book today, though, is about the kinds of work farmers do. Can you find any lists on our semantic map that describe the work of a farmer? Yes, *field chores* and *animal chores* represent good choices. Let's talk about these words before we turn to our chapter."

Focusing the discussion directs students' attention to particular words on the map. This is quite appropriate when the semantic map is used as an activity to develop vocabulary prior to reading a story, book, or other reading selection. You may wish to use semantic mapping for general vocabulary development as well (e.g., using a newspaper article, a popular television series, or a school event as the central concept). Focusing may not be a necessary part of a general vocabulary lesson.

8. Postreading activities might also include the development of a semantic map. Fourth-graders may be studying chapters on the transmission and alteration of light beams in their science text. A semantic map could serve as an excellent review mechanism and would help students organize concepts and vocabulary about the properties and movement of light beams.

Perhaps the discussion of semantic mapping exercises can be enhanced by sharing a variety of additional lesson ideas.

1. *Building Readiness for Semantic Mapping.* Some children may profit from readiness activities in which familiar topics are used to generate rather simple semantic maps. Practice exercises of this type give children a chance to experience the brainstorming, interaction, and discussion so essential to successful semantic mapping activities. Confidence is built as children experience success with topics that are almost second nature to them. The popular *Star Wars* space movies, comics, cartoons, and books might serve as a basis for a semantic map. Following the procedures we have given for the development of a semantic map, the network in Figure 4.3 might evolve.

Students may label the categories on the semantic map as follows:

1. Spacecraft
2. Human characters
3. Robots
4. Space equipment
5. Monsters, etc.

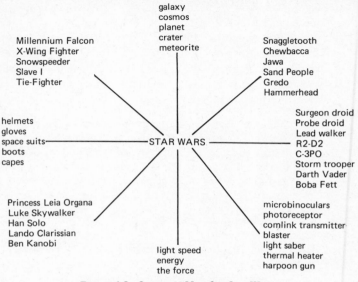

```
                              galaxy
                              cosmos
                              planet
   Millennium Falcon          crater              Snaggletooth
   X-Wing Fighter             meteorite           Chewbacca
   Snowspeeder                                    Jawa
   Slave I                                        Sand People
   Tie-Fighter                                    Gredo
                                                  Hammerhead

                                                     Surgeon droid
   helmets                                           Probe droid
   gloves                                            Lead walker
   space suits ────────── STAR WARS ──────────       R2-D2
   boots                                             C-3PO
   capes                                             Storm trooper
                                                     Darth Vader
                                                     Boba Fett

   Princess Leia Organa                          microbinoculars
   Luke Skywalker                                photoreceptor
   Han Solo                                      comlink transmitter
   Lando Clarissian                              blaster
   Ben Kanobi                                    light saber
                              light speed        thermal heater
                              energy             harpoon gun
                              the force
```

Figure 4.3. Semantic Map for *Star Wars*

The discussion following creation of the semantic map might be directed with queries such as:

> "What was the *Millennium Falcon* used for in the Star Wars movie series?" "Can you tell me what a *meteorite* (*crater, galaxy,* etc.) is?" "How do the characters use *light sabers?*" "Who was the bravest (cruelest, most hated, intelligent) character?"

Although this activity may be initially used as a readiness builder for more intense vocabulary exercises, the vocabulary generated in these high-interest areas does help to create a fascination with words. You may wish to use this semantic map as a springboard to artistic endeavors such as creative writing, play writing, or telecasting (videotaping a show). Extending the information secured in a semantic mapping exercise to expand all communication skills fits in well with the emphasis on total language experience we stressed in Chapter Three.

2. *Semantic Mapping as a Review Technique.* Semantic maps serve as a good format for review and reinforcement in any subject area. Let's join a group of junior-high students and their teacher as they work together to prepare for a mid-term examination in home-economics class. Today the class is reviewing vocabulary and concepts acquired during their lessons on food preparation. The teacher has selected the broad label *cooking* as the key vocabulary item in order to encourage the development of a very inclusive map that will serve as a resource in independent review by the students. Figure 4.4 illustrates the map on cooking.

Labeling of the categories would result in:

1. Range-top equipment
2. Utensils

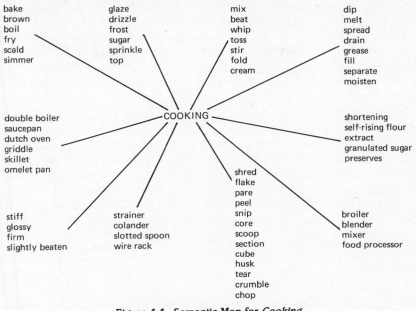

Figure 4.4. Semantic Map for *Cooking*

    3. Methods of mixing
    4. Preparation of ingredients
    5. Decorating/Garnishing

Discussion, aimed at review and reinforcement, would probably include teacher-directed questions such as: "Tell me, what is the difference between *creaming* and *folding* (*scalding* and *boiling*, *glazing* and *frosting*, etc.)?" "Show me the correct way to *toss* these salad mixings." Given an illustrated worksheet, the teacher may ask students to label cooking utensils with appropriate words from the chart.

    The semantic map just discussed has served the unique function of guiding a review lesson. Vocabulary essential to reading or conversing in topics related to food preparation was reviewed and reinforced.

SEMANTIC FEATURE ANALYSIS

Figure 4.1 demonstrated the class, example, and property relationships that exist among concepts. Through semantic mapping or through the type of feature analysis that will be described in this section we can quickly see that the English language is remarkably precise. Practically speaking, there is no such thing as an identical synonym. No two words have exactly the same range of meaning, for if they did, one of them would likely fall out of use. As the language has developed and expanded, certain words have come to replace others and some words have taken on new meanings.

But it is very important for children to grasp the fact that the term *synonym* refers to "something like," not "the same as." Until one clearly realizes this truth, a good deal of semantic precision is lost to children as they both read and write. We have found semantic feature analysis a worthwhile activity for two reasons. First of all it helps to demonstrate clearly the uniqueness of each individual word, and secondly it is useful for direct instruction to add "something-like" synonyms to the individual's vocabulary.

Semantic feature analysis, like semantic mapping, draws on a reader's prior knowledge (and the ways it is organized) and stresses the relationship of concepts within categories. Semantic feature analysis differs from semantic mapping in one major way; instead of exploring how words are *alike*, students explore how related words *differ* from one another. Analyzing semantic features of words helps students master important concepts and has been shown to have great potential for expanding vocabulary (Stieglitz and Stieglitz 1981; Johnson, in press).

Semantic feature analysis involves the following steps:

1. Select a category *(shelters)*
2. List, in a column, some words within the category *(tent, hut)*
3. List, in a row, some features shared by some of the words (small, exquisite)
4. Put pluses or minuses beside each word beneath each feature
5. Add additional words
6. Add additional features
7. Complete the expanded matrix with pluses and minuses
8. Discover and discuss the uniqueness of each word
9. Repeat the process with another category

Semantic feature charts (or grids) are quite simple to develop. Again, start with a list of known words that share some features. For example, you might begin with types of shelters if the words are known to the children: *villa, cabin, shed, barn, tent.* These words are listed in a column on the chalkboard or on paper. Next, have the children suggest features that at least one of the words possesses. These features are listed in a row across the top of the board or paper. Then have the children fill in the matrix (grid) by putting pluses or minuses beside each word under each feature as is shown below in Figure 4.5.

After this has been completed, two more activities can occur: the children may be asked to suggest more words that share some of these features *(apart-*

	large	small	exquisite	lovely	rustic
villa	+	−	+	+	−
cabin	−	+	−	−	+
shed	−	+	−	−	+
barn	+	−	−	−	+
tent	−	+	−	−	−

Figure 4.5. Semantic Feature Analysis: *Shelters*

ment, *mobile home, hut, igloo*) and then to suggest more features shared by some of these words (has wheels, made of ice, multifamily, several stories high). Unless you have enormous chalkboards or lots of paper in your room, you will likely run out of space or time before you will run out of features or words. Next have the children complete the remainder of the matrix by adding pluses and minuses. Finally, help them discover that no two words have the identical pattern of pluses and minuses, thus no two words are identical in meaning. With even the most synonymous pairs or clusters of words the pattern will eventually become different once enough semantic features (either class, example, or property relations) have been listed. In addition to discovering the facts of the uniqueness of words, children learn new words within a category and new semantic features they perhaps had not thought about.

Children asked to list the semantic features of the word *carrot* might very quickly mention "something to eat," "something to cook," "something to chew" but eventually might add "something to plant," "something to sell," "something to cut," and so on. In other words, they begin to discover what they already know but didn't immediately think of, and they begin to view words in more complete and precise ways.

Semantic features can be constructed with any categories of words. We recommend that you begin with categories that are concrete and within the experience of your pupils and then progress to more abstract or less familiar categories. Beginning categories might include:

games	vegetables	pets
occupations	food	clothing
tools	buildings	animals
plants	conveyances	plants

Later categories could include:

moods	
feelings	modes of communication
commands	entertainment
sizes	musical instruments
shapes	machines

The categories of words in our language would comprise a lengthy list as would the words and features within many categories.

We favor the use of pluses (+) and minuses (−) to indicate whether or not a word *usually* has a given feature, even though we realize that many features of words are not truly dichotomous but exist, rather, in varying degrees. As children learn to read better and become more skilled with feature analysis, it is appropriate to substitute a scale of numbers (Lichert-type of 0 to 10 for example) for pluses and minuses.

We recommend that you duplicate a large stack of grid sheets to use with individuals or small groups in semantic feature activities (see Fig. 4.6).

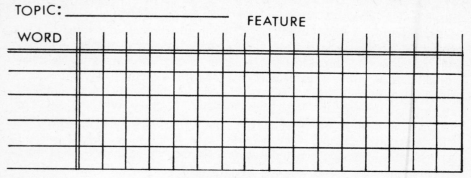

Figure 4.6. Grid Sheet

Semantic feature analysis has been a successful activity for learners from preschool through college. Preschool teachers would, of course, develop oral lessons and may elect to use symbols such as "happy" or "sad" faces instead of pluses or minuses in filling in the semantic feature grid.

☺ ☹

Semantic feature analysis works as well with content-area textbooks and materials as it does in building general vocabulary. Suppose that a science class is in the process of studying reptiles and amphibians. The teacher's goal is to help students learn the characteristics that differentiate members of the two different species. What might a semantic feature chart contain? Early in the unit, major classes of reptiles and amphibians could be listed in the left-hand column of a prepared grid sheet (see Fig. 4.7). A few major features representing concepts to be studied could be entered in the row across the grid. Children fill in the matrix, using pluses or minuses. Question marks indicate the class has not yet been introduced to the information requested by the chart.

Once the grid has been completed, children examine the pattern of pluses and minuses that were filled in for each target word. The ensuing discussion becomes the major instructional device. As the unit of study progresses, grid

	reptile	amphibian	4 legs	scaly	clawed feet	cold blood	lungs
turtles	+	−	+	+	+	+	+
lizards	+	−	+	+	+	+	+
snakes	+	−	−	+	−	+	+
alligators	+	−	+	+	+	+	+
crocodiles	+	−	+	+	+	+	+
frogs	−	+	+	−	−	?	?
toads	−	+	+	−	−	?	?
salamandars	−	+	+	−	−	?	?

Figure 4.7. Semantic Feature Analysis: *Reptiles* and *Amphibians*

work can be expanded to include additional features (tailed, lays eggs, dangerous, poisonous, lives on land, tropical, has ear openings, eats insects, lives in captivity, etc.). New specific grids could be developed to include such topics as a study of the seven families of salamanders, poisonous snakes, and extinct forms of reptiles.

A general vocabulary lesson can also draw on the semantic feature technique. Let us suppose that a teacher wanted to introduce five new vocabulary words and decided to use the theme "Feelings about School" as a vehicle to help children relate to new words in a personal manner. The five vocabulary items are:

> AGOG — highly excited, full of intense interest
> > The children were *agog* watching the magician perform tricks.
> AMBIVALENT — having mixed feelings about something
> > Joey was *ambivalent* about choosing a career as a veterinarian; he liked being with animals but could not stand to see them hurt.
> APATHETIC — indifferent, not caring, having no interest
> > Johnny's *apathetic* attitude toward the baseball game got his team members upset.
> LACKADAISICAL — lacking spirit or enthusiasm
> > The students were *lackadaisical* after their school team lost the state basketball tournament.
> PROVOCATIVE — tending to arouse thoughtfulness or curiosity
> > The science experiment was *provocative* — it got all the children thinking about new experiments to do.

Subsequent teaching procedures might include the following.

1. *Introduction of the Semantic Feature Analysis Activity.* Explain that an activity, semantic feature analysis, will be used to show how vocabulary words are alike and different by examining features or characteristics the words *usually* share or *usually* do not share. For each word on the grid, decisions will have to be made. If a word is usually true or usually describes a feature, a plus will be made in the grid; if the word is usually not true or does not apply, a minus will be entered in the grid. A working grid may be displayed on the chalkboard or by using an overhead projector.

2. *Definition of Vocabulary Words and Other Unfamiliar Words.* Distribute individual grids with the words *excited, agog, proud, ambivalent, apathetic, lackadaisical,* and *provocative* listed in the left-hand column and the entries "Things That Happen in School" listed above the rows (see Fig. 4.8). Discuss each of the seven entry words (one at a time) and have the children decide whether to record a plus, a minus, or a question mark in each of the six boxes on the group grid that is displayed in front of the classroom. When the grid has been completed, review the meanings of each of the seven vocabulary items. Examine the pattern of features recorded on the grid.

3. *Addition of a Word and a Feature to the Grid.* Ask the children to think of one or two additional words to add to the vocabulary list displayed on their individual grid worksheets (e.g., to *agog, ambivalent,* etc., they might add *curious, fascinated, worried, delighted*) and to add a couple of features to the list

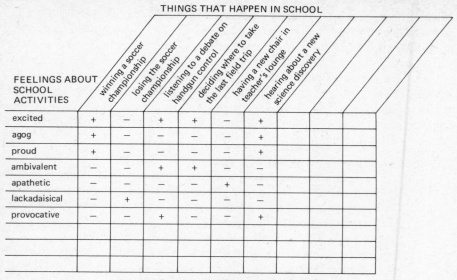

| THINGS THAT HAPPEN IN SCHOOL | | | | | | | | | |
FEELINGS ABOUT SCHOOL ACTIVITIES	winning a soccer championship	losing the soccer championship	listening to a debate on handgun control	deciding where to take the last field trip	having a new chair in teacher's lounge	hearing about a new science discovery			
excited	+	−	+	+	−	+			
agog	+	−	−	−	−	+			
proud	+	−	−	−	−	+			
ambivalent	−	−	+	+	−	−			
apathetic	−	−	−	−	+	−			
lackadaisical	−	+	−	−	−	−			
provocative	−.	−	+	−	−	+			

Figure 4.8. Semantic Feature Analysis: *School*

"Things That Happen in School" (e.g., *taking a field trip to the historical society, having a bake sale, electing class officers*, etc.).

4. *Independent Work* Allow children five or ten minutes to complete their individual grid worksheets, reminding them that all pluses and minuses should be recorded. Remind them that the word *usually* is an important term to remember. Also remind them that question marks can be used if they feel uncertain about a particular box.

5. *Class Discussion.* Allow time for group sharing of the individual entries children have made. Add some selections to the chalkboard or projected grid and fill in the pattern of pluses and minuses, involving the entire group in the activity.

6. *Review of the Entire Vocabulary List.* Review each vocabulary item, noting the pattern of pluses and minuses on the grid. Have the children define each word in terms of situations or expressions drawn from personal experiences.

Reading comprehension improves when textual material is integrated with the experiences, prior knowledge, and attitudes previously stored in a reader's mind. We consider comprehending to be a task of "building bridges from the new to the known." Semantic feature analysis is an excellent process for building the vocabulary needed for successful comprehension in reading.

ANALOGIES

Analogies, the most difficult of the vocabulary processes, require students to portray word meaning through comparisons. Relationships between words are shown as the students create thought patterns. In the example *ice cream : pickle ::*

sweet : sour, the concept of "opposites in sensation" is portrayed. In the analogy *wine : bottle :: crackers : box*, the relationship of "object-function" is demonstrated.

There are several additional common categories of analogies that you will find useful in developing vocabulary exercises.

1. Characteristics: *Rain* is to *wet* as *sun* is to *dry*.
2. Part/Whole: *Leaf* is to *tree* as *feather* is to *bird*.
3. Whole/Part: *Cup* is to *handle* as *clock* is to *hands*.
4. Location: *Teacher* is to *classroom* as *sailor* is to *ship*.
5. Action/Object: *Run* is to *track* as *swim* is to *pool*.
6. Agent-action or Object: *Teacher* is to *students* as *doctor* is to *patients*.
7. Class or Synonym: *Smell* is to *sniff* as *see* is to *look*.
8. Familial: *Uncle* is to *nephew* as *aunt* is to *niece*.
9. Grammatical: *Hear* is to *heard* as *look* is to *looked*.
10. Temporal or Sequential: *Fifth* is to *first* as *twenty-fifth* is to *fifth*.
11. Antonyms: *Smile* is to *happy* as *frown* is to *sad*.

Analogy activities based on these categories are bound to have a positive effect on children's inductive and deductive thinking ability as well as the potential to build skill in reading through vocabulary enrichment.

We believe that analogies provide yet another means of making a connection between new knowledge and that which is already known. Even preschoolers can play oral word games based on these powerful organizers. Four- and five-year-olds can complete analogy exercises such as:

Calf is to *cow* as *puppy* is to _____.
Milk is to *cup* as *applesauce* is to _____.

Teachers find that analogies are extremely helpful when new concepts are being introduced in the classroom. For example, suppose a group of third-grade children has learned that a meteorologist is a person who studies weather. During a subsequent lesson, they find that a zoologist is a person who studies animals. The analogy "*meteorologist* is to *weather* as *zoologist* is to *animals*" summarizes the important comparison between these two new vocabulary items.

There are several techniques to use in designing practice exercises on analogies. Perhaps the most common practice sheet lists three parts of the analogy and asks students to choose or create a fourth (*gasoline : automobile :: electricity : _____*). At times, teachers list the first two items in the analogy sentence and students must select an appropriate set of word items to complete the analogy (*scissors : cut :: _____ : _____*). The activities that follow are techniques you may wish to adapt in your own classroom as you plan for direct instruction in vocabulary.

1. The ability to understand the relationship of ideas represented by words depends on a student's power of logical thinking. Conceptual relationships are demonstrated as students work practice exercises such as the following:

a. _____ is to *woman* as *boy* is to *man*.

b. _____ is to cow as *milk* is to *kitten*.

c. *Two* is to _____ as *duet* is to *trio*.

2. Expansion of meaning vocabulary is the purpose behind the activities outlined below; however, you may design similar activities to teach specialized content vocabularies in mathematics, science, or social studies.

a. Related Word Lists. The children's task is to match words in the two lists or to add additional words to each list.

Tool	Function	Object	Composition
hammer	cut	car	wood
saw	grip	book	metal
vice	pound	desk	glass
axe	chop	dish	paper
		_____	_____
		_____	_____

b. Supply the Titles. This activity is very much like the one just given except that this time a matched list is provided and the children supply appropriate titles for each list.

_____	_____	_____	_____
shoe	head	orange	dairy
gloves	foot	potato	fruit
hat	waist	cheese	meat
belt	hand	hot dog	vegetable

c. Traditional Analogies. Perhaps the traditional analogy pattern is used most frequently. Either of the four slots can be left open. Teachers of young children may find it necessary to work with just one position at a time. Analogy activities can include a list of word choices to use in sentence completion, or the children may be required to supply their own answers.

cow : moo :: horse : _____
(bark, neigh, chirp, quack)

quart : gallon :: _____ : dollar
(penny, dime, quarter, half-dollar)

rug : floor :: _____ : bed
(lamp, blanket, pillow, clock)

d. Fill in the Blanks. Analogies can be used in several formats. The following are a few additional examples we have found useful in vocabulary development.

A _____ is like a _____ only smaller.
   (calf)   (cow)
   (baseball)   (softball)
   (minnow)   (fish)

A _____ is like a _____ only shorter (or *smoother*, or *hotter*,
   (foot)   *(yard)*
etc.).
Yellow is to *green* as *white* is to _____.
United States is to *Canada* as *Saudi Arabia* is to _____.
Robin is to *worm* as *spider* is to _____.
A *secretary* works in a _____. A *nurse* works in a _____.
A _____ lives in a *hive*. A _____ lives in a *cave*.
A *conductor* works on a _____. A *stewardess* works on a _____.

    3. Logical thinking can be practiced through use of analogies, especially with upper-grade and secondary students. A variety of decoding methods can be used to solve word problems. Students could be asked to justify the correctness (or incorrectness) of an analogy by using their own words to explain the relationship between word pairs, or they may be asked to complete the analogy. The key to success is that the analogy must be completely understood by the student.

    a. *Etymologist* is to *word origins* as *entomologist* is to *insects*.
       The students should recognize that an etymologist studies words and an entomologist studies insects.
    b. *Magnanimous* is to *vindictive* as *resolute* is to *timorous*.
       Students must realize that *magnanimous* is the opposite of *vindictive* while *resolute* is an antonym of *timorous*.
    c. *Inflexible* is to *pliant* as *rigid* is to *yielding*.
       The students should think that *inflexible* means "rigid" and it is the opposite of *pliant*, which means "yielding."
    d. *Flamboyance* : *unpretentiousness* :: *resplendence* : _____.
       (*simplicity, planchette, epicure, duplicity*)

A FINAL WORD

Semantic mapping, semantic feature analysis, and analogies are three instructional processes that have great potential for increasing the vocabularies of elementary school children. Empirical research evidence (Johnson et al., 1982), testimonials from educators (Ignoffo 1980; Stieglitz and Stieglitz 1981), and common sense tell us that classification ability is critical to concept development and that the strategies presented in this chapter help students learn new words through classification.

    As emphasized in Chapter Three, activities are not intended to be ends in themselves. The activities must be based on vocabulary items that children will be using immediately in reading, writing, or content-area instruction. Learning words for any reason other than to use them directly in a communication-based activity is an invalid use of instructional time.

REFERENCES

Barrett, M. T., and Graves, M. F. "A Vocabulary Program for Junior High School Remedial Readers." *Journal of Reading* 25 (1981): 146–50.

Becker, W. C. "Teaching Reading and Language to the Disadvantaged—What We Have Learned from Field Research." *Harvard Educational Review* 47 (1977): 518–43.

Block, K. K. "Vocabulary Development: A Problem in Learning and Instruction." Pittsburgh: Learning Research and Development Center, 1976. Unpublished manuscript.

Collins, A. M., and Quillian, M. R. "Retrieval Time from Semantic Memory." *Journal of Verbal Learning and Verbal Behavior* 8 (1969): 240–47.

Davis, F. B. "Fundamental Factors of Comprehension in Reading." *Psychometrika* 9 (1944): 185–97.

Hayes, D. A., and Tierney, R. J. "Developing Readers' Knowledge through Analogy." *Reading Research Quarterly* 17 (1982): 256–80.

Hunt, C. L., Jr. "Can We Measure Specific Factors Associated With Reading Comprehension?" *Journal of Educational Research* 51 (1957): 161–71.

Ignoffo, M. F. "Thread of Thought: Analogies as a Vocabulary Building Method." *Journal of Reading* 23 (1980): 519–21.

Johnson, D. D. "Expanding Vocabulary through Classification." In *Reading Instruction and the Beginning Teacher: A Practical Guide*, edited by J. F. Baumann and D. D. Johnson. Minneapolis: Burgess Publishing Company, 1984.

Johnson, D. D.; Toms-Bronowski, S.; and Buss, R. R. "Fundamental Factors in Reading Comprehension Revisited." In *Reading Research Revisited*, edited by L. Gentile and M. Kamil. Columbus, Ohio: Charles Merrill, 1983.

Johnson, D. D.; Toms-Bronowski, S.; and Pittelman, S. D. *An Investigation of the Effectiveness of Semantic Mapping and Semantic Feature Analysis With Intermediate Grade Level Children.* Program Report 83-3. Madison, Wisconsin: Wisconsin Center for Education Research, University of Wisconsin, 1982.

Lindsay, P., and Norman, D. *Human Information Processing.* New York: Academic Press, 1972.

Pearson, P. D., and Johnson, D. D. *Teaching Reading Comprehension,* New York: Holt, Rinehart and Winston, 1978.

Spearritt, D. "Identification of Subskills of Reading Comprehension by Maximum Likelihood Factor Analysis. *Reading Research Quarterly* 8 (1972–73): 92–111.

Stieglitz, E. L., and Stieglitz, V. S. "SAVOR the Word to Reinforce Vocabulary in the Content Areas." *Journal of Reading* 25 (1981): 46–51.

5
Developing a Meaning Vocabulary: Part III

Language is central to our lives at all stages of development (Dale 1980). During the school years and beyond, extensive, specialized vocabularies become essential tools for learning (Thomas and Robinson 1977; Herber 1978; Barrett and Graves 1981). Through the study of word meanings students can become more capable, perceptive readers. In this chapter we will discuss how three resources, the dictionary, thesaurus, and etymology, can be used to help children manipulate vocabulary and, as a result, develop greater semantic precision and become more effective, efficient language users.

Words influence our thoughts and our ability to understand information received orally and through written channels. Without knowledge of word meanings, we would perceive words as mere *noises*, which would fail to serve as aids to communication. The phenomenal feat of language acquisition has been put into proper perspective by Helen Keller, who became deaf and blind in infancy:

> As the cool stream gushed over one hand she [Helen Keller's teacher] spelled into the other the word *water*, first slowly, then rapidly. I stood still, my whole attention fixed upon the motions of her fingers. Suddenly I felt a misty consciousness as of something forgotten—a thrill of returning thought; and somehow the mystery of language was revealed to me. I knew then that "w-a-t-e-r" meant the wonderful cool something that was flowing over my hand. That living word awakened my soul, gave it light, hope, joy, set it free! . . .
>
> I left the well house eager to learn. Everything had a name, and each name gave birth to a new thought. As we returned to the house every object which I touched seemed to quiver with life. That was because I saw everything with the strange, new sight that had come to me. (Keller 1954, p. 36)

As a classroom teacher, you will want to make continual efforts to encourage students to "give birth to new thoughts"—to expand their conceptual powers. A broad, extensive vocabulary will be a valuable asset as children attempt to comprehend academic, functional, and recreational reading materials. The dictionary and the thesaurus are valuable vocabulary resources and are useful for the study of word histories, etymology. We will describe these three components of vocabulary instruction and suggest instructional activities that emphasize building skills through total language encounters.

Let us begin by providing dictionary definitions of the three terms.

Dictionary—"A reference book containing an explanatory alphabetical list of words, as   a) A book listing a comprehensive or restricted selection of the words of a language identifying usually the phonetic, grammatical, and semantic value of each word, often with etymology, citations, and usage guidance, and other information.   b) Such a book listing the words of a particular category within a language." (*American Heritage Dictionary*, 1979, p. 366)

A "book that explains the words of a language, or some special kind of words. It is arranged alphabetically. You can use this dictionary to find out the meaning, pronunciation, or spelling of a word." (*Scott, Foresman Beginning Dictionary*, 1976, p. 159)

Thesaurus—"A book of selected words or concepts, as a specialized vocabulary for music, medicine, or the like. A book of synonyms and antonyms." (*American Heritage Dictionary*, 1979, p. 1336)

"1. A treasury or storehouse; hence 2. a book containing a store of words, as a dictionary or, especially, a book of classified synonyms and antonyms." (*Webster's New World Dictionary of the American Language*, Encyclopedia Edition, Vol. 2, 1966, p. 1513)

Etymology—"1. The origin and historical development of a word, as evidenced by study of its basic elements, earliest known use, and changes in form and meaning; semantic derivation and evolution 2. An account of the history of a specific word." (*American Heritage Dictionary*, 1979, p. 451)

Dictionaries and thesauruses yield different kinds of information and are organized in different ways. Very simply, dictionary entries are arranged alphabetically and contain information about word meanings and pronunciations, among other things. Entries in a thesaurus are arranged topically and contain lists of antonyms and synonyms organized by subgroup and grammatical function (remember *synonym* refers to "something like" not "the same as"). The study of word origins, etymology, encompasses dictionary use but goes beyond the dictionary to include a variety of interesting books and reference materials. In the next sections we describe features of each of these three resources in more detail, offer some cautions, and suggest some instructional activities.

THE DICTIONARY

abracadabra	gobbledygook
roly-poly	mollycoddle
whippersnapper	goober
gewgaw	helter-skelter
bamboozle	peccadillo

Are these words nonsense words? Slang? Or are they perfectly good, colorful words which just sound somewhat silly? Do they constitute gobbledygook? A good dictionary might tell you.

Of the more than 5000 different types of reference materials that are available to learners of all ages we believe that a good dictionary possesses tremendous potential for the expansion of one's vocabulary. Over four decades ago, Thorndike said:

> The ideal dictionary for a young learner is a book which will help him learn the meaning of any word that he needs to understand, the spelling of any word that he needs to write, and the pronunciation of any word that he needs to speak. It will give him the help that he needs when he needs it, with a minimum of eyestrain and fatigue. It will give him a maximum of knowledge and skill and power for reading, writing, and speaking for every minute that he spends. It will fit him in due time to make proper use of a dictionary for adults. (Thorndike 1935, p. vi)

Many dictionaries contain five discrete categories of information: guides to locating words, alphabetized entry words, pronunciation keys, abbreviation and symbol lists, and special sections.

1. Guides to Locating Words. The principal guide to the location of words is the alphabetical arrangement of the entry words: *a* words are at the beginning, *m* words are near the middle, and *z* words are near the end. Thus, knowledge of the alphabet and alphabetical order are prerequisite skills to dictionary usage. Some children who know, for example, that *ape* comes before *man*, which precedes *zebra*, may have difficulty with *fulcrum, fulfill, full,* and *fulsome.* The guide words that appear at the top of each page in nearly all dictionaries, are a very useful feature for word location. Printed in boldface type, the guide words are the first and last entries on that page.[1] Other locational aids pertain to different words with the same spelling and different spellings of the same word. Some words sharing the same spelling have two or more entirely different meanings. The words *bear*, meaning "to carry," and *bear*, meaning "an animal," are entirely different words. Words such as these are printed and defined separately and are marked with a superscript (bear[1], bear[2]). Identical words with variant spellings *(enclosed, inclosed)* are defined or cross-referenced under both entries.

2. Entry Words. Entry words are the heart of a dictionary. Entered alphabetically, each word listed presents information about the word's pronunciation, grammatical form class, and meaning(s). Comprehensive dictionaries often include sample uses (contexts), inflected forms of the word, derived words with affixes, word origins, and idiomatic expressions:

> **glow** (glō) verb 1. to shine brightly and steadily esp. without a flame. 2. to have a bright or ruddy color. 3. to be exuberant or radiant, as with pride.
> noun 1. a light produced by or as by a body heated to luminosity. 2. brilliance or warmth of color, esp. redness. 3. a sensation of physical warmth. 4. a warm feeling of emotion.   OE glōman   (American Heritage Dictionary, p. 306).

3. Pronunciation Keys. The pronunciation of each entry word in a dictionary is shown just after the word. Phonetic symbols, syllabic divisions, and stress marks to show accent comprise the key. Dictionaries variously use the

---

[1]For example, *henpeck—heretical; repress—repulsive.*

International Phonetic Alphabet, some other phonetic symbol system, or a diacritical marking system to indicate letter-sound correspondences. Most dictionaries present a full pronunciation chart at the beginning or end of the book, and a
concise (shorter) pronunciation key on each page. Since Americans speak a variety
of regional or social dialects, dictionaries sometimes present two or more pronunciations for a word: *roof (rōof, rŏof); greasy (grē′ sē), (grē′ zē)*. Remember that all
dialect pronunciations are valid and the pronunciation listed first is not the "pre-
ferred" pronunciation. The following full pronunciation key is taken from the
Scott, Foresman Beginning Dictionary (1976).

Full Pronunciation Key

The pronunciation of each word is shown just after the word, in this
way: ab bre vi ate (ə brē′ vē āt).

The letters and signs used are pronounced as in the words below.
The mark ′ is placed after a syllable with primary or heavy accent, as
in the example above.

The mark ′ after a syllable shows a secondary or lighter accent, as in:
ab bre vi a tion (ə brē′ vē ā′ shən).

a	hat, cap	ô	order, all
ā	age, face	oi	oil, voice
ä	father, far	ou	house, out
b	bad, rob	p	paper, cup
ch	child, much	r	run, try
d	did, red	s	say, yes
		sh	she, rush
e	let, best	t	tell, it
ē	equal, be	th	thin, both
ėr	term, learn	ŦH	then, smooth
f	fat, if	u	cup, butter
g	go, bag	ù	full, put
h	he, how	ü	rule, move
i	it, pin	v	very, save
ī	ice, five	w	will, woman
		y	young, yet
j	jam, enjoy	z	zero, breeze
k	kind, seek	zh	measure, seizure
l	land, coal		
m	me, am	ə	represents:
n	no, in		a in about
ng	long, bring		e in taken
			i in pencil
o	hot, rock		o in lemon
ō	open, go		u in circus

4. Abbreviation and Symbol Lists. Because many words are used repeatedly in a dictionary, they are abbreviated for the sake of efficiency and to save space. Thus most dictionaries include a list of abbreviations and symbols used frequently. Many of the abbreviations pertain to word etymologies (origins) and grammatical function.

The following is a short list of abbreviations and symbols typifying the entries found in good dictionaries:

abbrev., abbreviated	e.g., for example
adj., adjective	esp., especially
adv., adverb	est., estimated
Afr., African	etem, etemology
Am., American	ff., following
c., circa (about, approximately)	G., German
cf., confer (compare)	in., inches
colloq., colloquial	* hypothetical
compar., comparative	‡ foreign word
Dan., Danish	< derived from
deriv., derivative	? perhaps; uncertain

Abbreviation and symbol lists often contain as many as 200 entries. We certainly do not recommend that children be required to memorize such lists (many entries will never be used in their lifetimes), but they should become familiar with the location and purpose of the list as an occasionally needed reference.

5. Special Sections. Every dictionary contains some special sections and, generally, the more comprehensive the dictionary, the more such supplements are included. Special sections may be:

Tables of weights and measures	A description of the language
Foreign monetary units	Forms of address
Common given names	States of the United States
Flags of the United Nations	Precious stones
Full-page maps	Common flowers
Full-page illustrations	The Constitution of the U.S.
The Declaration of Independence	

So we can see that a dictionary contains an enormous amount of information. Of greatest pertinence to the purpose of this book are the word meanings presented for each entry, for that is the major purpose of a dictionary — to provide the definitions of words. Of lesser importance is the information offered about word pronunciation, grammatical function, and word origin, although all are potentially useful and often interesting. We find the dictionary to be of little use as an aid to spelling and have long been troubled by well-meaning teachers who admonish children to "Look it up in the dictionary" when they cannot spell the word. How can you look up a word you cannot spell? Obviously, if one has an approximate idea of the spelling, and perhaps knows the first three or four letters, a dictionary can be helpful in verifying the presumed spelling.

But, again, the essence of dictionary usage is to obtain definitional precision — to learn the meanings of new words or to learn "new" meanings for old words. The instructional suggestions presented in this chapter will be directed to meaning search and acquisition. We do not wish to ignore the importance of pronunciation and spelling. Words such as *con'duct* and *con duct', de'sert* and

---

SAMPLE COLUMN

1 Guide word ——————————— **clambake**

2 Entry word ——————— **clam·bake** (klăm′bāk′) *n-* a shore picnic at which clams, lobsters, corn, etc. are cooked on hot stones covered with seaweed. ——— 7 Pronunciation *(note stress marks)*

8 Part-of-speech label ——— **clan** (klăn) *n-* 1 group of families, the heads of which claim common ancestry and have the same surname, especially in the Scottish Highlands: *He wears the tartan of the Mac-leod clan.* 2 group of people closely united because of similar backgrounds or by common interests or sympathies; a set; clique. ——— 9 Numbered definitions

10 Example

clang (klăng) *n-* loud, harsh, ringing sound like metal being struck. *vi-: The bell* clanged *loudly. vt-: The drummer* clanged *a cymbal.* ——— 11 Definition by example

6 Prefix ——————— **co-** *prefix* with; together; joint: *to co-operate.*

2 Abbreviation ——————— **C.O.D.** (sē′ō′dē′) collect on delivery.

4 Different Spellings ——————— **co·ed** or **co-ed** (kō′ĕd′) *Informal n-* a woman student at a coeducational college.

col·leen (kŏl′ēn′) *Irish n-* girl; young woman.

13 Labels ——————— **coloratura soprano** *Music n-* high-pitched female voice having great range and flexibility; also, a singer having such a voice.

com·mu·ni·cate (kə myōō′nə kāt′) *vt-* [**com·mu·ni·cat·ed, com·mu·ni·cat·ing**] to pass on to another; convey; impart; transmit: *to communicate a message; to communicate a disease. vi-* to send and receive information, ideas, etc.: *They communicate easily.* ——— 14 Inflected forms

16 Run-on entries ——— **communicate with** to be connected with; also, to adjoin. ——— 15 Idiom

com·pla·cent (kəm plā′sənt) *adj-* 1 uncritically, often smugly, satisfied with oneself or one's lot; self-satisfied: *He was quite complacent about his good fortune.* 2 showing or expressing this feeling: *a gentle, complacent smile.* **—adv- com·pla′cent·ly.**

17 Usage ——————— ▶Should not be confused with COMPLAISANT.

com·pli·men·ta·ry (kŏm′plə mĕnt′ə rē, -mĕn′trē) *adj-* 1 giving approval or praise: *Her remarks on the new house were complimentary.* 2 given free: *a complimentary ticket.* **Hom-** complementary. **—adv- com′pli·men′ta·ri·ly.** ——— 7 Variant pronunciations

5 Homophone cross-reference

3 Superscript number for homographs ——— ¹**cow** (kou) *n-* 1 full-grown female bovine mammal, domesticated for its milk. 2 female moose, elephant, whale, etc. [from Old English *cu.*] ——— 12 Illustration

Cow, about 5 ft. high

7 Pronunciation Key ——— ²**cow** (kou) *vt-* to subdue by frightening; intimidate: *He cowed them with a show of strength.* [from Old Norse *kūga* having no connection whatever with ¹cow.] ——— Word histories

fāte, făt, dâre, bärn; bē, bĕt, mēre; bīte, bĭt; nōte, hŏt, môre, dŏg; fūn, fûr; tōō, bŏŏk; oil; out; tar; thin; **then**; hw for wh as in *what*; zh for s as in usual; ə for a, e, i, o, u, as in *ago, linen, peril, atom, minus*

8A

de sert' are dependent upon pronunciation for meaning. Similarly, words such as *fair—fare*, *maid—made*, and *great—grate* are dependent upon spelling for meaning.

Students need to know what kinds of information are available to them from a dictionary, and they must know how to use this valuable reference tool. They need to know alphabetical order, to the second, third, or even fifth or sixth letter of a word. They need to know the time-saving effectiveness of utilizing the guide words at the top of each page. It is helpful for them to know the pronunciation key and the list of abbreviations. They especially need to know that the varied word meanings and usages can be found there.

In Chapter Seven we will show the potential power of phonic, structural, and contextual analysis in word identification. But there will be times, probably frequently, when the reader will need to consult a dictionary to discern or affirm the intended meaning of a word in the context provided.

We encourage you to keep a proper sense of perspective as you approach dictionary instruction. It is not the sole authority or even the principal method for gaining word meanings. One of the important concepts that needs to be conveyed to students is that dictionaries *record* language rather that *dictate* it. Dictionaries are written by humans who wish to describe what exists. They are subject to human error, and, because of rapid language change, they are, to some degree, out of date on the day they are published. Dictionary work need not be viewed in the skill and drill "Look it up and copy the meaning" sense that it too often has. A number of the suggestions we present later can generate enthusiasm for using the dictionary as a valuable tool in solving problems.

There are numerous dictionaries available and prepared for children and scholars of all ages (see pp. 87–88). Beginning with the earliest stages of reading instruction, picture dictionaries such as *My Little Dictionary* (Scott, Foresman 1964) and the *Storybook Dictionary* (Golden Press 1966) are useful introductions to the functions and purposes of a dictionary and how to use one. Adult dictionaries such as the *American Heritage* (Morris 1979), *Webster's New World* (Guralnick and Friend 1966), and the *Oxford Dictionary* (Murray 1923) are very comprehensive references. An excellent dictionary for elementary school children is the *Holt School Dictionary of American English* most recently published in 1981. Page 8A, reprinted on the previous page, is a sample column showing 17 keys to the word entries.

THE THESAURUS

The thesaurus is, in our opinion, a highly useful aid to classroom vocabulary instruction. Unfortunately, it does not seem to be found and used in very many classrooms. For some reason teachers to not seem to readily consider it as a teaching tool, with the result that many students even in the intermediate and high-school grades are totally unfamiliar with its contents or its possibilities. Yet, in many ways, the thesaurus is less complicated than a dictionary since it emphasizes only one aspect of words, their meanings through synonyms and antonyms. The thesaurus can be a tremendously useful aid in expanding students' reading, writing, and speaking vocabularies. It can be of invaluable help in suggesting new words, more colorful or interesting words, less common words, and more precise words for the many tired, overused words in a child's lexicon. The examples on pages 58–61 (which contain words relating to feelings, smells, and religion) are reprinted from among nearly 150 pages in *Words To Use, A Junior Thesaurus* written by Patrick Drysdale (1971), an elementary school thesaurus that we recommend to teachers with whom we work.

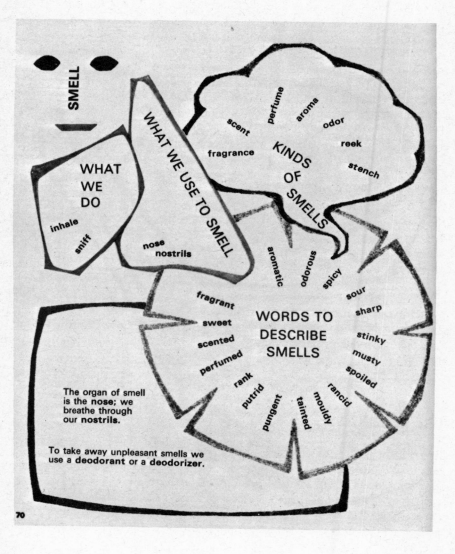

The specific intent of a thesaurus, and the way in which it is significantly different from a dictionary, was most articulately expressed in 1852 by the "Father of the Thesaurus," Peter Mark Roget:

> The present work is intended to supply, with respect to the English language, a desideratum hitherto unsupplied in any language; namely, a collection of the words it contains and of the idiomatic combinations peculiar to it, arranged, not in alphabetical order as they are in a Dictionary, but according to the *ideas* which they express. The purpose of an ordinary dictionary is simply to explain the meaning of the words; and the problem of which it professes to fur-

nish the solution may be stated thus: — The word being given, to find its signification, or the idea it is intended to convey. The object aimed at in the present
undertaking is exactly the converse of this: namely, — The idea being given, to
find the word, or words, by which that idea may be most fitly and aptly
expressed. For this purpose, the words and phrases of the language are here
classed, not according to their sound or their orthography, but strictly according
to their *signification*. (Roget 1965)

Simply then, a dictionary goes from word to meaning while a thesaurus
goes from meaning to word. A thesaurus generalizes while a dictionary
particularizes.

Peter Roget was born in England of French and Swiss parents in 1779 and
he died at 91 in 1869. His scholarly attainments are too vast to mention in this

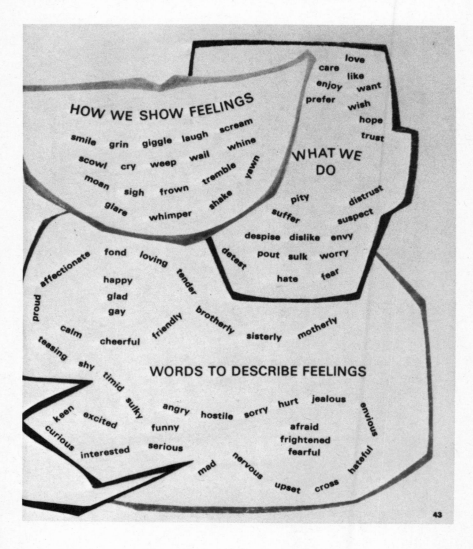

small volume, but we think you might be interested in his stated motivation (in 1852) for undertaking the monumental task of creating a thesaurus.

It is now nearly fifty years since I first projected a system of verbal classification similar to that on which the present Work is founded. Conceiving that such a compilation might help to supply my own deficiencies, I had, in the year 1805, completed a classed catalog of words on a small scale, but on the same principle, and nearly in the same form, as the Thesaurus now published. I had often during that long interval found this little collection, scanty and imperfect as it was, of much use to me in literary composition, and often contemplated its extension and improvement; but a sense of the magnitude of the task amidst a multitude of other avocations, deterred me from this attempt. Since my retirement from the duties of Secretary of the Royal Society, however, finding myself possessed of more leisure, and believing that a repertory of which I had myself

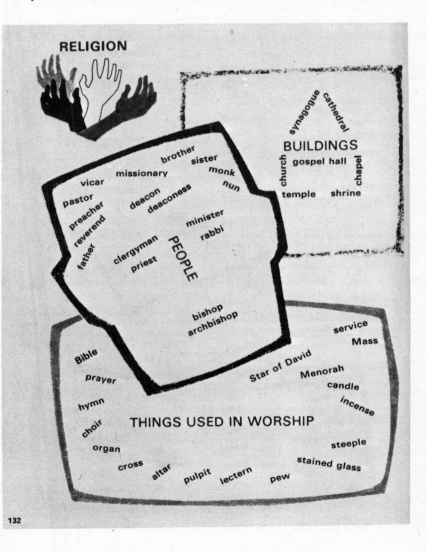

132

experienced the advantage might, when amplified, prove useful to others, I resolved to embark on an undertaking which, for the last three or four years, has given me incessant occupation, and has, indeed, imposed upon me an amount of labor very much greater than I had anticipated. Notwithstanding all the pains I have bestowed on its execution, I am fully aware of its numerous deficiencies and imperfections, and of its falling far short of the degree of excellence that might be attained. (Roget 1965)

To most people who know *Roget's Thesaurus* (and they are largely college students) the work is viewed as a massive collection of synonyms with an index, which is very useful if you are searching for an alternate word or are in need of a word to label an idea. To create his thesaurus, Roget established six classes (Abstract Relations, Space, Matter, Intellect, Volition, and Affections) and divided each into a range of three to eight sections (that is, Matter: Matter in General, Inorganic Matter, and Organic Matter). Each of these sections was further divided into a number of categories (for example, Matter in General into: Materiality, Immateriality, Universe, Gravity, Levity). Under each category were numbers of synonymous and antonymous words and phrases.

In the 1965 edition of *Roget's Thesaurus* by St. Martin's Press (Roget 1965), 629 pages are devoted to the text (the classes, sections, categories, and words) and 772 pages to the index. If one were interested in selecting words related to *hate*, for example, they would find six optional entry points listed under *hate* in the index. The first of these is "*dislike* 861 vb." In entry 861 of the text *dislike* is presented (together with lists of synonymous words and phrases) in four ways—as a noun, an adjective, a verb, and an interjection. Under the *vb* entry is an array of words and phrases, some of which are: *dislike, loathe, resent, despise, abominate, abhor,* and *hate.*

We have dealt with *Roget's Thesaurus* at some length because it was and is the most significant adult thesaurus of English and it has been the pattern for the many others that have followed. It has gone through "scores of reprints, new editions (some unauthorized), imitations and adaptations demanded by generations of users, a demand still continuing after more than a hundred years." (Roget 1965, p. vii)

So a thesaurus is, in essence, a list of words classified according to their meaning, and carefully indexed and cross-referenced. Unlike a dictionary, which seeks to define a word in all its meanings *in one place*, a thesaurus starts with a meaning (not with a word) and presents words that represent some aspect of that meaning—in a context. A number of thesauruses are available commercially, including those written for elementary school children, such as *Words To Use, a Junior Thesaurus* (Drysdale 1971), from which we included excerpts earlier, small abridged paperback editions, and large thumb-indexed desk editions such as *The St. Martin's Edition of The Original Roget's Thesaurus of English Words and Phrases* (Roget 1965). Thesauruses such as the latter are especially useful to teachers as source materials for direct vocabulary instruction.

We recommend that the thesaurus and the dictionary, together, be introduced to children as useful tools of reference and as sources of great interest and knowledge about words. This chapter presents teaching activities that we think exemplify both sound and useful instruction in the use of these vocabulary reference works. These activities are examples; most can be used across grade levels if appropriately modified. As we said previously, dictionary instruction, particularly with picture dictionaries, can begin at the very earliest stages of reading development. Instruction can continue throughout the elementary grades and beyond.

Both the dictionary and thesaurus need to be introduced as the valuable vocabulary sources they are for providing word meanings and for confirming a tentative judgment of a word's meaning achieved through the use of context, structure, and phonics. Of course, prerequisite skills for the use of both references are a knowledge of alphabetical order and an understanding of the component parts of both works.

INSTRUCTIONAL ACTIVITIES—THE DICTIONARY AND THE THESAURUS

We are indebted to many teachers for some of the suggestions that follow. In particular we wish to thank Mrs. Lynn Kepper, an experienced elementary teacher in Wisconsin, for providing a number of the suggestions that follow.

Choosing Meanings

Too many times children are simply asked to look up a word in a dictionary and find its meaning. A more interesting approach is to form questions that may pique their curiosity. The instructions may be as follows: "Can you answer these questions? You can use your dictionary when you need to."

1. How is a *flume* like a *gorge?*
2. Could you ride in a *smock?*
3. What is the same about a *raft* and a *coracle?*
4. Would you ever use a *kirtle?*
5. What does a *backbiting* person do?
6. How is a *skiff* like a *lugger?*
7. Which is a boat — *dingy* or *dinghy?*
8. Is a *codling* a small fish?
9. What do *fuchsia* and *mignonette* have in common?
10. How is *mother* related to *vinegar?*

Guide Words

Ask children to locate the guide words (using their class dictionary) at the top of the pages where each of the following words is found:

daily	extremely
ensign	handcuff

hunk   seize
medicine   toenail
pestle

Next, reverse the process. List pairs of guide words such as these:

told — ton
recycle — refer
stag — stake
flipper — flowery

Have the children: (1) find one or more interesting words on that page and use them in sentences; or (2) find surprise meanings for common words on that page. The purpose of both these activities is to give practice with alphabetizing and using guide words. Some teachers sponsor "races" in which the students race against themselves or each other in locating correct page numbers for words listed on the chalkboard or on a mimeo page. By using guide words, the students are to locate the listed words as quickly as possible. Since there is little "meaning" attached to this activity, we recommend using it sparingly.

Another guide-word activity involves asking students questions like the following: "If you were trying to look up the word *dog* and you found a page with the guide words *dogma* and *domicile,* you should: (1) turn toward the front; (2) turn toward the back; (3) look on that page.

Imported Words

In the following exercise, students are asked to use unabridged dictionaries to determine the origin of certain words.

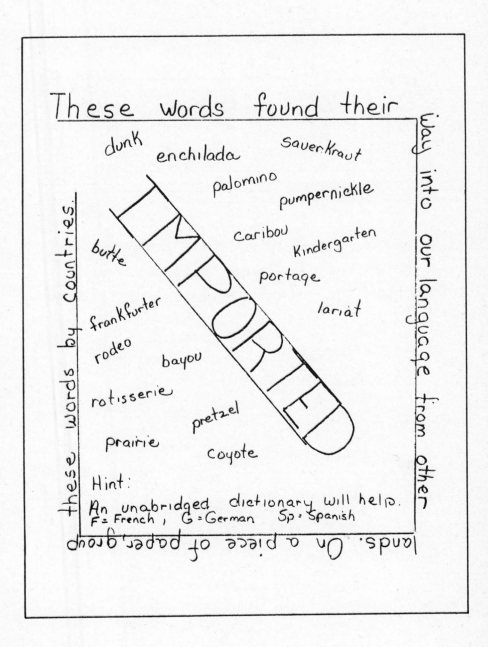

Greek Myths

Similar to the above activity is the following, which requires research in a good dictionary or more specialized reference.

Do some research on the names from Greek myths to find out how they acquired the meaning they have today.

atlas - Atlas   epicure - Epicurus

odyssey - Odysseus

tantalize - Tantalus

arachnid - Arachne

narcissus - Narcissus

echo - Echo

thespian - Thespis

zephyr - Zephros

stentorian - Stentor   panic - Pan

Acronyms

The following activity helps children acquire meanings and origins of common acronyms through the use of a dictionary.

Word Comparisons

The following exercise of word comparison is greatly enhanced by using a dictionary.

It's

Like

A

- - - - -

But

...

Some words can be defined by comparing them to other words (For example: A gondola is like a canoe, but it has a high prow and stern and is paddled by one person standing.) Try defining the words below in this way. Then select four words from your reading to do this with.

helicopter   dragonfly

antelope   skateboard   van

ravine   milkshake

Animal Families

The dictionary will be helpful to students in completing some of the following phrases. Some they will know from experience.

Most animal groups have very fancy names, such as a <u>swarm</u> of wasps, or a <u>school</u> of fish. Try to find the missing animal names below? (consult a dictionary

A colony of ___?___   A skulk of ___?___

A pack of ___?___   A pod of ___?___

A gaggle of ___?___   A herd of ___?___

A gam of ___?___   A drove of ___?___

A pride of ___?___   A bevy of ___

A skein of ___?___

Illustrating Words

This activity involves the use of a dictionary and some art supplies to help expand vocabulary.

Multiple Meanings

Have the pupils use their class dictionaries to decide *which* meaning of selected multimeaning words is appropriate in the contexts provided.

1. (a) The *bank* is closed.
   (b) The pilot will *bank* his plane.
   (c) She swam toward the *bank*.
2. (a) Tommy couldn't stay *long*.
   (b) I *long* for my old friends.
   (c) How *long* is the street?
3. (a) It surely is *cold* today.
   (b) Lisa's greeting was very *cold*.
   (c) Try not to catch a *cold*.
4. (a) I'd rather *stand* than sit.
   (b) They just can't *stand* each other.
   (c) Get me a newspaper from the *stand*.

Fifty-cent Words

Many children enjoy working with big, long, "hard" words. Using either a dictionary or a thesaurus, have them select synonymous words or phrases for such "50-cent" words as the following. Then have them construct parallel sentences using both the 50-cent and the 5-cent (synonymous) word.

serendipity	myopic	disencumber
gargantuan	gluttony	facilitate
puritanical	sybarite	caricature
euphemistic	angularity	ludicrous
cajolery	incomprehensible	parsimonious

Tummy Time

Children may need to use the dictionary to learn the meanings of some of the following gourmet terms. Have them create a menu using these terms, together with a short explanation of each.

shish kebab	mocha
consomme	filet
hors d'oeuvre	taco
au gratin	gumbo
à la mode	

Fictionary

An interesting activity for guessing—and later ascertaining—the meanings of new or unusual words is a game called Fictionary, described next.

> The picker picks a word s/he thinks no one will know.
> S/he writes down correct definition on a slip of paper.
> S/he spells it for everyone else.
> Each person makes up what s/he thinks is a possible definition, and writes it on a slip of paper. Try to make your definition sound like one from a dictionary, "one who . . . ," "the act of . . . ."
> Then the picker reads all the definitions. The rest of the group tries to guess the real definition. The picker then reads the correct definition.

Sounds and Meanings

Children should consult their dictionary to determine the two different pronunciations and meanings of each of the following words.

conduct	object
present	rebel
row	content
lead	desert
sow	subject
sewer	wind
relax	wound

Slanguage

Many words take on new meanings (connotative) over time. Words such as *grease*, *pot*, and *heavy*, mean different things to different people. Either as an individual or as a class project, many children enjoy creating their own slang dictionaries.

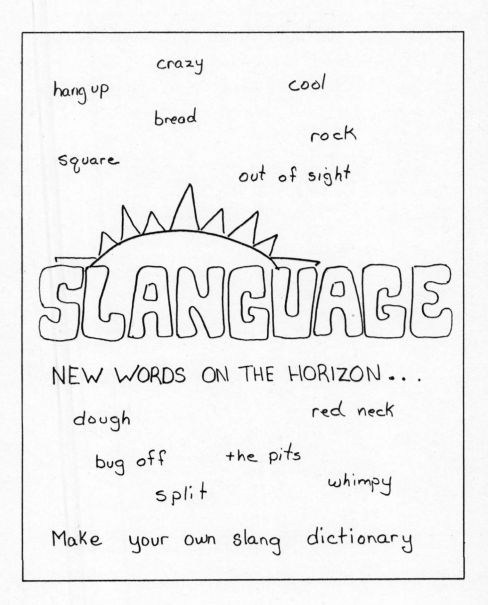

C.B. Talk[2]

The CB radio boom did a lot to create a "new language" found offensive to some and good fun to others. The following exercise capitalizes on the uniqueness of CB talk.

:) Make your own C.B. Slang dictionary. Use the words below and any more you know.   Or...

2) Write a C.B. radio conversation using the words below and others.

C. B. SLANG
AND COMPANY

Bear Trap

Hammer

Smokey

Clean

Super Slab

Pumpkin

Good buddy

Motor mouth

Copy

Juice

Advertising   Back door   Local yokel   Taking pictures

Big 10-4   Bear bite

Green stamp   Ears   Come on

---

[2]Adapted from Marge Frank (1976).

INSTRUCTIONAL ACTIVITIES—THE THESAURUS

Some of the foregoing activities pertain to the thesaurus as well as the dictionary. Likewise some of the following activities could be used with a dictionary.

Ranking Words

The children are asked to select sets of synonymous words from their thesaurus and rank them in some way, for example, according to seriousness, intensity, approval, degree, and size.

hostility	despair
rage	sorrow
anger	regret
annoyance	melancholy
joy	astound
pleasure	flabbergast
happiness	surprise
delight	astonish
cry	gaze
weep	regard
whine	observe
wail	watch
love	lean
like	skinny
care for	trim
adore	thin
ailment	fine
disease	fair
illness	okay
sickness	passable

The point being made is that synonymous words are not *exactly* alike in meaning. Ask the class to write or compose oral sentences (or pantomimes) that demonstrate the differences in these words.

Too Very Very[3]

Sentences such as the following, which contain the word *very*, can be made more interesting by consulting a thesaurus and selecting good replacements.

Can you find some words to replace these "very" words?

1. The mouse in the corner was <u>very little</u>.

2. We were quickly approaching the <u>very high</u> mountains.

3. The zoo keeper tried to get the <u>very big</u> elephant into his cage.

4. We watched the race cars go <u>very fast</u> at the Indy 500.

5. The <u>very old</u> building was thought to be haunted.

6. Sam was <u>very frightened</u> by the noises.

[3]Adapted from M. E. Platts (1970).

Tired Words

An expansion of the previous activity is done with such overused words as *happy*, *sad*, *mad*, *nice*, *mean*, *big*, *little*, and so on. This exercise encourages vocabulary replacement through the use of the thesaurus.

Words get tired too!

We're Overworked

HAPPY
gay
jolly

SAD
forlorn
mournful

MAD
cranky
cross

Use the thesaurus to find some words for each of the tired ones above.

Walking Words

The example that follows concerns vocabulary expansion of words that show walking. It can be modified for use with many other kinds of words:

talking words	looking words	thinking words
sitting words	touching words	laughing words
standing words	smelling words	eating words

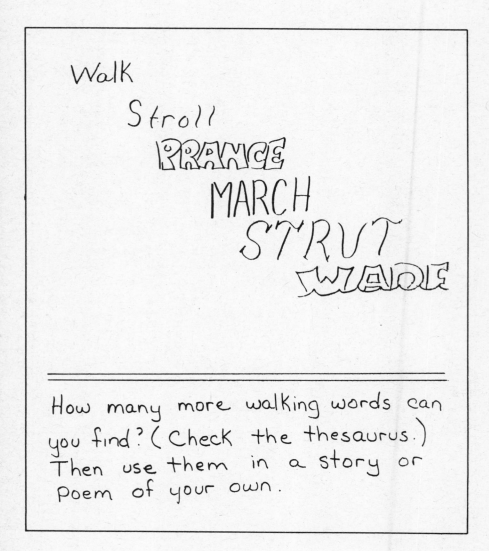

Walk

Stroll

PRANCE

MARCH

STRUT

WADE

How many more walking words can you find? (Check the thesaurus.) Then use them in a story or poem of your own.

Noise

This activity is included to show you another way of arranging a thesaurus activity. Many words (meanings that have lots of words associated with them) could be used in a similar way. Or, one word (e.g., *noise*) could be presented and the pupils' task could be to discover the associated words.

Ruckus

Bedlam

Boisterous

Racket

Roaring

Commotion

NOISE

Din

Flurry

Thunderous

Clamor

Shrill

Hubbub

These words can be found under *loud* and *noise* in the thesaurus. Select at least 8 to use in a poem. Try to find others

Thesaurus Is the Judge

The teacher divides the class into teams and assigns each team the same word. Each team compiles a list of words that are somewhat synonymous to the word the teacher has given them. The team with the most words (check the lists, using a thesaurus!) is the winner.

Simplified Sentences

Construct sentences that contain a number of "50-cent" words. Ask the class to use a thesaurus or dictionary to help them rewrite the sentence in simple English. They should then compare their new sentences. For example, "Inform the male adolescent contiguous to Bonnie that he is excessively loquacious" becomes "Tell the boy next to Bonnie that he talks too much."

Writing and Speaking

Perhaps the best use of the thesaurus as a tool for vocabulary development in reading is through the preparation of stories, essays, and speeches. Children should be encouraged to write stories and essays and to prepare speeches, and to consult their thesaurus frequently while doing so in a search for fresh, interesting, and precise words. As they use these new words in their writing and speaking, their vocabulary will grow and their subsequent reading comprehension will be greater.

We think that the thesaurus has been too long overlooked in classroom instruction. It has great potential value for the expansion of children's reading, writing, and speaking vocabularies. Its use can be as interesting as it is helpful, and we think every classroom should have a set of thesauruses appropriate to the level of the children.

Similarly, we value the use of a dictionary in vocabulary instruction and believe there should be a set of good dictionaries in each classroom. Too often, though, it seems that dictionary work has been dull, repetitive, and even frustrating (students are asked to look up the spelling of a word). We think that the kinds of dictionary and thesaurus instructional activities provided in this chapter are imaginative enough to encourage some interest in the two reference works. Perhaps from interest will come habit—not the habit of slavishly looking up every new word encountered, but, rather, the habit of turning to a dictionary or a thesaurus to verify a meaning, gain precision, and expand vocabulary. We would much rather see children make use of a combination of phonic, structural, and contextual analysis whenever it is possible. This is the goal of instruction with these two reference tools.

ETYMOLOGY

Etymology, the study of word histories or origins, should be introduced to most children during the middle school years, though some children will be ready earlier. Word origins seem to hold a special interest for most youngsters. Because our language is a living language, it is constantly in a state of flux, changing in sound, syntax, and word meaning. English-language users have borrowed thousands of words from other languages and have coined new words at a phenomenal rate to keep up with technological advances. Thus words like *candy, lemon* (Arabic), *cent, depot* (French), *burro, rodeo* (Spanish), *sleigh, cookie* (Dutch), and *noodle, semester* (German), are now common to the English language as are the relatively recent terms *astronaut, astrodome, supersonic, motor home, telegram,* and *disc jockey.*

Children should be exposed to the history of their language. Lessons on word histories can be based on a multitude of themes. One unit might encompass a comparison of our Modern English words with their Anglo-Saxon origins *(heaven—heafonum, right—riht)* while another set of lessons could examine words white settlers borrowed from Native Americans *(chipmunk, pecan, Illinois, moccasin, caucus)*. Older children might be asked to search for the spellings and pronunciations of words that are quite similar across several languages:

Modern English: *Mother*
French: *Mère*
German: *Mutter*
Italian: *Madre*
Norwegian: *Moder*
Russian: *Maht*
Spanish: *Madre*

Through this activity children discover that these languages do have similarities; further study will lead the class to discover that all seven languages mentioned above grew out of the same Indo-European base.

As you plan introductory lessons on etymology you may wish to try some of the following whole/small group activities.

1. Plan a trip to the IMC, school, or public library to explore reference materials on word histories. Dictionaries should be included in this study, but other good reference books provide interesting, very readable data on etymology. You may wish to examine the following books to learn how intriguing the study of word histories can be.

Adelson, Leone. *Dandelions Don't Bite: The Story of Words.* New York: Pantheon Books, 1972.

Asimov, Isaac. *Words from the Myths.* Boston: Houghton Mifflin, 1961.

Davidson, Jessica. *Is That Mother in the Bottle: Where Language Came From and Where It Is Going.* New York: Franklin Watts, 1977.

Epstein, Sam, and Beyrl Epstein. *The First Book of Words.* New York: Franklin Watts, 1954.

Fitzgerald, Cathleen. *Let's Find Out About Words.* New York: Franklin Watts, 1971.

Funk, Charles. *Horsefeathers and Other Curious Words.* New York: Harper and Row, 1958.

Pickles, Colin, and Lawrence L. Pickles. *The Beginning of Words: How English Grew.* New York: Putnam, 1970.

Wagner, Rudolph F., and Marvey H. Wagner. *Stories about Words.* Portland, Me.: J. Weston Walch, 1960.

————. *Stories about Family Names.* Portland, Me.: J. Weston Walch, 1961.

————. *Stories about Place Names.* Portland, Me.: J. Weston Walch, 1963.

Wolf, Cynthia G. *A Feast of Words.* New York: Oxford, 1977.

These and other books at a variety of reading levels can be checked out and used in a classroom interest center.

2. Create a bulletin-board display of many similar words drawn from the Indo-European language base. Ask children to contribute groups of words they have identified. Intermediate-level classes might investigate and prepare a series of reports on Indo-European cultures.

3. Use displays or transparencies of Old, Middle, and Modern English writings. Excerpts from the *Anglo-Saxon Chronicles* (Old English), *Canterbury Tales* (Middle English), and a selection from Shakespeare's writings (early Modern English) could be shared with the students. Students could look for any similarities these excerpts have with our modern English language. They will note that one major change is the simplification that has occurred in our language.

4. Assign groups of children to form Ethnic Exploration Teams. The team's task would be to search through reference books in the classroom interest center to find words the various ethnic groups have contributed to English as the United States was explored and settled.

5. Divide the class into any manageable number of groups. Randomly select lists of ten words from a book currently in use in the classroom. Distribute the lists to the children. The group must use a good unabridged dictionary to locate the origin of each term on their list and enter the term's origin on a tally sheet provided by the teacher. At the end of the group meetings, tally charts will be combined. Results will indicate the percentage of words borrowed from other languages and those of English origin.

Children will need to learn how to use the etymology notes in a dictionary. Most dictionaries include a list of abbreviations and will explain the conventions used in noting etymology. For instance:

Abbreviations

Am. Sp.	American Spanish
Brit.	British
OF.	Old French
Jap.	Japanese

Some dictionaries, such as the *American Heritage Dictionary* (Morris 1979), have eliminated abbreviations in etymologies. Etymologies appear in square brackets following the definitions in this dictionary. However, many other dictionaries do use abbreviations.

Conventional Listing

cipher [OF. *cifre* zero, fr. Ar. *sifr* empty]

(*Cipher* is derived from the Old French term *cifre* and it means "zero." It is also derived from the Arabic term *sifr* meaning "empty."

Before you ask children to work with word origins independently, examine the reference materials they will be using and explain the dictionary's policy of recording etymological information.

The study of word histories will help students develop word consciousness and an interest in word study. Words enter a language because they fulfill our need to communicate. Acronyms, for example, developed to permit us to use brief word forms to communicate ideas *(snafu, radar)* or lengthy titles (UNESCO, NATO). A study of acronyms might be used to initiate interest in etymology. Students might even enjoy creating their own acronyms for classroom or recreational activities.

Once the students in your classroom have been given an introduction to etymology, you will find many exciting projects are available for individual, small, or whole-group study. The following activities are just a few of the good vocabulary exercises you will want to try out in your classroom.

1. People's names and names of places have become commonly used words (Kean and Personke 1976). A lesson on word study could be based on the following list.

People's Names (both real and fictional)	Place Names
braille	bologna
chauvinism, colt	calico
gargantuan	frankfurter
gladstone	hamburger
macadam	italics
mackintosh	jeans
malapropism	jersey
martinet	marathon
panic	olympic
pasteurize	tweed

People's Names
(both real and fictional)

quisling
quixote
sandwich
silhouette
saxophone
vulcanize

For example, children searching for the history of the word *macadam* will find that a man named John L. McAdam, a Scottish engineer, developed a pavement of layers of small stones that is usually bound together with tar. The term *jeans* originated in Genoa (Middle English *Jene*), where the blue denim fabric was originally made.

2. Students discover something about etymology when they examine their own names. "What's in a Name?" is an activity children will enjoy pursuing. The procedure is as follows:

a. Assign students the task of researching the meaning and origin of their first names. Dictionaries will often supply this information; or your class could use a "name book," as it lists the derivations of many first names. For example, children will find over 10,000 girls' and boys' names in Bruce and Vicki Lansky's *The Best Baby Name Book in the Whole Wide World* (1979). Help children enter their names on a large chart that lists the etymological histories they have found.

> *Jessica* — Hebrew — wealthy
> *Matthew* — Hebrew — the gift of the Lord
> *Stacy* — Middle Latin — stable, prosperous
> *Jacinda* — Greek — beautiful, comely, hyacinth flower

(Once the word history chart has been completed you will have a wealth of words to use in a general vocabulary lesson!)

b. Provide a dictionary for each student for this next activity. Instruct the children to use the first two letters of their last name and find the first 30 words listed in the dictionary that begin with these letters. Examining the lists to see if there is some consistency in etymology, children may learn where their names came from. For example, if a child by the name of Denise Smith were to produce a list such as the following:

> *Smith*
> smack — Old English
> small — Old English
> small-age — Modern English
> smart — Old English
> smear — Old English
> smelt — Old English
> smile — Modern English
> smock — Old English

smirk — Modern English
(etc.)

what could she infer about her origins?

c. Discuss with students some of the ways last names have developed. Names ending in -*son* mean "son of . . ." — *Jacobson, Nelson,* and *Peterson* mean "son of Jacob," "son of Nels," and "son of Peter," respectively. Other last names, such as *English, French, Hill,* and *Waters,* may refer to a family's place of origin. Some last names *(Brewer, Taylor, Miller)* are derived from family occupations. Foreign-language dictionaries and conversations with parents and other relatives will help students as they attempt to analyze the origins of their last names. Check for resource books in your school library that deal with this topic. (See, for example, Wagner and Wagner 1961). In order to create a total language experience, students may present the newly acquired information in the form of a short story or report, chart, or poem. A fascinating bulletin board could be developed.

Some children may even become obsessed with the study of word histories. These budding "word historians" or future etymologists, should be encouraged to become involved in additional projects.

3. Students have fun speculating about the origin of words. They should be encouraged to discuss and debate their opinions and to check on the origins by using a good reference resource. It would be interesting, for example, to compare the relationship between origins of words and their modern-day usage. For instance, take the word *hamburger;* does it have anything to do with *ham?* What about *frankfurter* or *mustang?* How did these terms originate?

As an alternative, you may wish to write some statements about word histories on the chalkboard and discuss them with the students. Speculate on the correctness or incorrectness of the statements. Finally, ask students to check each of the statements in a reference book. Those like the following might be used:

a. Soccer probably began as part of training for battle.
b. The steam engine is named after Jacob Steam, a German inventor.
c. It is true that the sandwich is named after Lord Sandwich, who ate his meat on bread.

4. A humorous, extremely motivating activity is one that uses combined names and initials as puns. This type of exercise might be used to introduce etymology as well as to inspire interest in unusual words and names. Examples include *Ima and Ura Hogg, Dr. Waters* (urologist), *Mr. Groaner Digger* (undertaker), *I. C. Shivers* (iceman), *Justine Tune* (choir director), *U. R. Rong, Patty Hamburger,* and *June First.* Children should be encouraged to collect odd names from newspapers, telephone directories, and magazines. These could be used to develop many different activities—the possibilities are limitless, let your creativity flow!

5. As you browse through a dictionary it will become quite obvious that many of our words have Greek and Latin derivations. Some common word beginnings that indicate number or quantity are drawn from these languages. *Deca-* or *dec-* (ten), *hexa-* or *hex-* (six) *penta-* (five), and *hemi-* (one-half) are prefixes from

Greek words, while *cent-* or *centi-* (one hundred), *octo-* or *oct-* (eight), *semi-* (one-half), and *milli-* (one thousand) are prefixes from Latin words. This next activity will be interesting and challenging to students who have become familiar with these words parts.

> a. *Penta*gon is a _____ -sided figure.
> b. *Octo*pus is an _____ -armed animal.
> c. *Deca*de is a period of _____ years.
> d. *Centi*grade is divided into _____ degrees.

Perhaps as a follow-up activity, the children would enjoy locating these words in word-search puzzles, finding the given words from their descriptors; e.g., find the eight-armed animal *(octopus)* or find the one-hundredth celebration *(centennial)*.

6. Children will discover more about how our language grows and changes as they engage in the following exercises.

a. People in different parts of the country use a variety of words for common objects. For example, *bag, poke,* and *sack* are terms denoting an object used to carry things in, and *spider, skillet,* and *frying pan* are words commonly used to identify a special cooking utensil. Have children construct their own illustrated classroom dictionaries of regionalisms. As a resource, develop correspondence with children or adults in other parts of the country and make a game of composing lists of terms unique to the region. Do you like to eat *spuds* or *potatoes?* If you get thirsty, do you search for a *bubbler* or a *water fountain?* Do you like *meat cakes* or *meat balls* with spaghetti? Will you *carry your lady* or *take your girlfriend* to the football game?

b. The sports field has lent new meanings to old words. Words like *spare, fly, crawl, love, tackle, iron, glove, birdie,* and *stroke* have all taken on additonal meaning and thus built depth to their "word histories." Using books, sports magazines, and newspaper articles as a base, ask children to compile lists of words that take on new meanings in the sports arena.

c. Greek and Roman mythology have both added words to our English vocabularies *(volcanoes, herculean strength, mercury).* Lively research projects can be designed for students beginning at about the third-grade level. Direct students to search for terms and associated meanings drawn from the myths.

d. Slang terms *(trip, jive, spiffy, catch-you-later, goofing around, bummer,* and *neat)* enter the language with each new generation. Interviews with a cross section of parents, teachers, relatives, neighbors, and friends will yield interesting lists of words (e.g., "Fifties Slang," "Language of the Forties," etc.).

A FINAL WORD

Our goal throughout the pages of this book is to demonstrate strategies you can adapt as you work to help students increase their meaningful vocabularies. Direct instruction with an emphasis on total language involvement has been our central theme.

In the present chapter we have identified three resources that you will find valuable as you plan vocabulary lessons: the dictionary, the thesaurus, and etymology. Each resource provides a unique type of information about words. The dictionary lists words along with their spellings, pronunciations, meanings, etymologies, and grammatical classes. The thesaurus provides categories of words classified as synonyms and antonyms. The study of word origins, etymology, leads students through a variety of reference books in search of information on word history. Using each of these unique resources demands two types of instruction by the teacher: 1) instruction on how to locate and use the reference tools effectively; and 2) instruction that builds excitement for using words in a variety of communicative settings. In other words, our end goal is not to teach children to locate words or to play enjoyable word games; we are interested in helping children increase their *performance* vocabularies, the vocabulary used in communication.

REFERENCES

Barrett, M. T., and Graves, M. F. "A Vocabulary Program for Junior High School Remedial Readers." *Journal of Reading* 25 (1981): 146–50.

Dale, E. "Readings That Made a Difference: Serendipities for All." *Journal of Reading* 23 (1980): 586–88.

Drysdale, P. *Words To Use, a Junior Thesaurus*, New York: William H. Sadlier, 1971.

Frank, M. "10-4 for Teachers, Are Your Ears On?" *The Good Apple News*. Carthage, Ill.: Good Apple, Inc., 1976.

Guralnik, D. B., and Friend, J. H., eds. *Webster's New World Dictionary of the American Language*, 5th ed. Cleveland, Ohio: World Publishing, 1966.

Herber, Harold L. *Teaching Reading in Content Areas*, 2nd ed. Englewood Cliffs, N.J.: Prentice-Hall, 1978.

Holt School Dictionary of American English. New York: Holt, Rinehart and Winston, 1981.

Kean, J. M., and Personke, C. *The Language Arts: Teaching and Learning in the Elementary School*. New York: St. Martin's Press, 1976.

Keller, H. *The Story of My Life*. New York: Doubleday, 1954.

Kepper, L. *Creative Approaches to Vocabulary Development within an Individualized Reading Program*. Madison, Wisconsin: The University of Wisconsin, 1977. Unpublished Master's Thesis.

Lansky, Bruce, and Lansky, Vicki. *The Best Baby Name Book in the Whole Wide World*. Newton, Mass: Meadowbrook Press, 1979.

Monroe, M. *My Little Dictionary*. Chicago: Scott, Foresman, 1964.

Morris, W., ed. *American Heritage Dictionary*. Boston: Houghton Mifflin, 1979.

Murray, J. A., ed. *Oxford Dictionary*, 13 vols. London: Oxford University Press, 1923.

Platts, M. E. *A Handbook of Games, Activities, and Ideas for Vocabulary Enrichment*. Stevensville, Mich.: Anchor, 1970.

Roget, P. *St. Martin's Edition of the Original Roget's Thesaurus of English Words and Phrases*. New York: St. Martin's Press, 1965.

Scarry, R. *Storybook Dictionary*. Racine, Wis.: Golden Press, 1966.

Thomas, E. L., and Robinson, H. A. *Improving Reading in Every Class—A Sourcebook for Teachers*, 2nd ed. Boston: Allyn and Bacon, 1977.

Thorndike, E. L., ed. *Thorndike Dictionary*. Chicago: Scott, Foresman, 1935.

Thorndike, E. L., and Barnhart, C. L., eds. *Scott, Foresman Beginning Dictionary*. Garden City, N. Y.: Doubleday, 1976.

Wagner, Rudolph F., and Wagner, Marvey H. *Stories about Family Names*. Portland, Me.: J. Weston Walch, 1961.

6
Developing a Basic Sight Vocabulary

The ability to recognize whole words rapidly and fluently is absolutely essential to a successful reading experience (La Berge and Samuels 1974; Durkin 1978; Kibby 1979; and Ehri and Wilce 1980). Even initial reading instruction ought to include many opportunities for children to interact with whole words put into meaningful written sentences. The purpose of this chapter is to discuss the types of whole words children need to learn and to recommend effective techniques for teaching these words.

Whole words that can be recognized and pronounced instantaneously by a reader, without any mediated decoding processes (see Chap. Seven), are termed *sight words*. Sight words or *sight vocabulary* refers to the ever-expanding pool of words a reader recognizes when they are encountered within context or in isolation. These words have been stored in a visual memory bank and can be recognized easily. Upon entering school most children can read very few words (*Sesame Street*, *Pepsi*, *McDonald's*, etc.) even though they use and understand thousands of words in spoken language. Most of you, on the other hand, can fluently and rapidly read tens of thousands of different words. For the most part, you have acquired this massive sight vocabulary by frequent exposure to words.

Which words should teachers help children record in their sight vocabulary banks? There are at least three categories of basic sight words we feel children should commit to memory. They include: 1) high-frequency words, 2) self-selected/key vocabulary words, and 3) selection/critical words.

High-frequency words are among the most important basic sight words a child must learn (Fry 1980; Hayden 1981). This first category encompasses a relatively small corpus of words that occur so often in printed material they are essential to fluent reading, especially in the beginning stages. Many sight words are neither meaningful nor picturable and are, thus, uninteresting to children. Yet, they are important function words (Cunningham 1980). Children have to learn to recognize high-frequency sight words instantly. A reader who stumbles over words in this category (or relies on phonics or other word-identification skills) will have a great deal of trouble comprehending written material.

We also favor the practice of helping children learn to read words drawn from their own speaking vocabularies. *Self-selected*, or *key*, *words* are filled with meaning, whereas many of the high-frequency words we have just discussed are devoid of meaning. Engage a child in conversation about a favorite book and you might gather a set of words such as *Peter Rabbit, Flopsy, Mopsy, Cotton-tail, garden, sad,* and *frightened.* These words will be highly interesting and quite meaningful to the young learner. They will be learned easily, with techniques we will describe in this chapter.

The third category of basic words you will teach children to read are those words found in the basal reader and other textbooks used in your classroom. These words parallel the *selection/critical* vocabulary we introduced in Chapter One. As you will recall, selection/critical words are those words that carry meaning in any particular selection. At the beginning reading level, a sentence like *Billy has a red wagon* contains two vocabulary words (*Billy* and *wagon*) that are central to the meaning of the selection. At a more advanced level you will find an increasing number of specific meaningful vocabulary items children need to learn to read in order to comprehend their assignments.

Children need to learn to read whole words early in the reading program. That is not to say we discourage the teaching of phonics or other mediated word-identification skills. A child's sight vocabulary, in fact, forms a basis for teaching mediated word-identification skills in a meaningful fashion. (A discussion of those essential word-identification skills will be presented in Chap. Seven.) Given an early exposure to sight words selected from the three categories we have just introduced, children can begin reading complete sentences from the outset of instruction. We will demonstrate how these early sight word lessons might be developed so that children view reading as a communication process rather than a task of mastering isolated skills. Remaining true to our original intent, these lessons are based on the principle of language as a total experience and emphasize direct instruction.

DEVELOPING PRINT AWARENESS

Children cannot benefit from instruction in sight vocabulary (or any other skill in reading) until they have discovered some of the essential relationships between their oral language and the printed language. A number of research studies have examined what youngsters do know about reading (Meltzer and Herse 1969; Read 1971; Calfee et al. 1972; Ehri 1975; Richeck 1977; Mason 1980; Hiebert 1981). A review of the literature reveals the fact that some youngsters are unaware of the process we call reading. They do not recognize that a reader gets information from a page of print (Hiebert 1981). Children may not even understand what a word is or that language sounds can be represented by graphemes (Downing and Oliver 1973–74; Clay 1979; Ehri 1979). Children need to gain some idea of the nature of a "word" in language before we proceed with instruction in reading. They should be able to think about language as an object, as something that can be studied, and be cognizant of the fact that the flow of oral language can be segmented into words.

Downing (1979) claims that some children are in a state of "cognitive confusion" when they enter school. They are unable to benefit from early instructional attempts because they do not understand the function of print nor have they discovered the "code" of our writing system. Teachers can help children develop the essential concepts of literacy, or "code-consciousness" before formal reading instruction begins (Templeton 1980; Mass 1982; Agnew 1982). We suggest that you examine several of the references on print awareness cited in this section.

Youngsters can learn concepts of print from meaningful exposures to reading. Environmental situations and concrete learning tasks might form the basis of lessons designed to foster code-consciousness in youngsters. You might wish to implement the following techniques.

1. Read books to young children on a regular basis. The following read-aloud activities are designed to actively involve the child in discovering printed language.

a. Discuss the "title of each book and its author/illustrator while pointing to words on the book's cover. Ask the child to point to and "read" the name of the book. Place three or four books by the same author on a table. Show the child that the author's *name* appears on each cover — that the *words* and *letters* are the same on each book.

b. Use alphabet and number books to help the child discover that symbols have names and can be identified by that name. (Some children will intuitively gain early phonics information from these lessons designed to simply build print awareness.)

c. Read books with repeated sentence patterns as often as you can. Children learn that book language is predictable. They can memorize the book language and will often "read" pages effortlessly. On occasion, sweep your finger along the lines of print to develop the idea of directionality in print.

d. Read books that are rich in vocabulary and varied in syntactic form. These books will, among other things, help children recognize that "book language" is more formal than speech — an important aspect of print awareness.

2. The child's everyday environment can be used to develop code-consciousness by labeling children's things (cubbies, paintings, etc.).

a. Gather objects and pictures that are likely to be recognized by youngsters (a McDonald's cup, Sesame Street shirt, Atari advertisement, milk carton, etc.). Give children a chance to "read" the *words* and name any *letters*. Ask them to tell something about one of the items/words. Print the *sentence* on a chart:

> Matt likes to eat at *McDonald's.*
> Susie's brother got an *Atari* for his birthday.

Talk about the *words, letters,* and *sentences* recorded on the board without requiring children to read the script unless they request the opportunity. Using the language of instruction while you are creating written sentences will help the children gain an understanding of these often confusing terms. Point out words that "begin" the same way (*basket,* birthday; *Matt, McDonald's*) and "end" the same way (*Matt, eat, at, got*). Point out "short words" *(an, at, to)* and "long words" *(brother, birthday, McDonald's).* Take advantage of every available cue that might encourage the children's developing awareness of print.

b. Ask children to help you equip a classroom grocery store with a set of commonly used packaged-good items (Jell-O, Morton's salt, Campbell's soup, Cheerios, butter, etc.). Print up a set of word cards corresponding to each item. Children "shop" for items on the grocery shelf by 1) matching the printed word card to the actual object; 2) reading the word card to a storekeeper, who locates the correct object; 3) printing a list of needed grocery items and reading the list or handing the list to the storekeeper. The activity can be expanded to a sentence-awareness activity (oral or written) by using the cloze technique. Print *I want to buy some* _____. on a sentence strip card. The student shopper "says" or "reads" the card and completes the sentence with any item on the store's shelf or with any word card representing the food items.

3. Lessons can also be designed to raise children's metalinguistic awareness.

a. Oral cloze sentences can be developed and used in game-type situations. Children complete the sentences using any word they wish. Put a cloze sentence on the board: *I wish I could eat* _____. Print each child's word choice on a card as the word is given. By this procedure children are shown, for example, that oral language can be segmented into individual words, that words can be recorded in print, that letters are used to write words, and that words are printed from left to right. The possibilities for linguistic discovery are limitless when meaningful, nonthreatening lessons are designed.

b. Letter/word naming, letter/word matching, letter/word printing games also help increase children's awareness of print. The words used in discussion and demonstration of game directions are frequently as valuable to alleviating a child's cognitive confusion as are the games themselves.

The above activities represent just a few ways you can help youngsters discover the mysteries of printed language. Repeated exposures to print in natural, meaningful settings offer children valuable opportunities to learn about the nature and structure of our writing system. All of our suggested activities have sought to surround the child with print — to encourage learning without placing any demands or pressures on children or fostering competition of any type. Code-consciousness develops gradually. For many children, these activities will simply bring to awareness concepts of print that have been developing subconsciously throughout the preschool years. We believe that informal activities such as these will serve as excellent precursors to the reading-skill-development lessons children inevitably face as formal reading instruction begins.

BASIC VOCABULARY FOR BEGINNING READING

High-Frequency Sight Words

There has been a long history of attempts to form word lists of words that are important to learners, as evidenced by the more than three thousand entries in the bibliography of *Vocabulary Studies* (Dale 1965). Basic word lists have been constructed for a number of purposes and have derived from a variety of sources. Word lists have been compiled from sources such as the speech of young children, school essays and themes, language of bilingual adults, comic book words, computer analyses, award-winning children's literature, college profanity, and phonic regularity. But most word lists have been constructed on some basis of frequency of occurrence.

Johnson's Basic Vocabulary for Beginning Reading

Johnson's basic vocabulary of sight words was developed on the basis of a given word's high frequency in children's spoken language and high frequency of appearance in general printed English.

The basic vocabulary includes words from two sources — the spontaneous speaking vocabulary of children in kindergarten and first grade and from a compilation of 500 frequently used words occurring in printed English. Many of the words selected occur in materials commonly used in beginning reading instruction. A few of the words do not occur in these materials, but probably should if one's goal is to expose children to words that young readers often say or hear.

Words that had a high frequency on one of the lists, but were not high on both under the criteria established, were not included. For example, such words as *state* and *during* have a high frequency in printed English but occur very infrequently in the oral English of young children. Conversely, words such as *apple* and *bathroom* are often used by children but occur infrequently in print. Thus words such as these were not included in Johnson's list.

A total of 306 words met both criteria: 276 of the words had been used at least 50 times by the kindergarten children, and the remaining 30 had been used at least 50 times by the first-grade children.

Several pilot studies and field investigations were conducted with the basic vocabulary. The earliest study used a flash-card approach to test children's knowledge of the words, and the second test equated flash-card performance with group test performance. Studies with 225 first- and second-grade children have shown a correlation range of .86 to .91 between performance on the group tests and on an individual flash-card test.

Two forms of the group test were then validated, based on a sample of nearly one thousand first- and second-grade children from all socioeconomic groups who were taught with a wide variety of reading programs. Based on this study, the word list was divided into two grade levels according to the percentage of children who correctly recognized the words. The 180 first-grade words were known by at least 70 percent of the first-grade subjects. The remaining 126 words were known by a minimum of 65 percent of the second-grade subjects.

Table 2 contains an alphabetical listing of the 180 first-grade words and Table 3 lists the 126 second-grade words (see pages 94 and 95).

Unlike many word lists, which stem directly from basal series, these words were selected on the basis of oral usage and printed frequency, rather than because of their occurrence in basal readers. We would much rather see basal

TABLE 2
Johnson's First-Grade Words

a	day	I	off	table
above	days	if	old	than
across	did	I'm	one	that
after	didn't	in	open	the
again	do	into	or	then
air	don't	is	out	there
all	door	it	over	these
am	down	its		they
American		it's	past	think
and	end		play	this
are		just	point	those
art	feet		put	three
as	find	keep		time
ask	first	kind	really	to
at	five		red	today
	for	let	right	too
back	four	like	room	took
be		little	run	top
before	gave	look		two
behind	get	love	said	
big	girl		saw	under
black	give	make	school	up
book	go	making	see	
boy	God	man	seen	very
but	going	may	she	
	gone	me	short	want
came	good	men	six	wanted
can	got	miss	so	was
car		money	some	way
children	had	more	something	we
come	hand	most	soon	well
could	hard	mother	still	went
	has	Mr.		what
	have	must		when
	he	my		where
	help			which
	her	name		who
	here	never		why
	high	new		will
	him	night		with
	his	no		work
	home	not		
	house	now		year
	how			years
				yet
				you
				your

TABLE 3				
Johnson's Second-Grade Words				
able	different	last	real	water
about	does	leave	road	were
almost	done	left		west
alone		light		while
already	each	long	same	whole
always	early		say	whose
America	enough	made	says	wife
an	even	many	set	women
another	ever	mean	should	world
any	every	might	show	would
around	eyes	morning	small	
away		Mrs.	sometimes	
	face	much	sound	
because	far	music	started	
been	feel		street	
believe	found	need	sure	
best	from	next		
better	front	nothing	take	
between	full	number	tell	
board			their	
both	great	of	them	
bought	group	office	thing	
by		on	things	
	hands	only	thought	
called	having	other	through	
change	head	our	together	
church	heard	outside	told	
city		own	town	
close	idea		turn	
company		part	until	
cut	knew	party	us	
	know	people	use	
		place	used	
		plan		
		present		

readers utilize words common to oral and printed English rather than the opposite approach, which seems to us to be a cart-before-the-horse way of thinking. Nonetheless, five widely used basal reading series were analyzed to determine the occurrence of the words in their first- and second-grade materials. This analysis showed that 99 percent of the Johnson words occurred in at least one of the series, but 93 percent of the first-grade words and 87 percent of the second-grade words occurred in *all five series*. Thus teachers who use basal readers can feel confident that these sight words are likely to occur in their program.

Words with More than One Meaning

There is a basic problem with most sight-word lists based on frequency tabulations, and that is with words having more than one meaning. Johnson (1974, p. 61) noted this: "Too many sight word lists contain only the printed word without a description of its function or meaning. Obviously, lists would be improved if the high-frequency meaning were indicated where appropriate." Hunter (1975, p. 253) made the same point: "Finally, this writer found that word lists do not account for the meanings of words used in context. This writer believes that, in the future, more attention to semantics must be given if one is to accurately compare and interpret the word lists compiled from either spoken or written vocabulary."

Many sight-vocabulary lists contain such words as *well*, *part*, *saw*, and *back*. But because the lists are based on word counts rather than word meanings, the users of such lists are not sure which meaning is intended. In other words, many multimeaning words probably would not be found on sight-word lists in the first place, if they were single-meaning words. For example, a word like *back* would probably appear on a sight-word list due to the accumulated frequency of its occurrence across such diverse meanings as those exemplified in the following sentences, rather than because one of the meanings was of considerably high frequency:

> She has a strong *back*.
> They went in *back* of the school.
> Which candidate will you *back*?
> When will she come *back*?
> Have you learned to *back* the car out of the garage?

In a recent examination of 9000 words of high frequency for elementary school children, Johnson, Moe, and Baumann (1983) found that 72 percent of them (6530 words) are multimeaning.

Balch (1976) analyzed six sight-word lists. She alphabetized each list and checked each word in the *Webster's New Collegiate Dictionary* to determine whether it represented more than one meaning. Words were counted as multimeaning if the dictionary included more than one specific denotative definition. Table 4 indicates the word lists she examined, the total number of words on each list, and the number and percent of multimeaning words on each list.

We can see from Table 4 that the percentage of multimeaning words ranged from 23 percent on Durr's and Johnson's lists to 42 percent on Moe's and Otto-Chester's lists. These percentages are sufficiently high to cause a good deal of confusion to teachers who use the lists. Which meanings are they to teach?

Table 5 lists the 71 multimeaning words found in the basic vocabulary presented in this chapter. Some of the words clearly have a primary meaning and a more obscure secondary meaning (*American*, *boy*, *office*, *will*). Others, though, have more than one highly frequent meaning (*left*, *change*, *cut*, *kind*, *like*, *over*,

TABLE 4
Percent of Multimeaning Words in Each of Six Lists

Word List	Total Words	Multimeaning Words	Percent of Total
1. Dolch Basic Sight Vocabulary (1936)	220	57	26
2. Durr: 188 Words of More than 88 Frequencies (1973)	188	44	23
3. Harris-Jacobson (1972)	333	135	40
4. Johnson: A Basic Vocabulary for Beginning Readers (1971)	306	71	23
5. Moe: 200 Words of Highest Frequency (1973)	200	88	42
6. Otto-Chester: Great Atlantic and Pacific Sight Word List (1972)	500	209	42

TABLE 5
Johnson: A Basic Vocabulary for Beginning Reading
Multimeaning Words (71 out of 306 = 23 Percent)

1. about	19. end	37. like	55. put
2. air	20. even	38. long	56. red
3. America	21. five	39. love	57. right
4. American	22. feet	40. may	58. room
5. art	23. found	41. mean	59. saw
6. back	24. front	42. might	60. school
7. board	25. go	43. miss	61. set
8. book	26. hand	44. number	62. show
9. boy	27. hands	45. off	63. sound
10. by	28. hard	46. office	64. still
11. called	29. head	47. open	65. table
12. can	30. home	48. over	66. top
13. car	31. house	49. part	67. turn
14. change	32. just	50. party	68. way
15. close	33. kink	51. place	69. well
16. company	34. last	52. play	70. while
17. cut	35. left	53. point	71. will
18. down	36. light	54. present	

turn). We recommend that teachers use written and oral contexts to present the variant meanings felt to be appropriate for the children being instructed. For example, probably all first graders should be taught the two major meanings of *may*, but few first graders need to get into the fine points of parliamentary procedure to learn how to *table* a motion.

Children at even the earliest stages of reading need to learn that many words have more than one meaning. Since about one- to two-fifths of the basic sight words they will be taught (depending on the list a teacher uses) are multimeaning, great care must be taken to teach those meanings. If that is done, children's vocabularies ought to expand accordingly, and it follows that they will begin to develop a "set for diversity" with regard to word meanings.

Self-Selected/Key Vocabulary

Self-selected words represent another category of basic sight vocabulary we think teachers should help readers develop. These "key" vocabulary items are most often taught as a means of introducing children to reading but have also been used in remedial reading. Key vocabulary items are drawn from a child's oral language. Learning to read these words is not difficult for most children because they have been involved in the selection process and have chosen words that carry a high personal interest value. As Geoffrion (1982, p. 665) has stated: "Successful reading and language instruction must be derived from the child's experiences and knowledge about the world."

Key vocabulary differs from the high-frequency vocabulary introduced in the previous section in one important way — each key word children select will be a "content" word or meaning-carrying language unit. Given an opportunity to prepare a batch of homemade fudge, a group of five-year-old children may select words like *fudge, chocolate, sugar, creamy, boil, delicious,* and *silky* as their key words. Asked to list favorite words, individuals may list *skateboard, cotton candy, Honda, dirt bike,* or *Spiderman*. A quest for the tastiest flavors of ice cream could yield *butter pecan, mint-chocolate chip, spumoni,* or *licorice*. Words like *it, to, the, with,* and *come* are never selected as key words.

What is the value of eliciting these random words and helping children commit them to memory? Key vocabulary words provide a bridge between what children know about oral language and what we must teach them about written language. As sight-word banks grow there are limitless opportunities to introduce children to "real" reading. Key words, combined with high-frequency function words, can be used to create sentences children can read almost immediately. For example, examine on the following page the brief lists of words Beth, Amy, and Eric have been learning early in their reading program.

As soon as a few words have been learned by children, small groups can work together to create and read sentences such as:

1. Beth likes chocolate ice cream.
2. Amy likes vanilla ice cream.
3. Eric likes peach ice cream.

Children will read their own sentences and even those created by classmates since

Children's Names	High-Frequency Words All Are Learning	Recently Gathered Key Vocabulary per Child
Beth	the, can, see, likes, is, want, eat, and	ice cream, fudge, chocolate, cotton candy
Amy		ice cream, vanilla, delicious, roller skates
Eric		ice cream, peach, Honda, creamy

the frames are so similar. As the children continue to work together, sentences like the following might emerge:

1. Can Beth eat the chocolate candy?
2. Amy and Eric want vanilla and peach ice cream.
3. Is vanilla ice cream delicious, Amy?
4. Eat the creamy peach ice cream, Eric!
5. Beth likes the roller skates, Amy.

Practice with the key and high-frequency vocabulary advances children's reading quite rapidly.

Key vocabulary development serves several purposes:

1. Whole words are introduced early in the child's reading program and put into meaningful sentences; therefore, from the beginning, reading instruction makes sense to children. Opportunities to write sentences incorporating key words, high-frequency sight words, and words children spell out using their own "invented" orthography have been shown to promote reading development (Chomsky 1979; Lancaster et al. 1982).

2. Print awareness, or code-consciousness, is developed for some children as the teacher uses instructional jargon (*letter, word, sentence, first word, beginning sound*, etc.) while printing words, sentences, and short paragraphs. Children have additional opportunities to rediscover the code of written language, its function, *and* features.

3. Some of the essential, though meaningless, structure words from the high-frequency vocabulary list are practiced in natural sentence patterns. Children aren't likely to segment these functional words (markers, connectives, prepositions) from content words in the speech flow (Blachowicz 1978). Continual exposure to function words in whole sentences will help children understand their function and will help secure a permanent place for them in visual memory.

Words children choose to learn to read will not just be magically deposited in a visual memory bank. Like the high-frequency words or any other category of words, key vocabulary items must be taught and reinforced. The following procedures will help your children learn and retain key words.

1. MOTIVATE children prior to word selection. An object, film, book, or discussion might be used to stimulate the children's thinking.

2. ELICIT meaningful words with direct probes: "Jill, which flavor of ice cream would you like me to print on your card this morning?"

3. PRINT words on personal word cards, noting as many unique features as possible: name the letters, indicate the beginning of the word, the ending of the word, double letters, etc.

4. READ the word, put it on a list on the chalkboard or chart, and have the child read it.

5. PRACTICE using the word in oral and written sentences. Teachers and children should all be involved in creating sentences for practice. Plan many activities in which children write words they have selected for their key vocabulary. Encourage them to print sentences using invented spellings to supplement known high-frequency and key words as they create sentences.

6. REVIEW words as often as possible, using any appropriate sight-vocabulary games or activities (see activities at the end of this chapter).

a. File key vocabulary words in a personal word bank. A bank may consist of a piece of yarn to hold "keys," a metal file bank, or a sturdy plastic container. Some teachers require that key words be filed alphabetically as a means of building predictionary and phonics skills.

b. Have children practice key words frequently. Group exercises can be planned for brief gaps that occur in any school day—the few moments before recess or lunch, for example. Ask children to place all words from their word banks on the desk tops. Each child holds up personal word cards as the teacher quickly calls out categories: "words that begin with s," "word for a color," "word that names a person," "word that names something to eat," etc.

c. Early creative writing activities can be initiated. Put a cloze sentence on the chalkboard. Hold a contest where you ask children to write as many different sentences as possible by using words from their personal banks to complete the sentence.

> Examples:
> I can _____ and _____.
> I like to _____.
> My favorite food is _____.

Illustrations can be added if time allows. As you will note, high-frequency words are again practiced along with key vocabulary.

Teachers who wish to learn more about teaching reading through using key vocabulary techniques should consult these excellent reference materials:

> Nessel, Denise D., and Margaret B. Jones. *The Language-Experience Approach To Reading: A Handbook for Teachers.* New York: Teachers College Press, 1981.

Stauffer, Russell G. *The Language-Experience Approach to the Teaching of Reading.* New York: Harper and Row, 1980.

Van Allen, Roach, and Claryce Van Allen. *Language Experience Activities.* Boston: Houghton Mifflin Company, 1982.

Van Allen, Roach. *Language Experiences in Communication.* Boston: Houghton Mifflin Company, 1976.

Veatch, Jeanette, et al. *Key Words to Reading: The Language Experience Approach Begins.* Columbus, Ohio: Charles E. Merrill, 1973.

Selection/Critical Words

Progress in reading could not occur if children were simply taught and drilled on high-frequency words accompanied by key vocabulary. They must receive instruction that prepares them to read library books, textbooks, magazines, newspapers, and other print in their environment. Printed language contains innumerable words children will need to commit to memory to become fluent readers. Basal readers feature regular vocabulary lessons. Words children must learn are identified, and teaching techniques are suggested. Most authors of instructional materials designed for content-area teaching also identify specialized vocabulary. Most of these latter materials, however, do not offer ideas on vocabulary learning. News magazines, articles, or library books used for classroom instruction do not often highlight words children need to learn to read; teachers need to examine these resources carefully to determine words needing special attention. Direct instruction of vocabulary must be given if children are going to learn words from basal readers, content textbooks, or ancillary classroom materials.

TEACHING A SIGHT VOCABULARY

Five-Step Teaching Plan

We advocate a five-step teaching plan that can be adapted to teaching words from each of the three groups of sight words we have identified. Students of any age level will benefit from lessons based on this plan. Note once again that we emphasize direct teaching and total language involvement throughout the five steps.

1. Seeing. The word is written on the chalkboard, a flash card, or a piece of paper and *spoken in an oral context*. With appropriate words *(book, table, chair)* we recommend labeling the objects themselves in the classroom. With other words *(children, party, house)* we recommend labeling a picture that exemplifies the word. However, many basic sight words are not picturable, and with them the following steps become very important.

2. Discussing. After the word has been written, it should be read aloud by the teacher and by the children. Some words lend themselves to short discussions related to the children's environment, experiences, and interests. But, again, many basic sight words do not lend themselves to interesting discussions, and the next step is highly useful.

3. Using. Children are next asked to use the word in a sentence or two or to suggest synonymous words or phrases. Remember, most basic sight words are already in the speaking/listening vocabularies of young children, even though they cannot yet read them. Since many basic sight words *(the, of, which)* cannot really be discussed, it is important they be used and reused in sentences by the children so that they clearly see the function and purpose of the words. As much as possible the sentences they generate ought to be written on the board and compared, to help them see the roles played by such words as *and, then,* and *with.*

4. Defining. Providing a definition of a word is often much harder for a child (or an adult for that matter) than providing a synonym or using the word in a sentence. Again, many basic sight words are not easily definable *(have, it, let).* But whenever possible, children should be led from using to defining — in their own words, not those of a dictionary, "What does this word mean to you?"

5. Writing. Finally, the children should be encouraged to practice writing the words, both alone and in various contexts; for writing a word reinforces learning the word. Many teachers have their pupils keep word books or personal dictionaries in which they write new words, their meanings or synonyms, and sample sentences containing the new words.

To reinforce and review sight vocabulary, the use of games, worksheets, and *a good deal of silent and oral reading should be used.*

Multimeaning Activities

We have pointed out that many words have more than one meaning. Many children find it enjoyable to learn the different meanings of some of the basic sight words presented in Table 5 as well as many other new words they will be taught. Activities such as the following can provide practice with these "oddities."

1. Double Trouble. Draw pictures to illustrate the double meaning of at least five of these words.

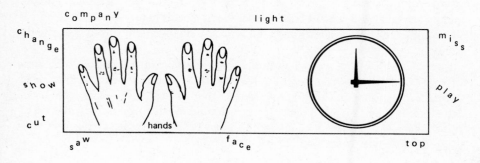

2. Use *back* in as many different ways as possible. Write a sentence illustrating each.

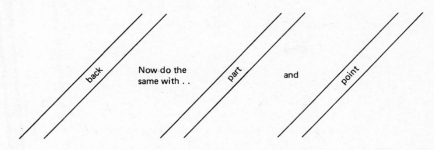

3. How many meanings can you think of for these words?

air   feet   may
can   hard   open
end   kind   red

How many of them can you use in a story?

Vocabulary Games

Many teachers use instructional games to reinforce the learning of new sight words. Hundreds of games are available from commercial publishers, but many games can be quickly and inexpensively made in the classroom. We prefer games made up by teachers or pupils to commercial games because they can be made more relevant to the instructional needs, experiences, and interests of the children in the class.

A great many of these instructional games are simply modifications of other popular children's games. Virtually any word can be taught or reinforced with practically any children's game. *We urge teachers to construct games that can be reused* or changed slightly to achieve different purposes. Board games, for example, take some time and effort to make, so it is desirable to create them in such a way that they may teach different words at different times. A typical game designed to reinforce learning of basic sight words might look like the one on page 104.

This game, Speedway, requires two players. Draw a large oval racetrack with a start and finish line. The racetrack is divided into sections with printed drill words in them. The players' toy cars are placed at the track's starting line. The two players each have a deck of word cards that match the words on the racetrack. The players shuffle their cards well and place the deck face up in front of themselves. The first player reads the top card on the deck. The toy car may be moved up if the word read is the same as the word in the first space of the track; otherwise, the player cannot move and the other player gets a turn. The first player to go around the track to the finish line wins the game.

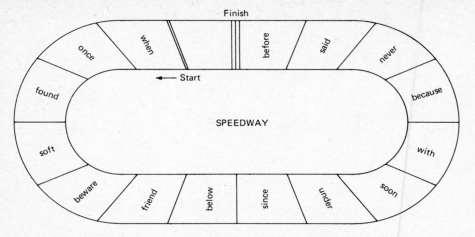

The point is this: the game board could easily be reused for other purposes. Small cards could be made to fit the board spaces, and each set of cards could be used over and over again for different purposes. One set of cards might contain other sight words, or perhaps phonics patterns (see Chap. Seven) you wish to work on.

There are many types of games that lend themselves to vocabulary instruction. The major types of games are described next. You are urged to choose the types of games of most interest to your pupils and to use the games to teach or reinforce all kinds of new words.

Track Games

Track games are designed in the tradition of such popular children's games as Candy Land, Horse Race, Chutes and Ladders, Monopoly. The game Speedway (described above) is an example of a track game. In all such games players begin at a starting point, proceed along a track by demonstrating certain word knowledge, and try to reach a goal to win the game. Small spinners or dice usually determine the number of spaces moved. Each space contains instructions or key words. Track games are based both on chance (the number of spaces moved) and competition (the ability to correctly complete the tasks). Listed below are the names of several track games whose titles will suggest to you the variety of themes that can be adapted according to interests, important topics, seasons, or events. Remember, virtually all track games lend themselves to vocabulary development.

Escape from Haunted Forest	Busy City
Turtle Race	Building a House
Hurdles	Going to the Zoo
Win the Election	Be My Valentine
Jumping Fences	Ski and Skate
Buried Treasure	Tunnel Race

Easter Egg Hunt
Stock Car Game
Make a Date
Through the Zoo
Trim the Tree

Home at Last
Crossing Bridges
Firecrackers
Pop the Balloons
Baking Cookies

We encourage you to be as artistic and creative as possible when making games, and to involve your pupils in game construction. Not all of us are skillful artists, but by clipping pictures from magazines or tracing objects, it is quite possible to "dress up" games so that they are appealing to children.

Board Games

Most track games utilize game boards, and there are several other types of board games as well. Popular board games that can be modified for instructional purposes include Clue, Bingo, The Game of Happiness, Football, and Baseball. The variety of board games is as infinite as your imagination (or the shelves of the local toy store) and as with track games, they can be used to teach and review new words.

Possible titles for board games include:

Treasure Hunt
Word Baseball
Vocabulary Checkers
Blend Backgammon
Crossword Puzzle
Word Football
Alphabet Detective

Word Bingo
Matchmaker
Cat and Rat (Tic-Tac-Toe)
Spin a Sound
Masterpiece
Picture Puzzle
Tiddly Winks

The design and complexity of board games can be as great or as simple as you wish to make them. Below is an illustration of a very simple football game intended to reinforce learning of sight words.

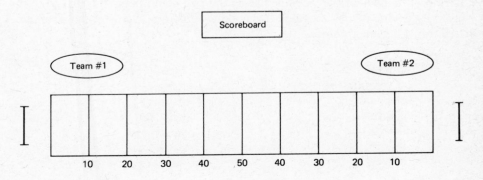

WORD FOOTBALL

This game can be played by two players or two teams. Its object is to score touchdowns and extra points. Each team has a pile of cards shaped like footballs. On each football is written a sight word. Kickoff begins with the flip of a coin. The receiving team chooses a card and says and defines or uses the word. If correct, the team advances ten yards and selects another card. If incorrect, the team does not move and the other team has the ball. Touchdowns are scored when a team moves the length of the field. Extra points are added by using the "scoring" word in an additional sentence. For older children, the game can be modified to allow for defensive as well as offensive strategies.

Feed-Through Games

Feed-through games consist of a large object cut out of poster paper or painted on tagboard with an opening through which can be fed a slip containing the desired words or patterns. For example:

In this case, the object is a large colorful frog. The strip is the frog's tongue. As the child pulls the tongue from the mouth, the words are read. The child's teacher (aide, classmate, or friend) continues to feed the "tongue" through as the words are read correctly. Very young children (through about age seven) thoroughly enjoy feed-through games as a way of practicing words and patterns they have been taught. In the example above, the frog could be used over and over again by having many "tongues" listing other important words. Other ideas for feed-through games include:

Object	Feed-Through Strip
any animal	tongue
elephant	trunk
giraffe	head and neck
flower	stem
train	flatbed car
beaver	tail

Object	Feed-through Strip
sandwich	ingredients
duck	beak
dachshund	body
horn of plenty	ingredients
piggy bank	coins
pitcher	juice

The best use of feed-through games is to help the child review words or patterns already learned.

Other Games

There are many other kinds of games that can be easily adapted to teach or reinforce vocabulary: card games such as Checkers, Old Maid, Rummy, Crazy Eights, and Go Fish; television show games such as Concentration, Hollywood Squares, 25,000 Dollar Pyramid and High Rollers; physical activity games like Fish Pond, Hop Scotch, Twister, Simon Says, Musical Chairs, and Pin-the-Tail-on-the-Donkey; and other children's favorites such as Dominoes, Racko, and Scrabble can be adapted to vocabulary instruction.

Direct instruction such as the use of the five-step approach described earlier, and activity sheets and games can be helpful in teaching and reviewing sight vocabulary. We believe, though, that *nothing is a replacement for reading*. Children need to read and reread the words in meaningful contexts if the words are truly to be incorporated in their sight vocabularies. Just as no skill has any intrinsic value unless applied, extremely few words have any value in isolation. We encourage teachers, through the use of books, magazines, and experience stories, to provide abundant opportunities for their pupils to read the new words they are learning.

Visual Memory Activities

Some children are helped to learn basic sight words through practice with visual memory activities. The following exercises can be used to provide practice with the visual appearances and memorization of these key words.

1. Direct Copying. The pupils are presented with lists of sight words (usually done on ditto or spirit masters) with the complete word on the top, followed by the same word with letters omitted. The task is simply to copy the missing letters to complete the word:

though	morning
th_ _ _h	m_ _ _ _ _g
_ _ _ugh	mor_ _ _ _
_ _ou_ _	_ _ _ _ing
_ _ _ _ _ _	_ _ _n_ _ _

2. Word Searches. The pupils look at the word at the left of the page and then circle the letters in the correct order to spell the word:

though   x y l f (t) r x f (h) l c (o)(u) n p h a i f (g) t (h)

A variation of the word search is to have the pupils circle all instances of the word at the left:

though   thrxh(though) yrsf(though)ty   kroughy(though) nthro(though)

3. Rapid Recognition. In this activity the teacher rapidly goes through a set of flash cards containing several "look-alike" words as well as the target word *(though, through, rough, thought).* Each time the child sees the target word he or she responds by saying the word.

A FINAL WORD

A large sight vocabulary is essential for fluent reading. Helping children build a vast sight vocabulary may seem like a tremendously challenging feat — it is. It demands a *great deal* of talented teaching, or as the White Queen in Lewis Carroll's *Through the Looking Glass* would say: "It takes all the running you can do, to keep in the same place. If you want to get somewhere else, you must run at least twice as fast as that" (1979).

Certain words appear so frequently in print that they are essential for beginning reading development. They are worthy of intense direct instruction in the early grades and with older children who do not read well. We believe that Johnson's basic sight vocabulary (Tables 2 and 3) represents a good corpus of basic sight words children ought to know. Key vocabulary items, personally selected by children, form another set of words that will be valuable as reading instruction progresses. Selection/critical words represent the third group of words children must commit to visual memory.

In this chapter we have provided techniques to help you teach sight vocabulary. Direct teaching of whole words in meaning-based lessons was emphasized throughout. Many active, child-involvement games were suggested as ways to review and reinforce sight vocabulary. Active involvement seems to help children retain words (Dickerson 1982).

In the next chapter we will move beyond basic sight-word instruction and into the mediated word-identification skills. Children must master both *mediated* and *nonmediated* word-identification skills in order to become good readers.

REFERENCES

Agnew, A. T. "Using Children's Dictated Stories to Assess Code Consciousness." *The Reading Teacher* 35 (1982): 450–54.

Balch, M. C. *A Problem with Sight Vocabulary Lists: Multi-Meaning Words.* Madison, Wisc.: University of Wisconsin, 1976. Unpublished Master's Thesis.

Blachowicz, C. Z. "Metalinguistic Awareness and the Beginning Reader." *The Reading Teacher* 31 (1978): 875–82.

Calfee, R.; Venezky, R.; and Chapman, R. "How a Child Needs to Think to Learn to Read." In *Cognition in Learning and Memory*, edited by L. Gregg. New York: John Wiley and Sons, 1972.

Carroll, L. *Through the Looking Glass—Illustrations*. Rev. ed. Edited by G. Ovenden. New York: St. Martin's Press, 1979.

Chomsky, C. "Approaching Reading through Invented Spelling." In *Theory and Practice of Early Reading*, Vol. 2, edited by L. B. Resnick and P. A. Weaver. Hillsdale, N.J.: Lawrence Erlbaum, 1979.

Clay, Marie, *Reading: The Patterning of Complex Behaviour*. Auckland, New Zealand: Heineman Educational Books, 1979.

Cunningham, P. M. "Teaching *Were, With, What,* and Other Four-Letter Words." *The Reading Teacher* 34 (1980): 160–63.

Dale, E., *Bibliography of Vocabulary Studies*, 5th ed. Columbus, Ohio: Ohio State University, 1965.

Dickerson, D. P. "A Study of Use of Games to Reinforce Sight Vocabulary." *The Reading Teacher* 36 (1982): 46–49.

Dolch, E. W. "A Basic Sight Vocabulary." *Elementary School Journal* 36 (1936): 456–460.

Downing, J. *Reading and Reasoning*. New York: Springer-Verlag, 1979.

Downing, J., and Oliver, P. "The Child's Conception of a Word." *Reading Research Quarterly* 9 (1973–74): 568–82.

Durkin, D. *Teaching Them to Read*. Boston, Mass.: Allyn and Bacon, 1978.

Durr, W. K. "Computer Study of High Frequency Words in Popular Trade Juveniles." *The Reading Teacher* 27 (1973): 37–42.

Ehri, L. "Word Consciousness in Readers and Pre-readers." *Journal of Educational Psychology* 67 (1975): 204–12.

Ehri, L. C. "Linguistic Insight: Threshold of Reading Acquisition." In *Reading Research: Advances in Theory and Practice*. Vol. 1, edited by T. G. Waller, and G. E. Mackinnon. New York: Academic Press, 1979.

Ehri, L. C., and Wilce, L. S. "Do Beginners Learn to Read Function Words Better in Sentences or in Lists?" *Reading Research Quarterly* 15 (1980): 451–76.

Fry, E. "The New Instant Word List." *The Reading Teacher* 34 (1980): 281–89.

Geoffrion, L. D. "Reading and the Nonvocal Child." *The Reading Teacher* 35 (1982): 662–69.

Harris, A. J., and Jacobsen, M. C. *Basic Elementary Reading Vocabularies*. New York: MacMillan, 1972.

Hayden, B. J., Jr. "Teaching Basic Function Words" *The Reading Teacher* 35 (1981): 136–40.

Hiebert, E. H. "Developmental Patterns and Interrelationships of Preschool Children's Print Awareness." *Reading Research Quarterly* 16 (1981): 236–60.

Hunter, D. L., "Spoken and Written Word Lists: A Comparison." *The Reading Teacher* 29 (1975): 250–53.

Johnson, D. D. "A Basic Vocabulary for Beginning Reading." *Elementary School Journal* 72 (1971): 29–34.

———. "Word Lists That Make Sense—and Those That Don't." *Learning Magazine* 4 (1974): 60–61.

———, Moe, A., and Baumann, J. *The Ginn Wordbook for Teachers: A Basic Lexicon*. Lexington, Mass.: Ginn and Co., 1983.

Kibby, M. W. "Passage Readability Affects the Oral Reading Strategies of Disabled Readers." *The Reading Teacher* 32 (1979): 390–96.

LaBerge, D., and Samuels, S. J. "Toward a Theory of Automatic Information Processing in Reading." *Cognitive Psychology* 6 (1974): 293–323.

Lancaster, W.; Nelson, L.; and Morris, D. "Invented Spellings in Room 112: A Writing Program for Low-Reading Second Graders." *The Reading Teacher* 35 (1982): 906–11.

Mason, J. M. "When Do Children Begin to Read: An Exploration of Four Year Old Children's Letter and Word Reading Competencies." *Reading Research Quarterly* 15 (1980): 203–27.

Mass, L. N. "Developing Concepts of Literacy in Young Children," *The Reading Teacher* 35 (1982): 670–75.

Meltzer, N., and Herse, R. "The Boundaries of Written Words as Seen by First Graders." *Journal of Reading Behavior* 1 (1969): 3–14.

Moe, A. J. "Word Lists for Beginning Readers." *Reading Improvement* 10 (1973): 11–15.

Otto, W., and Chester, R. "Sight Words for Beginning Readers." *The Journal of Educational Research* 65 (1972): 435–43.

Read, C. "Preschool Children's Knowledge of English Phonology." *Harvard Educational Review* 41 (1971): 1–34.

Richeck, M. "Readiness Skills that Predict Initial Word Learning Using Two Different Methods of Instruction." *Reading Research Quarterly* 13 (1977): 201–22.

Templeton, S. "Young Children Invent Words: Developing Concepts of 'Word-ness.'" *The Reading Teacher* 33 (1980): 454–59.

7
Developing Word Identification Processes

If we taught vocabulary only by teaching individual words, reading instruction would be extremely inefficient, laborious, and dull. Instead, we want to help children learn to use three major types of word-identification skills. By using these skills, often in combination, children will very quickly and continuously expand their reading vocabulary and increase their reading ability.

Before examining the typical list of "word-attack skills" found in most reading methods textbooks and instructional teacher's manuals, it would seem appropriate to consider the usual catch-all labels often used interchangeably to denote word-identification skills. It would seem useful to select one label that most closely represents our purpose, and use it in the remainder of the book. The five most frequently occurring labels found in the literature are: *decoding, word analysis, word attack, word recognition,* and *word identification.*

The term *word identification,* we think, is the most accurate description of the kinds of things to be outlined in this chapter and expanded in the following chapters.

1. *Decoding* is too restrictive a term. It implies explicit concern for breaking the letter-sound correspondence code and for phonics only. While we have no quarrel with phonics, and indeed have devoted an entire chapter to it, we believe the term *word identification* encompasses phonics and much more.

2. *Word analysis* is a broader term than *decoding* but is still too restrictive. It suggests that word meaning can be discerned by analyzing the word — and only the word — itself. It suggests provision for phonic analysis and structural (morphemic) analysis, but confines the unit of analysis to the word.

3. *Word attack* has no inherent meaning related to reading that we can see, although it does portray a rich metaphorical, militaristic image of what we ask children to do with some words.

4. *Word recognition* implies encountering again something already known. Smith (1971) provides a useful distinction between recognition and identification:

"Identification" involves a decision that an object now confronted should be treated in the same way as a different object met before: that the two should be put into the same category. There is no implication that the object being identi-

fied should itself have been met before. "Recognition," on the other hand, liter-
ally means that the object now confronted has been seen before although it does
not require identification. We *recognize* a person when we know we have seen
him before, whether or not we can put a name to him. We *identify* a person
when we put a name to him, whether or not we have met him before." (Smith
1971, p. 106)

5. *Word identification* seems to us to be the most accurately comprehensive term available to encompass the various grapho-phonic, morphemic, syntactic, and semantic generalizations and strategies readers employ independently to
expand their reading vocabulary and comprehend printed discourse.

To help develop a rationale for the topics included elsewhere in this
book, and to explain why some others are excluded, it is necessary to consider the
eight usual subtopics found on most lists of word-identification skills. They are:

> sight words
> configuration
> phonics
> syllabication
> structural analysis
> picture clues
> contextual analysis
> dictionary skills

Those familiar with the above list of skills realize that a major point of
confusion is that while some are indeed skills that can be applied by readers when
encountering unfamiliar words, others are goals, habits, or instructional strategies.
Further confusion arises because some of the terms refer both to generalizations
and teaching methods, and still more confusion surrounds the great variance in
the usefulness of the stated "skills."

1. Sight words. To nearly all teachers of reading the term *sight words*
has three rather discrete meanings. First and foremost, it is the principal goal of
all instruction in vocabulary and word identification. Children enter school able
to read — on sight — only a handful of words, such as their name, *stop, exit*, and
so on. On the other hand, adults can read on sight up to 100,000 or more different
words. Some of those words were directly taught, while most were learned
through independent application of the various word-identification skills and
strategies. Secondly, the term *sight words* refers to one or another of the compi-
lations of high-frequency words that are essential to fluent reading *(the, and, but,
or)*. Primary-grade teachers and remedial reading teachers are those most concerned with teaching children a basic sight vocabulary. A rather short list of just
a few hundred words comprises the majority of all printed words used in children's and adult materials. Third, sight words are taught as an introduction to
common reading assignments in any school subject. These are usually the words
deemed potentially troublesome and because they may inhibit comprehension of
the subsequent reading assignment.

So whether the term *sight words* is used as a referent for the primary goal of instruction in word identification, as a way of labeling high-frequency words, or as a reference to direct vocabulary instruction, it is clearly not a generalizable, applicable word-identification "skill" children can use. However, sight-word instruction is highly important for reading development, as was explained in Chapter Six, which presents a basic sight vocabulary of 306 high-frequency words, discusses its origin, and provides instructional suggestions for sight-word development. Chapters Three, Four, and Five discuss a number of instructional strategies and activities for developing a "meaning" vocabulary. This is not to suggest that "sight" vocabulary is not also "meaning" vocabulary. Obviously, unmeaningful basic sight words would be of no use to anyone, and similarly, many "meaning" words become part of a reader's "sight" vocabulary. Rather, a separate chapter is included to permit us to more fully describe the rationale for the basic sight words we think are important.

2. Configuration. *Configuration* is not a word identification skill either. It is a term that refers to a practice used by some kindergarten, first-grade, and remedial reading teachers to help children learn sight words. The practice is designed to help children notice how certain words have graphically different shapes or appearances. This is usually done by drawing boxes around words to highlight their differences.

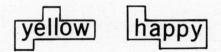

Some teachers point out the "tail at the end of *monkey*" or "the eyes in *look*." While such configuration practices may help children initially memorize a few sight words, the practice quickly loses utility as the child's sight vocabulary grows. Once a child knows book , look , and took , the little boxes are hardly of any help. Since configuration is not a useful word-identification skill, and since it has pratically no value except in the most initial stages of reading instruction, it will not be discussed further in this book.

3. Phonics. The term *phonics* (sometimes erroneously called *phonetics*) has caused confusion because it refers both to sets of letter-sound relationships, which, once learned, can be applied, and to a variety of strategies that can be used for teaching those relationships. We recognize the importance of phonics instruction. Children enter school with thousands of words they cannot identify in print in their speaking/listening vocabularies. By learning and applying the generalizations of letter-sound correspondence, children can expand their reading vocabularies. For example, many five-year-olds have the word *bed* in their speaking/listening vocabulary but cannot identify the word in print. By applying phonics generalizations they are helped to pronounce the word *bed*, thus rendering the printed form meaningful. Thus, the purpose of phonics is to help children pronounce words they have not seen before in print with the hope that once pronounced, the word can be matched to an already existing item in children's listening/speaking vocabulary.

4. Syllabication. *Syllabication* is probably the most misclassified and mis-

used of the word identification skills. Some reading authorities call it a phonics skill whose purpose is to help with pronunciation *(win/ter)*. Others call it a structural analysis skill whose purpose is to help identify meaningful parts of words such as roots and suffixes *(walk/ing)*. In either case syllabication often is not taught properly and involves drawing lines between syllables — a task that usually cannot be done unless the word is already known by the child. In other words, knowing a word often must *precede* identifying its syllables. For example, one syllabication rule says "divide before the consonant if the vowel is long *(ra/di/o)* and after the consonant if the vowel is short *(rap/id)*." Of what use is such a rule? One must know the pronunciation in order to divide correctly. Thus the act of dividing has served no useful purpose for reading. In this book, syllabication will be described as an aid to pronouncing unrecognized printed words when phonic syllabication generalizations may be used to ascertain the appropriate letter-sound relationships. Syllabication is also discussed in reference to such meaningful parts of words as roots, prefixes, suffixes, and inflected endings. In general it is our view that syllabication is of much more interest to poets and song writers than it is of help to children acquiring reading ability, and its use in classrooms ought to be considerably diminished.

5. Structural analysis. Unlike phonics, whose purpose is to help children pronounce unfamiliar printed words, the purpose of structural analysis is to help children analyze unfamiliar printed words by picking out already known meaningful parts of words. The smallest units of meaning in a language are called morphemes, and in English there are many thousands of them. Some morphemes are entire words, but some words contain more than one morpheme. The word *book* contains one morpheme while *books* contains two, *book* plus *plural (s)*; the word *bankers* has three morphemes; and so on. A first-grade child may be able to read the word *help* but will falter when encountering *helping*. By analyzing the word structurally for its meaningful components (morphemes), the child may be able to identify the unfamiliar word.

6. Picture clues. The inclusion of the term *picture clues* in lists of word-identification skills also creates some confusion. Picture clues are not generalizable skills per se but are rather a type of contextual analysis strategy that directs children's attention to pictorial materials as a means of identifying a word and comprehending printed text. As such, the use of pictures is mentioned briefly in reference to contextual analysis.

7. Contextual analysis. Using surrounding context to identify an unfamiliar word (that is, making an educated guess) is the most frequent word-identification procedure used by mature readers. Contextual analysis is typically defined as "figuring out a word by the way it is used in a passage." Context clues, if a reader knows how to use them, help define an unfamiliar word by providing syntactic, semantic, pictorial, typographic, and stylistic clues. Whereas phonics and structural analysis focus the reader's attention on the word (but for different purposes), contextual analysis focuses that attention beyond the individual word. In the present chapter (pp. 111–149), contextual analysis is presented more as a mindset, a way of thinking about and behaving toward reading, than as a finite set of discrete, generalizable skills. But contextual analysis is used for much more

than figuring out pronunciation and meanings for new words. Equally as important is its use in determining new meanings for old words. The very young child who knows her *back* from her elbow or her stomach, gradually learns that many things have a front and a *back*, and that to *back* a car out of the garage and *back* a political candidate are quite different concepts. Using context clues can help one learn that white elephants are not at all like "white elephants" and that dressing a child and dressing a chicken are quite different enterprises. As a powerful aid to vocabulary expansion, contextual analysis is an integral part of reading comprehension.

8. Dictionary skills. The use of a dictionary might more appropriately be viewed as a reference skill rather than a word-identification skill. Dictionary entries indeed provide useful information about word pronunciation, origin, and spelling. More importantly, a good dictionary can help a reader to verify a meaning he or she has tentatively assigned to an unfamiliar word. In Chapter Five, the dictionary and the thesaurus are treated as valuable references for vocabulary expansion.

The three types of word-identification skills that need to be taught are: 1) phonic analysis, 2) structural analysis, and 3) contextual analysis. *Phonics* is the term used for relating letters to sounds. Phonics instruction is concerned with providing the child with the means of *pronouncing* an unfamiliar *printed* word, and consequently recognizing it from one's oral/aural vocabulary. *Structural analysis* refers to learning the meaning of a new word by discovering *parts* of the word that are already meaningful. *Contextual analysis* refers to learning the meaning of a new word by the way it is used in a sentence or larger passage.

All three are very powerful word-identification skills. Good readers use all three skills regularly and almost automatically as they read new materials. As the skills are used, the child's reading vocabulary is expanded and reading efficiency increased.

Most of the elementary school teachers with whom we work teach a good deal of phonics in grades one to three and emphasize the skills of structural and contextual analysis from grades two or three upward. But we have taught high-schoolers who couldn't read very well because they had never mastered phonics, and we have also worked with first graders who capably used all three skills.

Children benefit from systematic instruction in word identification (Schell 1978). It would be convenient for teachers if we could provide an empirically sound scope and sequence for teaching these important skills; however, research on learning hierarchies in reading has been quite inconclusive to date (Samuels 1976; Bourque 1980). We will provide you with a body of information we feel should be taught (i.e., the content of phonics, morphemic units worth teaching) and then offer some guidelines for planning word-identification lessons. We suggest that you follow the skills hierarchy included in the basal reader used in your school district. The ordering of any basal hierarchy depends on the author's theory of reading, not on empirical data. Thus, as you gain experience, you may decide to alter the scope and/or sequence of skills presented to your students.

In this chapter we will once again emphasize direct teaching in a total language environment. It is our belief that you must carefully teach mediated word-identification skills to give children tools or techniques for identifying unknown words. Initially that means isolating each skill in order to help children focus their attention on the skill. Lessons on word identification, however, are not as straightforward as they may seem; each individual skill lesson must include a component we will call *teaching for transfer*. We certainly want children to master individual skills, but we insist that the only valid test of mastery is whether or not a child can apply individual decoding skills to reading connected text. In other words, a skill is not mastered until a child automatically uses the skill while reading (La Berge and Samuels 1974; Cunningham 1979). Children who can decode words quickly and accurately are freed to devote time and attention to reading for meaning. According to Downing (1982) *integration* is the key factor; children must practice using their skills in reading situations.

PHONICS: WHAT SHOULD BE TAUGHT

As you read books about reading and look at instructional materials for children, you will encounter several terms that mean about the same thing as the word *phonics*. These terms include *decoding, sounding out, unlocking,* and *cracking the code*. Whatever term is used, and we prefer *phonics*, the goal is to teach children:

1. The patterns of letter-sound relationships
2. The generalization that describes the patterns
3. The strategies for using both patterns and rules so that unrecognized printed words may be sounded out and pronounced

The following examples show the differences between pattern, generalization, and strategy:

> *Pattern:* The letter *c* nearly always represents the sound of /k/ as in *cup* or /s/ as in *nice*. (An exception is *cello*.)
>
> *Generalization:* The letter *c* is pronounced /s/ before *e, i,* or *y,* as in *cent, cider, cycle*. The letter *c* is pronounced /k/ before other letters, as in *candy, cotton, cupid, success*.
>
> *Strategy:* One instructional *strategy* is to teach the children several words with the letter *c* in them. Then the children are asked to look carefully at the words to discover the pattern and the rule (for example, *c* is /s/ before *e, i, y* in *cell, city, cyst*). A different

instructional strategy is to teach the rule directly
and have children use it to pronounce unfamiliar
words containing *c (cyclops, cemetery, cipher)*.

The phonics correspondences listed in Table 6 are the ones we have
found to be of highest value to young readers. Because of the nature of English,
there are exceptions to nearly every pattern and we do not recommend that you
teach directly the exceptions. Children can learn as sight words the words that
are exceptions. The patterns shown here are *not presented in any sequence*. You
may teach them in any order you prefer, but whatever sequence is used, these
patterns do need to be learned. Later in this chapter we present a table of common
"word families" that are built on many of the patterns listed in Table 6.

TABLE 6
Major Letter-Sound Correspondences[1]

For each pattern sample words are used to illustrate the letter-sound relationships
that need to be learned. Ocasionally a rule is given.

Consonants

b — book	k — king	qu — queen	w — water
d — dance	l — lemon	r — roll	x — xylophone
f — funny	m — money	s — sit *or* was	exam, tax
h — heart	n — new	t — top *or* nation	y — yes
j — job	p — party	v — violin	z — zebra

Other Consonants

c — cent	c — cat
city	cot
cycle	cup

Rule: *C* sounds like *s* before *e, i, y*, and sounds like *k* elsewhere.

g — gem	g — game
agile	gone
gym	guild

Rule: *G* sounds like *j* before *e, i, y*, and sounds like *g* elsewhere.

Double Consonants

digraphs

sh — shoe	th — thin	ch — chew
ph — photo	this	choir
ng — song	wh — while	chef

doubles

bb — rabble	nn — funny
dd — ladder	pp — happen
ff — jiffy	rr — narrow
ll — belly	vv — savvy
mm — dimmer	zz — dizzy
cc — buccaneer	gg — egg
accept	suggest

[1]Adapted from Smith and Johnson 1980.

TABLE 6 (cont.)

Rule: Except for *cc* and *gg*, two identical consonants have one sound.

blends	bl — black	br — brown	sc — scat
	cl — clue	cr — cry	scr — screen
	fl — flap	dr — draw	sm — small
	gl — glass	fr — friend	sn — snow
	pl — play	gr — ground	sp — spot
	sl — slow	pr — proud	squ — squeak
		tr — trap	st — stump
			sw — swing

silent letters	kn — knee	wr — wrong
	mb — comb	ten — fasten

Vowels

i — if	a — act	o — hot
mild	about	of
bird	ape	note
	want	off
	call	for
	star	
u — much	e — bed	
cute	jacket	
tube	blaze	
bull	often	
fur	she	
	her	

Rules: 1. "A vowel between two consonants is usually 'short'": *pin, cap, hot, bug, bed.*
2. "A vowel before two or more consonants is usually 'short'": *wish, graph, much, blotter, lettuce, happen, itch, hospital, cinder, bumper.*
3. "A vowel followed by a consonant plus *e* is usually 'long'": *pine, date, dope, cute, mete.*
4. "The letter *y* sometimes is a vowel and it has two sounds": *my; baby.*

Double Vowels

io — nation	ou — ounce	au — because
lion	though	laugh
ea — teach	soup	oo — moon
bread	would	book
great		
ai — pain	ee — see	ow — own
said	been	cow
ay — play		oi — coin

You might be wondering where to put your emphasis, since there are so many letter-sound relationships that need to be taught. The following sentences demonstrate our belief. First, try to read the first two sentences in which the consonants have been omitted. After that struggle try to read the two sentences in which the vowels are missing.

1. A _o_ _i_ _ _ _o_e _a_ _e_ _ _o _o_ _.
2. I _i_ _ _e_ _ _y _ _i_ _ _ea_ _ _e_ _e_.
1. _ r_ll _ng st_n_ g_th _rs n_ m _ss.
2. _ w_ll h _lp m_ ch_ld r_ _d b_tt_r.

The first two are impossible to read but the second two are quite easy. It is obvious that the consonants are the significant identifiers of words. We're not urging you to ignore vowels, but we do think the consonants are much more important.

Hundreds of different techniques have been used to teach phonics and all have been successful with some children. Most of these techniques are really quite similar.

PHONICS: SOME INSTRUCTIONAL DISTINCTIONS

Before we give our preferences concerning the teaching of phonics, it may be useful to examine the range of options open to us in presenting the content of phonics to children. A side benefit of this effort will be the clarification of a number of terms we often hear to describe phonics instruction.

Analytic Versus Synthetic

In synthetic phonics a child is taught a number of letter *sounds* — for example, *b*/buh/, *t*/tuh/, *e*/eeehhh/, and then how to blend those sounds into words, *bet*/buh-eeehhh-tuh//bet/. The emphasis is on going from parts to wholes, and the process of blending is critical to its success. In analytic phonics, the child is first exposed to a number of sight words. When a sufficient number sharing a common element have been introduced, a phonics lesson may proceed. For example, after introducing *dog, Dad, sad*, and *donkey* the teacher may give a lesson including a workbook page on the sound represented by the letter *d*. Rarely are sounds isolated in analytic phonics. Instead they are referred to by sample words. *D* does not represent /duh/ but refers, rather, to "the sound you hear at the beginning of dog." Furthermore it is rare to find blending activities associated with the analytic approaches. But in contrast with the part-to-whole strategy of synthetic phonics, the emphasis is on extracting common elements from known words — in short, whole-to-part. One note of caution: it is more accurate to view the terms as lying on opposite ends of a continuum rather than on opposite sides of a fence. Some materials are more synthetic than others, some lie near the middle, such as linguistic readers.

Systematic Versus Intrinsic

Chall (1967) uses this continuum to classify how various systems teach phonics. She called *systematic* those materials that tended to teach phonics rules early, systematically, and intensively, often before any sight words were introduced. She classified as *intrinsic* those materials that began with sight words and introduced phonics rules gradually as *one of several* cues available to attain meaning from the printed page. In short, there was a serious attempt to make the sparsely taught rules *intrinsically* meaningful to the reading task.

Notice that there is some overlap between the analytic-synthetic distinction and the systematic-intrinsic distinction. Almost any conceivable synthetic approach would have to be systematic. But while all intrinsic approaches would likely be analytic, not all analytic approaches would necessarily be intrinsic.

Rules Versus No Rules

The rules-versus-no-rules distinction has two levels of comparison. At one level you can distinguish between approaches that do or do not use the rules as *pedagogical* devices, mnemonics of a sort. At a second level, you can ask whether or not they require verbalization of the rule for complete mastery. Linguistic approaches neither use nor require them. *Phonetic Keys* (Sloop 1972) uses them but does not require verbalization. Some programs both use them and require verbalization for mastery.

Inductive Versus Deductive

The inductive/deductive distinction applies to both individual lessons and to total phonics programs. The inductive strategy begins the lesson with a corpus of words sharing some characteristic or characteristics. Through prompt and leading questions by the teacher, the children are led to discover the regularity among the examples or the distinction between two sets of examples. The deductive strategy, by contrast, starts the lesson with the rule. Then examples are added to illustrate its practice. Many times, one can find both inductive and deductive lessons and/or independent practice activities within the same series. The linguistic approaches are best described as inductive; however, they do not lead the child to the *verbalization* of a rule, only its *realization*.

Figure 7.1 summarizes the distinctions listed above, giving examples of published programs we think fit into the various categories.

GUIDELINES FOR TEACHING PHONICS

What follows represents the conclusions we have reached at this point in time regarding phonics instruction.

I. There is no program of teaching phonics that is so "pure" that it will be damaged if it is supplemented with materials designed for other programs. For example, an excellent supplement to a linguistic approach is the word-family phonics kit written by

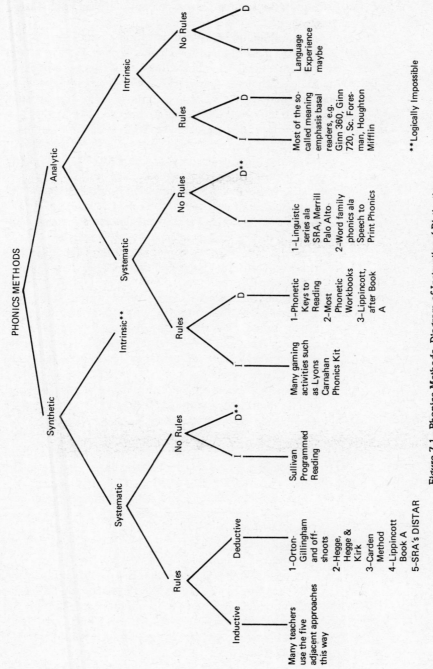

Figure 7.1. Phonics Methods: Diagram of Instructional Distinctions

**Logically Impossible

121

Murphy and Durrell, *Speech-to-Print Phonics* (1964). Interestingly, that kit is often used as a supplement to a traditional basal program.

II. We use the following strategy for teaching phonics.

  A. Begin with a word-family approach, that is, a set of words that share phonic elements illustrating the pattern being taught (see Table 7). Present the lesson in an inductive fashion, without rules. Why? We think it makes for a better lesson. Here is a step-by-step procedure you can follow:

    1. When the group has learned to read (as sight words) three or four words containing a particular sound or pattern, write them on paper or on a chalkboard *(Sandy, soup, self, Saturday)*. As a prerequisite, children must be able to discriminate either visually or by auditory means the *s* phoneme and letter.

    2. Ask the pupils to read each word aloud and to listen carefully to its beginning, medial, or ending sound.

    3. Next ask what the words have in common. (For example, the same beginning letter and sound in *Sandy, soup, self,* and *Saturday*.)

    4. Then ask the class to suggest other words having the same sound. Either you or the pupils may add to the list *(soda, supper)*. Some children will suggest words with different spellings of the sound *(cent, city)*. List them on the board separately and point out that some sounds have more than one spelling.

    5. Next ask them to read the entire list of words again and briefly discuss each word's meaning.

    6. Next, you may want to ask the pupils to write the words in their word books (self-dictionaries).

    7. If the pattern follows a rule, for example, *c* is pronounced /k/ before *a, o,* and *u,* ask the child to try to discover the rule.

    8. Then, together, you should make sentences which use the words containing the pattern.

    "Sandy likes soup."

    "I drink soda."

    "Saturday is my favorite day."

    The point is to put words back into a meaningful context. The meaning of the words and sentences should be discussed so your group never loses sight of the fact that the purpose of phonics is to help them read and understand.

  B. Assess skill mastery in an oral reading situation or with a paper and pencil test.

  C. For those who didn't achieve mastery, reteach the lesson but use the rules (refer to number 7) as a mnemonic device.

TABLE 7
Representative List of Word Families

ab	aim	an	are	at
ace	ain	ance	ark	atch
ack	air	and	arm	ate
act	ait	ane	arn	ave
ad	ake	ang	arp	aw
ade	alk	ank	art	ax
aft	all	ant	ase	ay
ag	alt	ap	ash	aze
age	am	ape	ask	
aid	ame	ar	ass	
ail	amp	ard	ast	
ead	eat	een	elp	esk
eak	eck	eep	elt	ess
eal	ed	eer	em	est
eam	eed	eet	en	et
ean	eek	eg	end	etch
eap	eel	ell	ent	ew
ear	eem	elm	ep	
ib	ig	ince	irt	itch
ibe	ike	ind	is	ite
ick	ile	ine	ise	ive
id	ill	ink	ish	ix
ide	ilt	int	isk	ize
ife	im	ip	iss	izz
iff	ime	ipe	ist	
ift	in	ire	it	
oach	obe	oll	oop	orn
oad	ock	om	oor	ort
oak	od	ome	oot	ose
oal	ode	on	op	ot
oam	oft	one	ope	otch
oan	og	oof	or	ote
oap	oid	ook	orb	ow
oast	oil	ool	ord	owe
oat	oke	oom	ore	ox
ob	ole	oon	ork	oy
ub	ug	ume	ur	ush
ube	uge	un	ure	usk
uck	ule	und	urn	uss
ud	ull	une	urt	ust
ude	ult	unk	us	ut
uff	um	up	use	ute
					uzz

D. Reassess.

E. For those who didn't achieve mastery, try the following:
   1. increase the number of practices
   2. increase the amount and frequency of individual feedback given
   3. take an entirely new track

F. Look for other problems, for example, motivation, readiness for the skill, inadequate auditory acuity, or visual perception.

III. All phonics approaches suffer from a lack of what we call *phonics-in-context* exercises. We firmly believe that when a skill is taught in isolation, it must be immediately *followed up* by sentence-level exercises requiring the use of the skill in context *before* the child is asked to use the skill in a real reading situation. Pearson (1976) discusses the rationale and the method for creating such activities. For example, after a lesson on silent *e*, give the child written or oral/written exercises such as:

The old $\begin{Bmatrix} \text{man} \\ \text{mane} \end{Bmatrix}$ used his $\begin{Bmatrix} \text{can} \\ \text{cane} \end{Bmatrix}$ to help him walk.

IV. Don't teach unnecessary phonics skills. We can think, offhand, on four commonly taught skills that cannot possibly contribute to independent word identification (the real goal of phonics instruction).

A. *Asking children to* place *diacritical marks on words.* Now, it is appropriate to teach children how to *read* diacritical marks, syllables, and accents. Those are important dictionary skills. But they are not helpful, without serious modification, as word-identification skills.

B. *Asking children to divide words into syllables.* Both this and the preceding skill are logically capable of being a help, but children do them backwards. They say the word, *then* they mark the vowels or divide the word. Thus, they are practicing useless habits. We have observed far too many bored and restless children drawing lines between syllables. While such line drawing may be useful in writing (dividing words at the end of a line), it has nothing to do with reading.

C. *Asking children to place accents on syllables.* This cannot be done *unless* the word is already known. There are no good *a priori* rules for determining accent. The word must be said first.

D. *Teaching erroneous rules such as "When two vowels go a-walkin' the first one does the talkin'"* (this means the first vowel is long and the other is silent). In a study of 61 vowel clusters Johnson (1970) found this rule to be true for only 4 clusters (*ai, ay, ee,* and *oa*) 75 percent of the time or more, and for 2 others (*ea* and *ow*) about 50 percent of the time. For the other 55 vowel clusters, it was rarely, or never, true. Such a rule is dangerous, for children will learn it! By the way, in the rule look at the only word with a vowel cluster (*does*).

V. As important as phonics knowledge is to a child, learning it can be dull and repetitious. We think that need not be the case. By varying your approach, and creating games and activities, your pupils can have fun with phonics.

You may want to have a "letter of the week" and ask your pupils to gather as many things as possible from around the house and neighborhood. If you can make a small table and bulletin board available, each week's collection could be displayed there. For example, during "*m* week," your class may display milk, money, mittens, a picture of Mary, M & M's, a mop, and so on. During *t* week, the display might include a turkey, a tent, tennis shoes, toilet paper, toys, and a table. *S* week might include Santa, Snoopy, snow (how to keep it from melting?), a saw, scissors, soap, and a can of soup.

Functional phonics is most appealing to young children from preschool though grade two. Its success is attributable, we think, to the fact that each sound is represented by concrete objects the child locates, touches, and handles.

In addition to locating and displaying the objects, the child is encouraged to practice writing the letters and the names of the objects he or she discovered. You may also have each child keep a record of the number of items displayed each week and perhaps prepare a chart. Self-competition is often highly motivating.

Some parents may be a bit dubious of this approach when the car keys are missing during *k* week, or the new golf clubs are out of action during *g* week, or there is no Pabst in the refrigerator during *p* week.

Again, so that phonics is always recognized as a key to reading with understanding, we recommend that the words be written, discussed, and used in oral and written sentences.

We discussed the use of games to teach vocabulary and described some types of games (including board games, track games, and feed-through games) that can be successfully used in reading instruction. We ask you to review those games and relate them to phonics skills. Any of the types of games that can be used to teach vocabulary can also be used to teach and review phonics skills.

Games can add the kind of variety necessary to keep phonics instruction from becoming dull. We encourage you to construct simple games and play with your pupils to add variety to the lessons. But we also caution you against the overuse of games. They have a tendency to fractionate the reading process and move children away from viewing reading as a meaning-getting process. Games used in moderation, as with so many things in life, can be healthy; used in excess they can be harmful.

VI. Don't classify phonic *processes* along with phonic generalizations. Most taxonomies of phonics skills include syllabication and blending right along with phonics generalizations. If they are to be useful, they have to be taught as *processes*. For example, in teaching syllabication it is not important that the child can accurately determine where to divide or the difference between an open and a closed syllable. This cannot be done accurately anyway; there is too much ambiguity in the rule system. What must be taught is a *set for syllabication*. In order to do that, the following steps are appropriate:

A. Teach the *concept* of the syllable from an *auditory* point of view, having the children clap out syllables with you as you say a multisyllabic word. Later have them count syllables as you say a word.

B. Teach a general concept of a syllable from a graphic point of view. One rule that does seem appropriate is that a syllable needs a vowel.

C. Combine steps *a* and *b* above. Have the written form in front of the children as they clap out or count out syllables.

D. Give practice in systematically pronouncing the parts of regular words.

Wash	No
Washing	Novem
Washington	November

You can do this as a chalkboard or as a tachistoscopic exercise. Notice that it emphasizes left-to-right attack and that it reinforces both the visual and the auditory notion of a syllable.

E. Highlight syllables in running text for oral (or silent) reading exercises by underlining them or putting dots between them. This works as a *process* practice technique.

F. In discussion and practice, emphasize the joint utilization of syllabication processes, context, and oral language in order to move from an approximation of an unknown word to its specification. Remember, phonics is only of use if the word is already within the child's oral/aural vocabulary.

VII. Whenever possible, require that mastery be achieved in a real reading situation. Rarely accept paper and pencil evidence for phonic skill mastery. Never accept rule verbalization. Require that the skill be transferred to a reading task. It can be done with silent reading, if you are a clever questioner. But it is simpler to do it in an oral reading situation.

VIII. Don't confuse phonics with reading. Too many children think that reading is what happens on workbook pages or dittoed worksheets. That's an attitude instilled by well-meaning educators who shiver with excitement at the sight of a "busy" child. Your students should know that phonics can *help* them with reading but that reading is what happens when they encounter the printed page and discover the meaning there.

STRUCTURAL ANALYSIS

Structural analysis is a skill through which children determine the meaning of an unfamiliar printed word by examining its meaningful parts. At first glance a reader may be stymied by the word *unimaginable*. But by using structural analysis, the child may discover the known word *image* and two familiar word parts, *un* and *able*. If the meaning is still not apparent, the additional use of contextual analysis will often help refine the meaning: "When Neil Armstrong was a child, it would have been *unimaginable* to him that he would walk on the moon." This chapter rests on the belief that one of the major goals of reading instruction is to help children develop independence in reading. This means developing the abilities to work out the pronunciation and the meaning of unfamiliar words on their own. While a good deal of help is often available from the context within which the word is found, frequently context is not sufficient, and the reader needs to use visual cues, the spelling of words and their parts, to search for meaning.

The purpose of structural analysis is to assist students to look for *familiar* meaningful word parts in words that are *unfamiliar* as a total unit. Thousands of English words are combinations of two other words. Words such as *stoplight*, *football*, *daytime*, and *overcoat*, may at first appear unfamiliar to young readers. Each of these is a compound word, meaning that it is composed of two short "root" words. In the new compound word, each root word retains at least the germ of its own meaning. It is quite likely that many of the root words are known even though the compound word is new to the child. By analyzing the structure of the word for meaningful parts of the words, children will often approximate the meaning of a new word.

Structural analysis does not apply only to compound words. Many words are formed from root words and prefixes; for example, *unhappy*, *disloyal*, *unicycle*, *reuse*, or from root words and suffixes, such as *fearless*, *enjoyment*, *loveable*, *childish*. Prefixes and suffixes are word parts that have meaning, but they have meaning only when they are attached to root words. Other meaningful word parts include what linguists call *inflections*: plural endings *(cats, dishes, babies)*, verb tenses *(walked, helped, walking, helping)*, comparisons *(big, bigger, biggest)*, and possessives *(John's, the girl's)*. Inflections differ from suffixes in that suffixes usually change the form class (part of speech) to which a word belongs, while inflections do not.

Thousands of new words can be added to children's reading vocabularies through the use of structural analysis, for many "new" words contain already known meaningful parts.

WORDS AND MORPHEMES

Structural analysis is sometimes referred to as morphemic analysis. The smallest units of meaning of a language are called morphemes and in English there are thousands of morphemes. The morpheme's function is to carry syntactic or semantic information. It is useful to view morphemes as comprising two classes, free and bound. Free morphemes are those that can stand alone to bear meaning — they are what most of us would call words. Bound morphemes, on the other hand, cannot stand alone, but must be attached to other morphemes. For example, the words *book* and *happy* are free morphemes, but the derived words *books* and *unhappy* each contain two morphemes — the free morphemes (*book* and *happy*), plus the bound morphemes (*s*, meaning "plural") and (*un*, meaning "not"). Bound morphemes are not restricted to affixes (prefixes, suffixes, and inflections); for example, the bound root *duc* appears in a number of words (*produce, reduce, induce, production*), but it cannot stand by itself as a word; it must be "bound" to other morphemes (usually prefixes or suffixes that cannot stand alone either) to form an isolable word. There are many such bound roots in English, many derived from Latin or Greek: *vis (revision, provision), pon (component, exponent), mit (admit, transmit, intermittent), scribe (prescribe, subscribe)*, and so forth. Thus a simple relational definition of a word could be shown:

> word = free morpheme *(book)*
> and
> word = free morpheme plus bound morpheme *(books)*
> but
> word ≠ bound morpheme *(s)*
> word ≠ bound root *(duc)*

Free and bound morphemes are often combined into larger meaning units referred to as derivatives, variants, and compounds.

Structural analysis, then, is the set of procedures readers use to examine meaningful elements within derivative, variant, and compound words. A middle-grade child may be familiar with the word *happy* and the prefix *un*, but may at first be troubled by *unhappiness*. By analyzing the structure of this longer word and recognizing familiar morphemes (free and bound) the child may be able to identify the unfamiliar word.

THE VALUE OF STRUCTURAL ANALYSIS

The beauty and advantage of morphemic analysis lies in the relatively high degree of consistency between letters, sounds, and meanings when words are analyzed at the morphemic level. For example, the word *laugh* is not easily analyzable if you look at the consistency between its component letters and sounds; both *au* and *gh* take variant pronunciations. However, as a morphemic unit, a root, *laugh* is quite predictable in both sound and meaning. Its pronunciation (lăf) and its meaning (to find amusement in something) are predictable and consistent whether it is used as a noun or a verb or whether it occurs by itself or in words like *laughing, laughable, unlaughable, laughed*, and so on. Hence analysis of words at the level of the morpheme is probably more rational and intuitively sensible than at the level of relating letters to sounds.

We believe structural analysis to be a highly important reading skill because though context *determines* the meaning of a word, it does not always *reveal* it. It is necessary to equip readers with all available strategies of word identification (structural and phonic) so they will not be required to guess wildly at the meaning of a word they do not recognize.

COMPONENTS OF STRUCTURAL ANALYSIS

Prefixes and Suffixes

We believe that one of the most useful techniques to employ in helping children acquire structural analysis ability is word building, or extensions. Later in the chapter we present several recommendations for accomplishing this. Accordingly, we do not believe it is helpful to teach long lists of prefixes and suffixes and to require memorization of their meanings. Some morphemes have more than one meaning (*un*wrap, *un*able, *un*willing) and some meanings (such as "not") are represented by more than one morpheme (*un*able, *il*legible, *dis*loyal, *in*active, *im*polite). Nonetheless there are some prefixes and suffixes that have invariant or nearly invariant meanings, or that play an important grammatical function, and thereby would be usefully learned (through extension, not memory) by children.

From a list of 68 prominent and commonly used prefixes, Deighton (1959) recommends teaching 10 that have invariant meanings[2] and several others with variant meanings but that occur with high frequency. Taking a cue from our own recommendations in Chapter Three (defining by example), read each of the following two lists and see if you can create a descriptive definition of these prefixes based upon the examples we have provided.

Invariant Prefixes

apo —	apoplexy, apogee
circum —	circumnavigate, circumvent
equi —	equidistant, equilibrium
extra —	extracurricular, extrasensory

---

[2]*Com*, while invariant, was not included because there are so many words in which the introductory letters *c · o · m* occur, but do not form the prefix *com*, e.g., *combination, come, comatose.*

intra —   intravenous, intramural
intro —   introspection, introvert
mal —   maladjusted, malapropism
mis —   misapply, misunderstand
non —   nonentity, nonprofit
syn —   synagogue, synapse, synonym

Variant (more than one meaning) but Common Prefixes

bi —   a) bicycle
           b) biannual
de —   a) dethrone, deactivate
           b) demerit, devalue
fore —   a) forewarn, forecast
           b) foreword, foreleg
in —   a) inept (also *ir*responsible, *il*legal, *im*material)[3]
           b) indoors
pre —   a) preschool, preadolescent
           b) precaution, prearrange
pro —   a) pro-war, pro-life
           b) proceed, project
semi —   a) semicircle, semiannual
           b) semiabstract, semiautomatic
re —   a) redraw, rearrest
           b) recall, reaction
un —   a) unable, unbecoming
           b) unlock, untie

Deighton discovered that of more than 100 common suffixes, 86 indicate invariably the part of speech of the word to which they are affixed, and most of the 86 provide additional clues to word meaning.

Noun Suffixes

Fourteen noun suffixes that indicate part of speech:

— ance, tolerance	— ness, wholesomeness
— ence, violence	— dom, freedom
— ation (-tion, -ion), starvation	— ery, drudgery
— ism, relativism	— mony, harmony
— ment, judgment	— ty, loyalty
— acity, tenacity	— tude, solitude
— hood, manhood	— ship, friendship

---

[3]Note that the prefixes *il*, *ir*, and *im* are only phonological variants of *in-*. They occur essentially because it is more natural to say *ir*responsible than *in*responsible.

Eight noun suffixes that indicate agent:

—eer, auctioneer	—ster, mobster
—ess, governess	—ist, cellist
—grapher, photographer	—stress, seamstress
—ier, financier	—trix, aviatrix

Twenty-four noun suffixes with specific meanings:[4]

—ana, Americana	—graphy, photography
—archy, monarchy	—ics, gymnastics
—ard (-art), drunkard	—itis, gastritis
—aster, poetaster	—latry, idolatry
—bility, susceptibility	—meter, speedometer
—chrome, ferrochrome	—metry, geometry
—cide, suicide	—ology, biology
—ee, payee	—phor, metaphor
—fer, conifer	—phobic, claustrophobic
—fication, glorification	—ric, meteoric
—gram, telegram	—scope, telescope
—graph, photograph	—scopy, bioscopy

In addition to noun suffixes, Deighton lists seventeen suffixes to form adjectives that have invariant meanings.

Adjective Suffixes

Seventeen adjective suffixes:

—est, brightest	—less, careless
—ferous, odoriferous	—able, laughable
—fic, scientific	—ible, -ble, edible
—fold, tenfold	—most, foremost
—form, uniform	—like, humanlike
—genous, autogenous	—ous, humorous
—scopic, telescopic	—ose, cellulose
—wards, backwards	—acious, tenacious
—wise, clockwise	—ful, beautiful

In addition to these prefixes and suffixes identified by Deighton (and obviously their usefulness and frequency varies considerably), we recommend direct instruction of the following inflected endings.

---

[4]Many of these morphemes are technically "combining forms" rather than suffixes per se. However, Deighton (and most educators) regard them as suffixes. Since we do not believe that students should be taught to distinguish such subtleties, we will accede to the conventional (albeit, inaccurate) wisdom.

Inflected Endings

Plural	*Comparison*
s —girls	er —taller
es— watches	est —tallest

Tense	*Possessive*
ed —jumped	's—Ann's
ing—jumping	s'—boys'
s —jumps	

Compound Words

On the surface, compound words seem to be simply two words put together. Closer inspection reveals that they are more complex.

First, many compound words appear as separate words when we write them. For example, *diesel truck* is written as two words whereas *steamboat* appears as a single word. But the meaning of *diesel truck* (truck powered by diesel) is similar to the meaning of *steamboat* (boat powered by steam). *Truckdriver* (someone who drives a truck) is often written as a single word, whereas *elevator operator* (someone who operates an elevator) is written as two. Linguistically, it would be inaccurate to regard *elevator* or *diesel* as adjectives modifying nouns, because they simply are not adjectives. A true adjective can appear as a relative clause. Hence *the black coat* can be paraphrased as *the coat that is black*. However, the *diesel locomotive* cannot be paraphrased as the *locomotive that is diesel*. Linguistically, entities like *diesel truck* and *elevator operator* are best regarded as compound nouns similar to *steamboat* or *truckdriver*.

Second, compound words differ in their underlying structure. For example, *whalebone* means "bone from a whale," but *fishhook* means "hook to fish with," not "hook from a fish." A *clothes closet* is a closet for clothes but *book review* is a review of a book, not *for* a book. While we do not recommend specific grammatical instruction for teaching compounds, we do recommend that you group similar examples for initial instructions. Hence we offer you the following structural break down of different types of compounds.

1. *B is of A.* There are numerous examples. A fishbone is a bone *of* a fish, and a coattail is a tail *of* a coat. Here are some others:

sunburn	handshake	mudslide	riverbank
nightfall	cottonball	heartbreak	
daybreak	logjam	potato chips	

2. *B is from A.* Goatskin is skin *from* a goat and hayfever is a fever *from* hay. Others:

sawdust	deerskin	horsehair
water spot	fever blister	cowhide
sunlight	moonlight	starlight

3. *B is for A*. A dog biscuit is a biscuit *for* a dog, and a dogleash is a leash *for* a dog. Others:

tire chain	wallpaper	tennis court	water bucket
beauty shop	dining room	potato peeler	bathroom
dishpan	cake pan	car thief	briefcase
golf course	bubble gum	tearoom	attic fan

4. *B is like A*. A boxcar is a car *like* a box, and bulldog is a dog *like* a bull. Others:

frogman	rock candy	cottontail
bottle fly	pigtail	tiger lily
ladybug	onion skin	crepe paper
cat women	cat burglar	Batman
catfish		

5. *B is A*. A nobleman is a man who *is* noble, and ice cream is cream that *is* ice.

dark meat	rapid transit	noble woman
blueprint	courtyard	White House
blackbird	bluebird	pipeline

6. *B does A*. A racehorse is a horse that *does* race, and a crybaby is a baby who *does* cry.

scrubwoman	printing press	towtruck	jumping bean
working man	loan officer	flying fish	race car

These lists (along with similar words) can be used by teachers to organize lessons about compound nouns. We do *not* recommend overemphasizing the common structure of these groups of compounds. Instead, we suggest a less formal approach:

1. Ask students questions like, "What would you call a woman who scrubs, a truck that tows, a bean that jumps, and so on?" Work with one category at a time.
2. Then reverse the process. Ask questions like, "If a scrubwoman is a woman who scrubs, then how would you define a loan officer, a tow truck, a race car?"
3. Then, ask questions like those in 1 and 2 across the above six categories of compound words.
4. Finally, as we have suggested for all our word-identification activities, it is advisable to have the students use several of these compound words in sentences. Have the students construct their own

sentences, or else give them modified cloze activities (see Chapter Six) in which they have to select one of the compounds to fit the context in the sentences you provide.

On the next several pages you will find classroom activities that emphasize word building, or word extension. Once your students have completed each activity, try to find ways to incorporate the vocabulary items in oral or written language activities. Remember, vocabulary lessons are not ends in themselves but are a means to improving verbal communication.

Word Building. List words and meaningful word parts in two columns. Ask your students to combine them to form new words and write the new words in column 3. For example:

Begin simply:

1	2	3
after	noon	_____
river	bank	_____
mail	box	_____

Then, the order should be varied:

rain	light	_____
foot	coat	_____
street	ball	_____

Then do the same thing with word endings and with prefixes:

young	ment	_____
fear	less	_____
enjoy	est	_____

un	marine	_____
sub	cycle	_____
bi	happy	_____

Then ask the children to use the new words in sentences or to write stories using the new words. Continue the activity with many other derived words.

Underlining. Read these paragraphs. Underline each compound word.

> Winter had come; snowflakes fell on the playground. At recess the children went outside for playtime. "Maybe there is enough snow to make a snowman," said Ben. Someone made a big snowball for the body. Another child made a small snowball for the head. Soon the snowman was finished.
>
> In the afternoon Grandmother came for a visit. She liked to make blueberry pancakes for others to eat. The children ate one after another. Jeff ate ten pancakes by himself. Grandfather could eat as many pancakes as anyone.

Word Puzzles. Another word-building activity is a type of puzzle. The group is supplied with meanings or synonyms (words that mean about the same thing) for the two root words, and are asked to discover and write the compound word. The following is an example.

> INSTRUCTIONS: See how well you can do with these puzzles. The answer to each problem is a compound word. Guess the word parts and then write the compound word.
>
> EXAMPLE: To live in a tent + earth = <u>campground</u>
>   (camp)   (ground)
>
> 1. automobile + to jump on one foot = <u>carhop</u>
> 2. animal with wings + part of the body used for thinking = <u>birdbrain</u>
> 3. lumber + to stroll = <u>boardwalk</u>
> 4. prepare food + bound group of printed pages = <u>cookbook</u>
> 5. object shot from a bow + part of body containing the brain = <u>arrowhead</u>
> 6. small, straight, pointed wire used for fastening + a round toy = <u>pinball</u>
> 7. to pull hard + vehicle used for water travel = <u>tugboat</u>
> 8. very warm + having been hit with a bullet = <u>hotshot</u>

Next ask the children to make similar word puzzles for you to solve. We have found that many elementary and junior-high school students enjoy doing this, and often create some very tough puzzles.

Compound words might be used to develop an activity to expand denotative (literal) word meanings. Simple compound words should be introduced initially (*mailman, airport, fireman, oatmeal, birthday, sandbox*). Help children to see that the words can be divided into two separate meaningful terms (e.g., *mail + man*, etc.) Follow-up activities might include:

a. Ask children to search through magazines to find pictures of items that can be combined to illustrate compound words. Horses pasted to a picture of a stage illustrates *horseplay;* a pat of *butter* stuck to the side of a coffee *cup* illustrates *buttercup;* a *cottage* mounted on to the tip of a *canoe* could represent *houseboat.* Humorous products will evolve during this exercise; excitement mounts as children attempt to guess and then spell the compound words classmates have created.

b. Choose compound words from children's reading/content-area materials. Develop a concentration game by printing the individual word parts on separate index cards. Number each card consecutively on the back side.

mail	oat	port	carrier
air	birth	fighter	meal
fire	sand	box	day

Shuffle the cards and place them facedown, in numerical order. Children take turns attempting to identify hidden compound words. To add a total language experience to this game, end the activity by asking each child to use his/her matched cards to create a meaningful oral or written sentence.

Contractions

Have the students make contractions with these words. Have them circle the letters they left out in writing their contractions.

Contractions with not
had not _____
was not _____
did not _____
have not _____
were not _____
would not _____
could not _____
should not _____
do not _____

Contractions with is
she is _____
it is _____
there is _____
where is _____
what is _____
that is _____

Contractions with will
he will _____
I will _____
they will _____
we will _____
you will _____

Contractions with were *or* are
we were _____
they are _____
you are _____

Contractions with had *or* would
we had _____
I would _____
they had _____
she had _____
he would _____
they would _____

Contractions with have
you have _____
I have _____
we have _____

Other contractions
I am _____
will not _____

Affixes

Word Building.   The following three activities involve word building by students through the addition of prefixes, suffixes, and inflected endings.

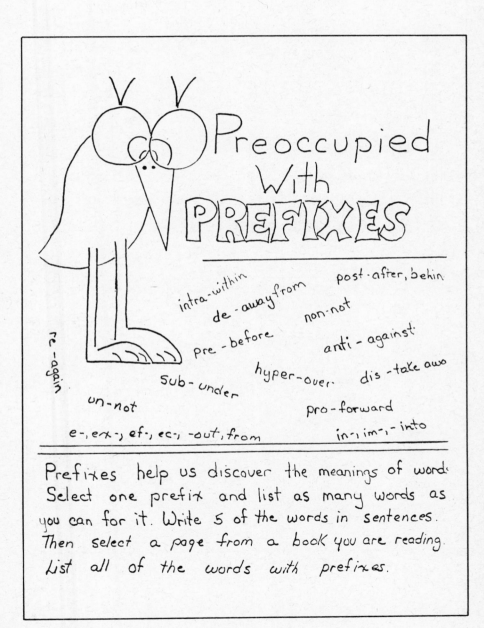

Preoccupied
With
PREFIXES

intra-within   post-after, behind

de - away from   non-not

re - again

pre - before   anti - against

hyper-over·   dis -take away

sub- under

un-not   pro - forward

e-, ex-; ef-, ec-; -out, from   in-; im-; - into

Prefixes help us discover the meanings of words.
Select one prefix and list as many words as
you can for it. Write 5 of the words in sentences.
Then select a page from a book you are reading.
List all of the words with prefixes.

SUFFIXES

...Change the meaning of root words. Write as many words as you can with these suffixes. Select 5 new words to use in a paragraph.

-er

-ology

-cian

-ness

-ian

-less

-ment

-ous

-ish

-ism

-able

-age

-ion

-ist

-dom

-ful

-fy

-ic

-y

-or

-sion

-tion

Inflectional

ENDINGS

Find 3 thing words (nouns) 3 describing words (adjectives) and 3 action words (verbs) from a book you are reading. For each word make as many new words as you can with the endings below.

-er

-ing

-es

-ed

-s

-less

-ly

-ful

-est

-ness

Create an Animal.[5]   Similar to "create a word," this activity demonstrates the power of morphemes in an entertaining way.

Distribute the following worksheet:

> Imagine you are a scientist exploring a wilderness that has never before been visited by man. Many unusual animals inhabit the area and it is your job to name them. But the names must be understood by scientists around the world, so we will have to use prefixes, roots, and suffixes that come from ancient languages— Latin and Greek—and are understood by people in many countries.
>
> The first animal you see is a
>
> Lineatus bicephalotriped.
>
> As soon as I looked at my chart I knew your animal must look like this:

> Here is a chart showing some of the terms that scientists use for naming living things. You may use any term as a prefix, root, or suffix.

Scientists' Vocabulary Chart

bi	—two	melano	—black
tri	—three	leuco	—white
quadro	—four	erythro	—red
pento	—five	bruno	—brown
mono	—one	lineatus	—lined
pedi	—foot	punctata	—dotted
cornis	—horn		
cephalus	—head		

> Now it is time for you to continue exploring the wilderness and find and name some more beasts. Draw each animal, too, so that any nonscientist will also know what the animal looks like.

Follow-up: Discuss other, more commonly used words in our language that derive from the roots in the chart. Use the student's own language experiences and/or the dictionary.

---

[5]We are indebted to Carol Welsch, a teacher in Madison, Wisconsin, for this suggestion.

CONTEXT CLUES

We continue our discussion of word-identification skills by turning to a very important strategy — contextual analysis. *Contextual analysis* and *context clues* are terms that refer to a reader's attempt to understand the intended meaning of a word by scrutinizing surrounding context, that is, "figuring out a word by the way in which it is used." In essence, using context means educated guessing. As we have seen, phonic analysis helps a reader define a word by pronouncing the word and discovering an already known auditory counterpart. Its focus is on the pronunciation of words. Structural analysis, the topic of the last section, again focused the reader's attention on the individual word, but the reader looked for *meaningful* word parts, rather than *pronounceable* word parts. With contextual analysis the focus moves beyond the individual word to other words, the structure of the sentence, and other features that can help pinpoint the meaning of the unfamiliar word. Context clues are very powerful and useful word-identification procedures (Gipe 1980).

As we have said before, and will again, rarely will the child use *only* phonics, or *only* structure, or *only* context. Two or three of the techniques are frequently used concurrently (Culyer 1979; Cunningham 1979) since two or three of the sources of information are almost always available within the target word or sentence. We agree with Jenkins, Longmaid, O'Brien, and Sheldon that: "Flexible hypothesis testing is thought to be a characteristic of good readers. . . . when a good reader sees an unfamiliar word s/he applies various phonic skills and tries different pronunciations until, with the help of context clues, the correct word is found" (Jenkins et al. 1980, p. 664).

Children benefit from direct instruction designed to develop a mindset or habit of using context in figuring out unknown words (Aukerman 1973). Contextual analysis, however, does not encompass a finite set of discrete *skills*. How, then, can teachers be expected to plan for instruction? A study of the literature reveals that learning from context has many dimensions. We will share several pertinent instructional implications drawn from the literature.

Gipe (1978–79; 1980) found that the context method was a most effective technique in teaching new vocabulary. Gipe found that the type of context used in vocabulary exercises was important. Familiar contextual settings are essential for successful lesson development. Multiple appearances of a new word in a variety of sentence patterns proved effective. Once children in Gipe's study worked with several sentences containing a new word, they were asked to create a meaning for the word by writing a new sentence. The application requirement seemed to assist word retention. Once words are taught and applied, Gipe suggests that a number of variable practice exercises be offered such as fill-in-the-blanks, matching of synonyms, dictionary exercises, etc. These activities serve as a means of reinforcing and reviewing words that have been taught.

An interesting theory of word identification has been described by Cunningham (1979). According to Cunningham's hypothesis, children identify unknown words by "searching through a store of known words and comparing the unknown [word or word parts] to the known [word or word parts]." Unfamiliar words are segmented into manageable units *(em ploy ment; arrange ment;*

em pire); the units are compared to known words or word fragments. The reader then recombines the units and tests the resulting word against concepts that are stored in oral language. Cunningham's research confirms nicely our often stated claim that instructional activities should build bridges between the new and the known. In this case, known base (root) words and affixes (prefixes and suffixes) should be identified and applied as children build or extend words and decode unfamiliar words. For instance, the base word *courage* could form the base of a word-extension activity that results in the creation of *discourage, encourage, courageous,* etc. A known prefix such as *semi- (semicircle)* could be used to assist in the decoding of *semiannual.*

Cunningham's research has been included in the section on context clues for one major reason; that is, decoded words must be reinstated into a meaningful language setting in order for their full meaning to come to light. The compare/contrast theory would make most sense (and be a most useful aid for children) if the difficult word were to be tested in context as a way of confirming meaning.

Sternberg, Powell, and Kaye (in press) claim that vocabulary training programs must help students recognize and use two subsystems of linguistic cues that hint at word meaning: *external cues,* those found in the context surrounding the word, and *internal cues,* those drawn from the morphemes within the word. (These are the cues we described in the section on structural analysis.) Word meaning can often be inferred by applying external and internal cues in unison.

External cues are text-related cues that can be classified into eight categories:

1. *Temporal cues.* Cues that imply the duration or frequency of an unknown word.
2. *Spatial cues.* Cues that tell something about the specific location of a word.
3. *Values cues.* Cues denoting the value (worth or desirability) of a word.
4. *Attribute cues.* Cues regarding a descriptive property of a word (e.g., size, shape, odor, color, feel, etc.)
5. *Functional cues.* Cues that tell of possible purposes, actions, or uses of a word.
6. *Enablement cues.* Cues regarding probable causes of or enabling conditions for a word.
7. *Class cues.* Cues that denote the class to which a word belongs.
8. *Equivalence cues.* Cues that refer to the meaning of a word or provide an antonym for the word.

An example of the use of some of these cues in textual analysis might help concretize our descriptive framework. Consider the sentence, "At dawn, *sol* arose on the horizon and shone brightly." This sentence contains several external contextual cues that could facilitate one's inferring that *sol* refers to the sun. "At dawn" provides a temporal cue, describing when the arising of *sol* occurred;

"arose" provides a functional cue, describing an action that sol can perform; "on the horizon" provides a spatial cue, describing where the arising of sol took place; "shone" provides another functional cue, describing a second action that sol can do; finally, "brightly" provides an attribute cue, describing a property (brightness) of the shining of sol. With all these different cues, it is no wonder that most people would find it easy to figure out that *sol* refers to the sun. (Sternberg et al., in press)

Text-related cues, according to Sternberg, Powell, and Kaye, vary in usefulness. If an unknown word appears often in the text, a student may be able to infer meaning from the variety of cues surrounding the multiple occurences of a word (i.e., temporal, spatial, value, etc.). Variability in the type of context cue should assist students' problem solving, although too much information could tend to "overload the circuits" for some students and reduce comprehension. Another point to note is that a reader's incentive to figure out a word's meaning is usually improved if a given unknown word is judged to be essential for understanding a passage. At times a reader may decide a particular word is not worth the decoding effort. The nature of a particular unknown word causes yet another concern. Some types of cues (temporal, spatial, etc.) will provide more value than others. In addition, it has been shown that context preceding an unknown word is of greater assistance than context following the word (Rubin 1976). The density of unknown words also influences the usefulness of textual cues. Most readers are overwhelmed when a passage contains a high density of unknown words. It is worth noting but not at all surprising to find that concrete words are easier to define than abstract concepts. Finally, the usefulness of textual cues will depend on the student's ability to retrieve, recognize, and apply past knowledge to the cue provided by an author.

Internal cues are those found within the word itself, such as prefix cues, suffix cues, and stem (base-word) cues. *Interactive cues*, those which result when a reader uses two or three of the previous cues (affix and stem) in combination, are also useful in inferring word meanings. Internal cues are influenced by a number of variables that have already been mentioned in regard to external cues. A reader's incentive to apply internal cues will likely increase if a word reappears frequently in a passage. Students are more likely to spend time on words that seem essential for passage comprehension. Too many unfamiliar words in a passage tend to overwhelm students and decrease incentive to use available cues. Some students may not recognize the effectiveness of noting internal cues. Multiple "decomposable" unknown words can prime students' awareness of the value of these in-word cues. Previously learned knowledge of words and word parts will assist readers' application of internal cues.

External and internal context cues can be of value to students as they attempt to infer word meaning. In the preceding paragraphs, a number of factors that influence the effectiveness of these cue systems have been outlined. You undoubtedly noted the value total language played in deciphering the meaning of unknown words. We hope that you will consider these external and internal cue systems as you design vocabulary-building exercises for children.

Context Clue Activities

The task of the teacher is to construct activities and situations through which children are given opportunities to develop the habit of examining surrounding context to make sensible guesses about the meanings of unfamiliar words. We would like to recommend several exercises you can use to help your students become more aware of the importance of surrounding context and develop a habit of making use of it.

1. Word meanings are learned more easily and retained longer if children restate the word's definition in writing. We suggest that you create a worksheet with a number of sentence problems, following our design.

Explain to the students that authors often provide clues or *signals* to the meanings of hard words. One signal includes the words *is* and *means*. Display these sentences with an overhead projector or on the chalkboard: *A foyer is the lobby of a hotel./To surmise means to guess an answer.* Work through one or two examples on the chalkboard: *A _____ decision is a decision that is made quickly.* Children may offer *hasty, speedy, quick, sudden*. Distribute the worksheet and give students time to complete the exercise.

Sample Sentences

a. A person who is fussy about what he eats is *finicky*.
   Finicky means _____.
b. A *rustic* setting is one that is simple and away from the city.
   Rustic means _____.
c. An *absurd* story is one that is foolish.
   Absurd means _____.
d. To *procrastinate* means to not do something right away.
   Procrastinate means _____.
e. To *grasp* the meaning of the sentence means to understand what is being said.
   To *grasp* means _____.

2. Select a set of vocabulary items you wish to help students learn. Create passages for the items that offer good cues to word meaning (see our samples below). Explain to the children that context refers to hints contained in a passage that help a reader understand an unknown word.

Display a *key word* card *(vagabond)* and read the passage containing the vocabulary word. Go through the paragraph with the children and underline words or phrases in the paragraph that help identify the meaning of the key item. Discuss the cues that have been identified. Distribute a worksheet containing key vocabulary items embedded in cue-rich paragraphs. After the children locate and underline all cues to word meaning, discuss each word's meaning. Review the entire set of words. Have children write a meaning for each item using their own words.

Sample Passages with Key Words

Alex had just arrived in our city. He had traveled around the country with no money for a long time. Alex decided to stay and look for work because he did not want to be a *vagabond* any longer.

Bernie wanted to *persuade* Kathy to vote for his best friend. He tried to convince her that his friend was the best one for the job. Bernie told Kathy everything he could think of that would make her change her mind.

The children were shopping in the men's clothing department for a present for their father. The children had planned to give him a shirt for his birthday, but some of the other types of *haberdashery* would also make a good gift. They finally decided on a beautiful blue tie.

3. Select a group of vocabulary items you wish to teach. Using the model we suggest below, create sentences that have a synonym or explanation of the unfamiliar word included. Explain to the students that authors often use *signals*, such as a phrase set off by commas, the word *or*, or a combination of commas and the word *or* to aid word meaning. Place examples on the chalkboard: *Jack was given an* equivalent, *or equal, portion./Sandra always uses a* pedometer, *an instrument for measuring the distance that one travels while walking, when she goes on her evening walks./The children were always* _____ *or bothering the dog.* Discuss how the author signals word meaning in each example. Distribute a worksheet using cue-rich sentences. Ask children to fill in the blanks with appropriate words and to circle the *signals* in each sentence.

Sample Sentences

a. She used a _____, a helpful tool, for cooking.
b. The old car is _____, or falling to pieces.
c. The child was _____, or discovered stealing cookies from the cookie jar.
d. The man stored tools in the _____, a shelter that is an open shed.

4. Many words have different meanings. The dictionary cannot indicate which meaning the writer intended; only the context can. Children can benefit from practice in comparing different meanings according to the use of the word in a sentence. You may find exercises like the following helpful:

Match the letter with the number.

1. Jane won a prize at the county *fair.*
2. Kenny just doesn't play *fair.* He cheats.

   a) a summer carnival   b) just, honest

1. Does your mother *conduct* the school band?
2. Marion was expelled from school for bad *conduct.*

   a) behavior   b) direct, lead

1. Edwinna plays *guard* on the team.
2. A lock may help *guard* against thieves.

a) protect   b) a ball-team position

5. Following the cloze procedure, words may be deleted systematically (every fifth or eighth word, for example) or by design (certain parts of speech for example). The child's task is to read the passage and supply the missing words. To do so, it is necessary to scrutinize the surrounding context — thereby developing the habit of using context. We invite you to supply the missing words in the following paragraph. The omitted words are listed below, but don't peek!

> I wish to begin _____ stating that I still _____ the some-what old-fashioned _____ that written words are _____ in read-ing. I know _____ is more fashionable to _____ concerned with syntactic structure, _____ nuances, and phonological relationships _____ important planks in bridging _____ gap from printed sur-face _____ to the writer's or _____ deep structures. And I _____ that they are important. _____ without words they are _____.

In the above paragraph every fifth word was omitted. The words you supplied may not be exactly the same as those which were deleted, but if they make some sense it indicates that you were making use of context cues. Here are the omitted words:

> by, hold, conviction, important, it, be, semantic, as the, structure, reader's, agree, yet, meaningless

The cloze procedure was first suggested by Taylor (1953) as a means of measuring the readability of written materials. The procedure stemmed from psy-chological studies of the Gestalt idea of closure, which refers to the impulse to complete a structured whole by supplying the missing element. In the case of reading, closure of the sentence is attained by filling in missing words.

6. Present context clues through the use of riddles and jingles, with the missing words supplied by the students. For example:

> I am small.
> I am brown.
> I like gardens.
> I eat lettuce and carrots.
> I am a ___(bunny___.

7. Junior and senior high school students in particular, and intermediate-grade children who are better readers, often enjoy demonstrating denotative and con-notative (that is, straight and hip, or conventional and slang) meanings of words through the use of context. Their task is to use words such as the following (and many more current and local ones they will be able to provide) in appropriate contexts. Their sentences or paragraphs can then be read to the class or exchanged with one another. They should be reminded that the context they use should indicate *which* definition of the word is intended.

in	trip	heavy
fuzz	split	pad
neat	weird	joint
hunk	acid	slam
tough	hangup	smokey
soul	turn on	ears
straight	tune in	rip off

8. A teaching activity such as the following might be highly useful in helping children expand their "set" for semantic diversity and thereby become more aware of the need to attend to context to discern the intended (though often infrequent) semantic attributes of even the most common words.

With this method children are presented with two or more sentences per word, each of which emphasizes a semantic attribute. Following each sentence are three choices related to feature emphasis. Later the teacher discusses the children's choices individually or in a group. The directions are: "Read the sentence sets below. Think carefully about what each sentence means. Put an X in front of the statement that helps you with the sentence meaning."

The fellow sniffed the food.
_____ In this sentence, the *price* of the food is important.
_____ In this sentence, the *smell* of the food is important.
_____ In this sentence, the *taste* of the food is important.
The fellow salted the food.
_____ In this sentence, the *smell* of the food is important.
_____ In this sentence, the *form* of the food is important.
_____ In this sentence, the *taste* of the food is important.
The adults bought the animals.
_____ In this sentence, the *price* of the animals is important.
_____ In this sentence, the *closeness* of the animals is important.
_____ In this sentence, the *hunger* of the animals is important.
The adults played with the animals.
_____ In this sentence, the *comfort* of the animals is important.
_____ In this sentence, the *price* of the animals is important.
_____ In this sentence, the *behavior* of the animals is important.

A FINAL WORD

At the start of this chapter we stated that the purpose of phonics instruction is to help children pronounce words they do not already recognize in print, with the hope that, once they hear the word, they will recall the meaning of it from their speaking and listening vocabularies. Because of the varied letter-sound relationships within the English language, many children find phonics difficult to learn. Thus, it is highly important for teachers to help those of their children who are having trouble with phonics. But phonic analysis is only one of the three important word-identification skills.

Thousands of English words are combinations of one or more root words or are words to which prefixes, suffixes, and other endings have been added. It would be a waste of time to attempt to teach each of these words as a sight word when children can identify so many unfamiliar words through the use of structural analysis. We believe that the more practice children have with subdividing unfamiliar words into meaningful parts (and building new words from known words and word parts) the more likely they will be to use structural analysis in their daily reading. Structural analysis is only one set of the word-identification skills, and has its limitations, since all words derive meaning from context. But it has value in vocabulary expansion both alone and when used in combination with context and phonics.

Contextual analysis is not a finite set of discrete generalizable skills that can be learned. Rather, it is an entire approach to reading. It is a robust word-identification procedure — and the one most frequently used by adult readers — to help determine the meanings of unfamiliar words. It can be used to identify new words, new or different meanings for already known words, and particular semantic attributes of words required for comprehension of the passage.

REFERENCES

Aukerman, M. D. "Acquisition and Transfer Value of Initial Training with Multiple Grapheme-Phoneme Correspondences." *Journal of Educational Psychology* 65 (1973): 28–34.

Bourque, M. L. "Specification and Validation of Reading Skills Hierachies." *Reading Research Quarterly* 15 (1980): 237–67.

Chall, J. *Learning to Read: The Great Debate.* New York: McGraw-Hill, 1967.

Culyer, R. C., III. "Guidelines for Skill Development: Word Attack." *The Reading Teacher* 32 (1979): 425–33.

Cunningham, J. W. "An Automatic Pilot for Decoding." *The Reading Teacher* 32 (1979): 420–24.

Deighton, L. C. *Vocabulary Development in the Classroom.* New York: Columbia University Press, 1959.

Downing, J. "Reading — Skill or Skills?" *The Reading Teacher* 35 (1982): 534–37.

Gipe, J. P. "Investigating Techniques for Teaching Word Meanings." *Reading Research Quarterly* 14 (1978–79): 624–44.

———. "Use of a Relevant Context Helps Kids Learn New Word Meanings." *The Reading Teacher* 33 (1980): 398–402.

Jenkins, B. L.; Longmaid, W. H.; O'Brien, S. F.; and Sheldon, C. N. "Children's Use of Hypothesis Testing When Decoding Words." *The Reading Teacher* 33 (1980): 664–67.

Johnson, D. D. *Factors Related to the Pronunciation of Vowel Clusters* (Technical Report #149) Madison, Wis.: Wisconsin Research and Development Center, University of Wisconsin, 1970.

LaBerge, D., and Samuels, S. J. "Toward a Theory of Automatic Information Processing in Reading." *Cognitive Psychology* 6 (1974): 293–323.

Murphy, H. A., and Durrell, D. D. *Speech-to-Print Phonics.* New York: Harcourt, 1964.

Pearson, P. D. "A Psycholinguistic Model of Reading." *Language Arts* 53 (1976) 309–14.

Rubin, D. C. "The Effectiveness of Context, Before, After, and Around a Missing Word." *Perception and Psychophysics* 19 (1976): 214–16.

Samuels, S. J. "Automatic Decoding and Reading Comprehension." *Language Arts* 53 (1976): 323–25.

Schell, L. M. "Teaching Decoding To Remedial Readers." *The Reading Teacher* 31 (1978): 877–82.

Sloop, Cornelia B., and Garrison, H. E. *Phonetic Keys to Reading*, 2nd ed. Oklahoma City: Economy Publishing Company, 1972.

Smith, F. *Understanding Reading: A Psycholinguistic Analysis of Reading and Learning to Read.* New York: Holt, Rinehart and Winston, 1971.

Smith, R. J., and Johnson, D. D. *Teaching Children to Read*, 2nd ed. Boston: Addison-Wesley, 1980.

Sternberg, R. J.; Powell, J. S.; and Kaye, D. B. "Teaching Vocabulary-Building Skills: A Contextual Approach." In *Classroom Computers and Cognitive Science*, edited by A. C. Wilkinson. New York: Academic Press, in press.

Taylor, W. L. "Cloze Procedures: A New Tool for Measuring Readability." *Journalism Quarterly* 30 (1953): 360–68.

8
Vocabulary Instruction in the Basal Reading Program

Words link minds together and allow communication to flow. A broad vocabulary is an indispensable tool for successful reading comprehension. Throughout this book we have emphasized the importance of vocabulary development and have provided a number of processes and techniques we hope you will use as you plan for vocabulary instruction. We recognize the fact that teachers use a wide range of books and other written materials as they design lessons for children; children's success with these instructional materials depends, in part, on their ability to understand the words authors have used to communicate ideas. In the present chapter we will demonstrate how teachers can enrich one type of instructional material, the traditional basal reader, by applying the vocabulary processes we have introduced throughout this book. Then, in Chapter Nine, we will focus our attention on vocabulary instruction in content-area materials. These chapters will conclusively demonstrate the necessity of direct vocabulary instruction in a total language setting.

We estimate that well over 90 percent of elementary-school teachers use basal readers as the major resource in reading instruction. There are many adequate basal programs on the market and all of them introduce and reinforce vocabulary. For example, note how vocabulary is highlighted in the Ginn Reading Program: "Words and skills are taught in meaningful contexts, with meaning established before reading a selection . . . pupils are involved in seeing, describing, using, defining and writing vocabulary words" (*Mystery Sneaker*, Teacher's Edition, p. T17). Figure 8.1 on the following page illustrates how the Ginn Reading Program emphasizes contextually based practice of new vocabulary words.

Most basal series provide sound activities for introducing and reviewing text-related vocabulary; however, we know that teachers are constantly searching for ways to make vocabulary study stimulating. We also know that not all children benefit from the same type of instructional designs. Alternative plans are needed to reteach and review words. Thus, we will include in this chapter a variety of suggestions for enriching the vocabulary component of the basal readers.

The vocabulary exercises we recommend serve two purposes: (1) chil-

Name

Use the new words next to each part to finish the story.
You may use some words more than once.

Robin looked at the car she had made from an old box. It
had four wheels and a _____**brake**_____ for stopping. It even
had a curved hood. _____**Robin**_____ started to paint the car.

"I'd like to go around the _____**world**_____ in this car," she
said to her friend Max. "But first I must _____**finish**_____
painting it."

"It is a long way around the _____**world**_____," Max
laughed. "How about starting with a race down the hill? I'm
sure I'll _____**finish**_____ first."

world

brake

Robin

finish

"We'll see who will _____**win**_____," laughed Robin as
she finished painting. She got into her car and Max got on his
bike. Robin asked Sue to be the _____**timer**_____. "Ready, get
set, go," she said.

_____**Robin**_____ and Max started down the hill. Robin's car
went very fast. She reached the end of the hill first and put on
her _____**brake**_____ to stop.

"I _____**won**_____!" Robin cried. "You made it in only one
minute!" cried Sue.

"I guess you did _____**win**_____," laughed Max. "That's a
fast car you made, Robin!"

won

timer

Robin

win

brake

VOCABULARY: word identification in context
BASIC WORDS: Robin, world, brake, timer, win, finish, won

Level 9 "Robin and the Sled Dog Race"

Figure 8.1. Contextually Based Practice of New Vocabulary Words: A Page from the Ginn Reading Program

dren *learn the basic words* needed to fully comprehend particular stories in their reading books; and, perhaps more important, 2) children *learn strategies for unlocking the meanings of unknown words* they meet in independent reading. With these exercises teachers can help children develop an insatiable curiosity for words that will last a lifetime.

In illustrating how our vocabulary processes can be applied to basal reading lessons, we have drawn sample lessons from the Ginn Reading Program, which itself includes many fine vocabulary teaching suggestions. In general, our lesson ideas can be used to supplement, expand, or enrich other exemplary teaching plans.

SYNONYMS

Figure 8.2 (p. 153) illustrates an introductory exercise designed to promote a better understanding of synonyms and antonyms. Our sample lesson is designed to create a better understanding of synonymous terms and to expand children's vocabulary as well.

Following completion and an in-class discussion/review of the workbook page shown in Figure 8.2, the following lesson might be used:

Step 1: Identify the four synonymous sentence sets.
Step 2: List the four pairs of synonymous terms (*errors/ mistakes; clever/smart; bad/terrible; tiny/small*) on the chalkboard.
Step 3: Elicit words from the reading group that have meanings "something like" the key items. For example:

errors/mistakes	clever/smart	bad/terrible	tiny/small
—blunder	—brainy	—horrible	—little
—flaw	—swift	—mean	—minute
—slip-up	—crafty	—awful	—wee
—miss	—intelligent	—bratty	—puny

Step 4: Ask children to work in pairs to rank each set of words according to intensity of meaning. 1 = most intense; 4 = least intense. (Note that groups of children will vary in assigning numbers to words.)
Step 5: Discuss the rankings with the entire group, noting differences in opinions.
Step 6: *Follow-up.* Each child must locate a new synonym for each of the four categories and write a sentence using each of the four new terms. During the next class meeting, sentences

Name

Read each pair of sentences. Circle the pair of sentences if they mean almost the same thing. Draw a box around those that have opposite meanings.

1. Gail made no errors on her homework.
   Gail made no mistakes on her homework.

2. The fox is thought to be a very clever animal.
   The fox is thought to be a very smart animal.

3. The weather was cloudy on the day of the race.
   The weather was sunny on the day of the race.

4. Lou couldn't go out because he had a bad cold.
   Lou couldn't go out because he had a terrible cold.

5. Some people like very plain meals.
   Some people like very fancy meals.

6. Kathy made tiny holes in the top of the box.
   Kathy made small holes in the top of the box.

7. Pablo lives on the east side of the city.
   Pablo lives on the west side of the city.

8. The store was crowded yesterday.
   The store was empty yesterday.

Additional Activity: List five pairs of words that have almost the same meaning.

VOCABULARY: vocabulary development
(synonyms/antonyms)

Level 9 "Alvin's Masterpiece"

Figure 8.2. Introducing Synonyms and Antonyms: A Page from the Ginn Reading Program

should be read and the new terms added to the
original list. The list could be entered into a class
vocabulary book to be used over and over again
in reading or writing lessons.

DENOTATION/CONNOTATION

A lesson stressing denotative word meaning can also double as a review lesson on
basic sight vocabulary. Examine the complete set of sight vocabulary words incorporated into a first-grade-level book shown in Figure 8.3 on page 156. The lesson
samples that follow serve several purposes: 1) basal sight vocabulary is reviewed;
2) denotative word meaning is expanded; and 3) children see how synonyms alter
sentence meaning to a slight degree. The children's task in the first exercise is to
read sentences that have been created with the basal vocabulary and to supply
synonyms drawn from their oral vocabularies for each underlined word. The
teacher records synonyms as they are given. Using the basic sight vocabulary
shown in Figure 8.3, the following sample sentences might be used:

> a. Ken, what are the *mean* dogs doing now?
>   (nasty, naughty, terrible, horrible)
>
> b. Can Ana help me *mix* the bread?
>   (stir, beat, blend, whip up)
>
> c. *Call* for help, the train is on fire!
>   (Yell, Scream, Telephone, Holler)

Words children supply could be written on word cards. Each card could be placed
over the appropriate underlined term so that the child could read the newly created sentence. Lessons such as the one just outlined provide children with an
opportunity to experiment with denotation.

Connotative word meanings also begin to emerge during early childhood.
Once again we can design a lesson using the basic sight vocabulary shown in
Figure 8.3. In addition to the textbook's vocabulary we will use *color words* since
they are usually recognized early during the first school year.

> Step 1: Develop sentences using basic sight words and color words
>   used *denotatively*.
>
>   a. Help me take this *blue* can out to my Grandma.
>   b. Dad thought the *green* bike may not race.
>   c. Ana will trick my dog with this *yellow* ball.
>
> Step 2: Demonstrate that color words are sometimes used to refer to
>   feelings or to describe how people act. Create simple sentences
>   using color words *connotatively*. Ask children to explain

Words in This Book

Level 4 introduces 49 words and maintains the 79 words introduced in Levels 1 through 3. The underlined words are introduced at this level. Words printed in second color can be decoded independently.

UNIT 1				
6. look	with	make	looks	46. want
Mom	8. here's	like	cat	47. trade
and	truck	bake	little	48. thing
Sara	now	bread	21. thought	fish
said	it	then	22. bone	49. Grandma
Ken	not	can't	I'll	take
I	big	get	23. drop	clay
see	good	go	24. that	hen
a	this	13. dog		51. something
fire	9. did	Jim	UNIT 2	52. pig
the	made	Ana	30. are	but
can	come	14. we'll	wheels	53. train
is	10. us	put	van	54. may
on	man	water	31. there	55. book
what	asked	out	32. doing	mean
we	she	15. bell	34. going	57. my
do	here	hop	up	58. Fox
7. have	11. Dad	16. dogs	36. fold	Coyote
to	in	dig	37. cut	59. me
call	Beth	run	39. read	am
for	does	play	race	60. back
help	he	17. some	40. day	62. from
will	work	18. trick	41. bike	63. beat
you	at	has	42. ride	
need	12. where	ball	mix	67
	eat	19. who	45. don't	

Figure 8.3. Sight Vocabulary Words: A Page from a First-Grade-Level Book

what the *color words* mean in sentences like the following:

a. Mom was *blue* when Sara did not help with the work.
b. Jim was *green* with envy when he saw Ken's new train. (Note: *envy* not on list of basic words)
c. "You are *yellow*," said Beth when Ana would not pet the little hen.

Step 3: Provide an instant follow-up by asking children to use the underlined words in denotative and connotative forms. You may wish to have an aide (parent or upper-grade student) assist you as you quickly record the sentences children create. Ask children to illustrate their sentences and place them on a bulletin board for further group sharing.

ANTONYMS

Study of antonyms not only expands and clarifies word meanings, but it also develops mental processes required when children meet contrasting ideas in reading assignments. Figure 8.4 (p. 158) offers children an opportunity to practice identification of antonyms (and synonyms). Note that key words in this basal lesson are *cheerful/unhappy; enormous/tiny; approaching/departing; wise/foolish;* and *succeed/fail.*

Step 1: List the four pairs of antonyms on a chart tablet. Hold a discussion on each pair, relating the words to the children's personal experiences. For example:

"We all enjoyed our class trip to the zoo last week. Jim, which zoo animals could we list as being *enormous* (elephant, rhinoceros, etc.). Sara, can you think of some *tiny* zoo animals? (snake, baby monkeys, etc)."

List all words on the board under the key vocabulary words (antonym pairs).

Continue the discussion, using the remaining three pairs of antonyms (things that make you feel *cheerful/unhappy*, etc.). Retain the word lists recorded on the chart tablet.

Step 2: On the following day, distribute an exercise that requires students to apply the contrasting concepts and words practiced in the previous day's lesson. The children's task is to read the sentence containing *one* word from the antonym pair and to

Name

A. Circle the word that means almost the same as the underlined word.

1. The spectators rose to their feet for the national anthem.
   players   (audience)   umpires

2. The grasshoppers were a menace to the wheat crop.
   solution   help   (threat)

3. Karen muttered something under her breath.
   shouted   (mumbled)   whistled

4. In her research, my mother employs the latest computers.
   repairs   (uses)   ignores

5. Warren was appointed to the student council.
   reported   introduced   (assigned)

B. Circle the word that means the opposite of the underlined word.

6. A group of cheerful children got off the bus.
   calm   (unhappy)   [laughing]

7. The small child had an enormous appetite.
   (tiny)   [gigantic]   [huge]

8. Through the fog I could hear footsteps approaching.
   [nearing]   (departing)   shuffling

9. It was wise of you to bring your umbrella.
   [smart]   (foolish)   [clever]

10. If you want to succeed, you must follow the directions.
    (fail)   conquer   [triumph]

Additional Activity: Go back to sentences 6–10. This time put a box around
   the word that means almost the same as the underlined word. Sometimes
   there is more than one answer.

VOCABULARY DEVELOPMENT: synonyms/
antonyms

Level 13 "A Wind to Sweep the World Clean"

Figure 8.4. Identifying Synonyms and Antonyms: A Page from the
Ginn Reading Program

select the word in parentheses that *cannot* be used to complete the sentence correctly.

a. Joan felt *foolish* when she forgot her math book at home. *(embarrassed, silly, proud)*
b. The *approaching* plane burst into flames just before it landed in the cornfield. *(departing, arriving, descending)*
c. An *enormous* elephant is coming out of the shelter. *(gigantic, puny, large)*

Once individuals have completed the exercise, discuss each example and decide why the choices were made for each sentence.

HOMOPHONES

Context clues provide the best hints to word meaning, thus, all lessons on homophones should draw on the examination of connected text. Since cues to the meaning of homophones lie in spelling patterns, not the sounds of the word, oral lessons will do little to promote development of reading vocabulary. The basal reader lesson shown in Figure 8.5 shows how direct instruction is used to conduct a review of homophones. Following a lesson such as that shown in Figure 8.5, children might enjoy the challenge of creating "hink-hinks" (see p. 29) with the homophones they have just studied.

Key homophonic pairs related to the lesson might be *beet/beat; sun/son; nose/knows; weighs/ways;* and *dye/die.* Riddles using the hink-hink pattern could be written, humorously illustrated, and placed into a class booklet for all to enjoy. Answers to the riddles (the homophonic word pairs) could be placed on a page in the back of the book. Children can be encouraged to contribute hink-hinks in addition to those based on the key vocabulary of the original lesson plan.

Sample hink-hinks:
What do you call an exhausted vegetable?
(a beat-beet)
What would you call a celestial male offspring?
(a sunny-sonny)

VOCABULARY

Vocabulary Development: Distinguishing between homophones (Review)

Write these words on the chalkboard and have them read: *flower, flour*. Then ask:

> What do you notice about these two words? (They sound alike.) What can you say about the way these words are spelled? (They are spelled differently.) What does the first word, *flower,* mean? (a blossom, the part of a plant that has petals and makes seeds) What does the second word, *flour,* mean? (the ground meal used in such baked goods as bread)

Ask volunteers to make up sentences of their own using the two words, *flower* and *flour*.

Review the fact that some words may sound alike but have different meanings and spellings. Write this on the chalkboard:

blue   blew
1. The breeze _____ the hat off my head.
2. Blanchard has a _____ pair of sneakers.

Have the words read and ask:

> What does the first word, *blue,* mean? (the color of the sky on a clear day) What does the second word, *blew,* mean? (sent out air) Which word fits into the first sentence? (blew) Which word fits into the second sentence? (blue)

Ask volunteers to write the correct word in each blank.

Figure 8.5. Direct Instruction in the Review of Homophones: A Page from a Basal Reader

MULTIMEANING WORDS

Multimeaning words are found in even the earliest levels of the basal reader. You will recall that a large number of words in the *Johnson Basic Vocabulary List* (see Chapter Six) had multiple meanings. Vocabulary lessons based on this category of words can begin very early in the child's reading career. We ask that you refer once again to the end-of-book vocabulary list presented in Figure 8.3. Note the large percentage of words that have two or more meanings (*look, see, fire, can,* etc.). At this early reading level, lessons on multimeaning vocabulary serve a number of purposes: 1) sight vocabulary words are reinforced, 2) word meanings are expanded, and 3) the child's level of linguistic awareness is raised. This latter point is quite significant to reading programs. Children have stored word meanings for years prior to learning to read. They have learned multiple meanings for numerous words (think of words like *run* or *set*, for example). Lessons like the one we propose here help children discover something they already know subconsciously. A child, for instance, shows us by verbal performances that *train* (a noun) refers to a vehicle, while *train* (a verb) is something one can do to a pet animal. Written exercises serve as a means of teaching the child that the word *t-r-a-i-n* is the code for both of these symbols. Lessons serve to raise linguistic awareness. Further, what we are doing is teaching the child to anticipate multiple word meanings during reading.

The example below could be used to introduce the concept of multimeaning vocabulary. (Note that all of the words in each sentence are drawn from the list in Figure 8.3; thus, sight vocabulary is reinforced.)

Step 1: Create and record sentences containing multimeaning words such as the following:

    a. The dogs can't run in this *race*.
    b. Can I *race* you to the van?

    c. My *fish* need to eat now.
    d. Beth, will you *fish* here with my Grandma?

    e. Ken is going to *train* his little Fox to ride.
    f. Hop on the *train* and get going!

    g. I want to go to the *play* that Jim is in.
    h. Who can see the dogs run and *play*?

Step 2: Ask volunteers to read the pairs of sentences and tell how the underlined words differ in each sentence. In these sentences one word in each pair refers to "something" (a noun) while the other word refers to "something that can be done" (a verb).

Step 3: Capable youngsters should be able to locate and write sentences with additional multimeaning words from the list. Perhaps children could work in pairs initially. Resulting sentences should be shared with the entire group.

SEMANTIC MAPPING

Semantic maps are valuable tools to use as lessons or units are introduced; maps can be expanded or focused during a unit of study and then used as a reference during review lessons. The sample lesson that follows illustrates how a semantic map can be used to: 1) introduce a story, 2) focus on selection/critical words, and 3) focus on new meanings for old words.

The Blind Connemara by C. W. Anderson is included in book-length form in Level 13 of the Ginn Reading Program, *Flights of Colors* (Clymer et al. 1982). The story tells of a young girl's devotion to a beautiful, white Connemara, an Irish pony, that becomes blind but that, with the girl's help, becomes a champion despite his handicap. Developing a semantic map on horses prior to assigning this story would not only teach and review vocabulary necessary for story comprehension, but the exercise would be an excellent device to use in motivating children to read the selection. The semantic map might yield the words shown in Figure 8.6 (see Chap. Four for guidelines).

Once words are listed in groups, categories can be labeled (riding clothes, ways horses move, horse-equipment, etc.). As the story is read, additional terms can be added to the original categories; a new category of selection/critical terms could be added; multimeaning vocabulary could be highlighted. Remember our key point on semantic maps — recording words is not the purpose behind map

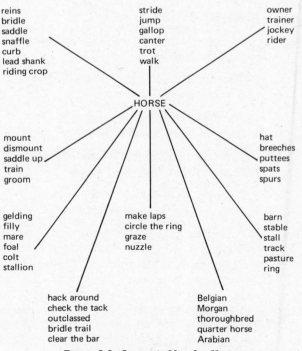

Figure 8.6. Semantic Map for *Horse*

development. We feel it is essential that words are discussed to be certain that children understand their meanings. Once the map has been completed, discussed, and revised and the story has been read, the class might be motivated to read some of the excellent books about horses. Vocabulary specific to the "horse theme" could be added to the semantic map. Retain the expanded semantic map in a large chart book for use in creative writing.

SEMANTIC FEATURE ANALYSIS

Basal reading lessons frequently focus on classifying words according to categories. The lessons shown in Figures 8.7 and 8.8 on the following pages demonstrate classification exercises common to basal programs. Teachers can enrich or reinforce these types of lessons through the development of semantic feature charts that go a step beyond categorical classification. Semantic feature exercises encourage students to look for slight differences in meaning between words in one category. (See Chap. Four for a step-by-step lesson plan using semantic feature analysis.)

How can semantic feature analysis be applied to these basal reader plans? By using semantic feature grids words (instruments) can be classified according to a general category (musical instruments) and then classified according to certain semantic features that some have and others do not have. By adding features children can learn, for example, how an organ and a piano are alike but differ, how a guitar, violin and, harp are similar and different (see Figure 8.9, p. 166).

Let us suppose that classification exercises similar to those in Figures 8.7 and 8.8 were part of a basal lesson accompanying a unit on animals. Following the text's categorization lesson, a teacher might lead children in the development of semantic feature grids such as the ones appearing in Figures 8.10a–c on pages 166 and 167. Specific vocabulary drawn from the textbook story would be used to develop the vocabulary lesson. Contributions to both the rows and the columns would ensure that the lesson concentrate on text-related vocabulary. Remember, semantic feature charts can be prepared before a lesson to motivate interest, teach vocabulary, and focus attention. Like semantic maps, they are also valuable sources of review and refinement of vocabulary concepts and as outlines for writing exercises.

VOCABULARY

Vocabulary Development: Classifying words according to category (Introductory Instruction)

Write the heading *Musical Instruments* on the chalkboard. Then ask pupils to name musical instruments. Under the heading, list the instruments they suggest. Pupils may mention the following:

piano	violin	drum
guitar	organ	harp
tuba	accordion	harmonica

To show the relationship of a category and its members, say:

> These words are items (point to the list of musical instruments) in a category (point to the heading).

Then read the following items, one group at a time. Ask pupils to name the category for each group:

eagles, owls, hawks (birds)
lemonade, water, milk (drinks)
happiness, anger, sadness (feelings)

To provide practice in classifying words according to category, distribute Skillpack page 34. Read the directions and do the first item with pupils. Then have them complete the page independently. Discuss answers and encourage pupils to do the Additional Activity.

Studybook page 45 also provides practice in classifying words according to category.

Figure 8.7. Classification Exercises: A Page from a Basal Reader, 1

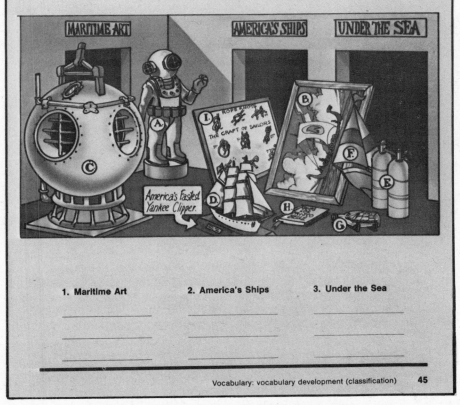

Cleaning Day at the Maritime Museum

The word "maritime" is used to describe something that has to do with the sea or ships. From that you can probably figure out what a maritime museum is. The picture below shows the main hall of the Pacific Maritime Museum. As you can see, some of the exhibits have been moved into the hall while the three showrooms are being painted. Each exhibit is lettered to enable it to be easily returned to its proper room. However, someone misplaced the master list, so you will have to discover where each exhibit belongs. Write the letter of each exhibit under the name of the room in which it belongs.

MARITIME ART

AMERICA'S SHIPS

UNDER THE SEA

ROPE KNOTS
THE CRAFT OF SAILORS

America's Fastest Yankee Clipper.

1. Maritime Art

_____

_____

_____

2. America's Ships

_____

_____

_____

3. Under the Sea

_____

_____

_____

Vocabulary: vocabulary development (classification)   **45**

Figure 8.8. Classification Exercises: A Page from a Basal Reader, 2

165

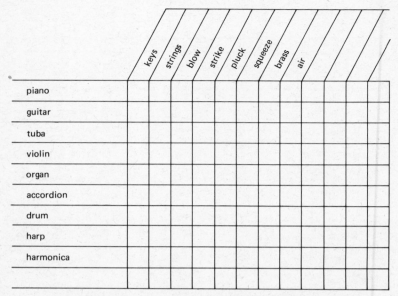

Figure 8.9. Semantic Feature Analysis: *Musical Instruments*

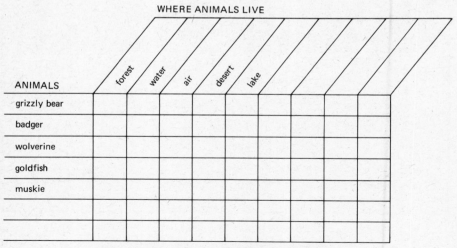

Figure 8.10a. Semantic Feature Analysis: *Animals*

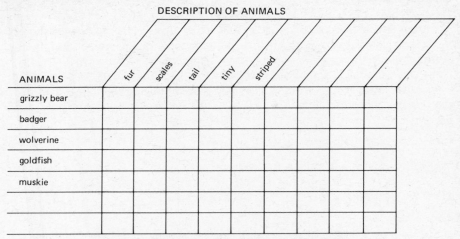

Figure 8.10b. Semantic Feature Analysis: *Animals*

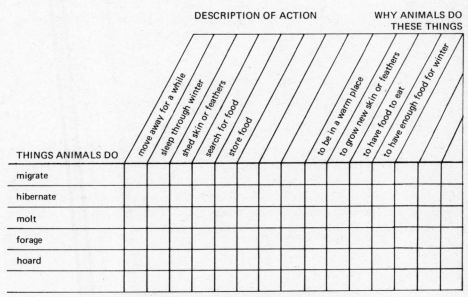

Figure 8.10c. Semantic Feature Analysis: *Animals*

ANALOGIES

Analogies are challenging for students and are a valuable resource for vocabulary reviews. Analogies permit practice in inductive and deductive thinking while embedding specific vocabulary items more soundly in the student's language system. The potential for application within basal reading programs is excellent, even at the lower levels. Word games such as the following could be drawn from the primary word list shown in Figure 8.3. (Children would be given the word list to use.)

EASY (Word choices are given.)

a. *Mom* is to *Dad* as *Sara* is to _____.
    (Ken, Ana, Fox)
b. *Bike* is to _____ as *book* is to *read*.
    work, play, ride

HARDER (Word choices are not given: children would search through basic sight words for choices.)

a. *Can* is to *man* as *to* is to __(do)__.
b. *Fish* is to *eat* as *(ball)* is to *play*.

At the middle- and upper-elementary-grade levels, the difficulty of the vocabulary increases dramatically and more words are available to use in lesson development. Analogies naturally gain depth in terms of the thought required in solving the word problems. Figures 8.11 and 8.12 (pp. 169–70) show a suggested technique for vocabulary review found in a basal reader. In addition, or as an alternative, to the basal lesson, the following lesson might be effective. (Refer to Chap. Four for additional designs for analogical sentences.)

SAMPLE SENTENCES

a. *(Towel)* is to *beach* as *blanket* is to *bed*.
b. *Knead* is to *(bread)* as *stir* is to *cookies*.
c. *(Minute)* is to *hour* as *second* is to *minute*.
d. *(Half)* is to *whole* as *teaspoon* is to *tablespoon*.

Note that our lesson incorporates the vocabulary presented in the basal reader. Students could be told to complete the analogies using the lesson's new vocabulary. Once the worksheet has been completed, a class discussion should focus on the relationship between word pairs. Students should justify the correctness or incorrectness of words the group has used to complete the analogical sentences. Teachers might consider developing analogies to use in an end-of-unit vocabulary review.

VOCABULARY

Word Identification: Using new vocabulary words

You may want to review briefly the meanings of the new vocabulary words, especially those pupils found difficult. Write these words on the chalkboard:

> towel   wheat   stir   half   tablespoon
> knead   minute   oven

In random order, read the Glossary definitions for each word. Call on volunteers to point to and read the word being defined. Then have pupils use each word in an oral sentence.

To provide practice with the new vocabulary words, distribute Skillpack page 13. Have pupils read the directions at the top of the page. Ask a volunteer to read the first group of words. Discuss how *minutes, second,* and *hours* fit into the same meaning category; elicit that *tables* does not belong. Direct pupils to cross out *tables* and to complete the rest of the numbered items independently. When all pupils have finished the page, review each item. Discuss how the words in each group are related and why the word that does not belong was crossed out. Have pupils correct any items they may have missed.

Figure 8.11. Vocabulary Review: A Page from a Basal Reader

169

Name

Find the word in each group that does not belong with the others. Cross it out.

1. minutes   seconds   hours   ~~tables~~

2. oven   sink   ~~tree~~   cupboard

3. towel   napkin   ~~lamp~~   sponge

4. kneading   folding   pushing   ~~talking~~

5. stir   ~~learn~~   mix   pour

6. tablespoons   teaspoons   cups   ~~baseballs~~

7. car   truck   ~~wheat~~   van

8. half   ~~green~~   whole   part

9. heat   warm   ~~stir~~   hot

10. tree   branch   twig   ~~towel~~

11. José   Charlie   ~~Pencil~~   Marsha

12. ~~towel~~   person   man   grandmother

Additional Activity: Write a funny sentence using some of the crossed-out words.

VOCABULARY: word identification
BASIC WORDS: towel, wheat, stir, half, tablespoons, kneading, minutes, oven

Level 9 "Mrs. Birdie's Bread"

Figure 8.12. Vocabulary Review: A Page from the Ginn Reading Program

DICTIONARY

We cannot directly teach all the words children will meet throughout their life-time. They will need to consult reference books to clarify vague word meanings or to identify unique or completely unfamiliar terms. Dictionaries are useful reference books only if students know how to use them effectively and efficiently. Most basal reading programs teach dictionary skills. These skills or subskills are essential for successful dictionary usage. First, students must be familiar with the type of material they can expect to find in a dictionary: guide words, entry words, pronunciation keys, etymological information, abbreviation and symbol lists, and special information sections (maps, illustrations, table of weights and measures, etc.). But most important, they must be able to find the unknown word they have come across in their reading, select an appropriate meaning from the several that are offered in the dictionary entry, and note how the word's meaning "fits" into the original reading context.

We believe that two distinct types of practice exercises must be included in regard to dictionary instruction: 1) exercises that help the child learn how to locate words and other information and 2) exercises that help children determine which dictionary definition best matches the original context of the unknown word. The former (skill-and-drill) type of exercises are usually found in abundance throughout basal readers; however, the latter type of exercise (meaning-focused) is not likely to appear often.

Our suggestion is that you supplement the traditional skill-and-drill exercises (alphabetizing, locating a word that means _____, etc.) with dictionary activities reflecting a total language perspective. At frequent intervals throughout the school year, identify sentences from the basal story that contain unfamiliar words. As a group, using personal copies of a good dictionary, work together to locate two or three of the hard words—discussing the location procedures as you go along. Read through the varied meanings and decide which is most appropriate to the original context. That means going to the textbook and reading a paragraph or so to check on the word's actual meaning. Then ask each child to locate a word from the textbook and to share the appropriate meaning from the several listed in the dictionary.

The following sentences, drawn from *The Blind Connemara* by C. W. Anderson (Ginn Reading Program, Level 13) illustrate the point we have tried to make. Many children would fail to comprehend this exceptionally fine story without recognizing the selection/critical and multimeaning words such as those in the following sentences:

1. There was just a hint of Irish *brogue* in the voice (p. 478).
2. "*Snaffle* or *double bridle?*" she asked (p. 481).
3. The white *Connemara* was *cantering* around the ring (p. 485).
4. He had everything, not only *conformation* but *disposition* and intelligence (p. 498).
5. The dog gave a sharp bark, and the Connemara *shied* into the bushes (p. 489).

6. When he felt the *crop* again he put on speed and jumped (p. 495).
7. "His *gaits* are perfect," he had said (p. 514).
8. The man in the brown *riding breeches* and leather *puttees* looked at the *bay* pony closely and put his hand under his *mane* (p. 478).

We realize that a lesson such as the one just described takes precious class time; however, we feel that it is a direct teaching technique well worth the teacher's and students' time and effort.

THESAURUS

A thesaurus contains a valuable treasury of words teachers and children will enjoy using in vocabulary development activities. In Chapter Five we offered several unique ideas for getting children "hooked on words" through using the thesaurus. Now we will demonstrate how basal reading lessons might be enriched through this rich resource tool.

Vocabulary exercises are most effective if they apply directly to practice in context. In the following activity, words and their meanings selected from a children's reading textbook are reinforced and expanded. Level 9 of the Ginn Reading Program includes the children's classic "Winnie-the-Pooh" by A. A. Milne (*Mystery Sneaker*, 1982, pp. 208–19). Throughout the story, Milne uses a number of *-ly* adverbs (*proudly, properly, politely, lovingly, loudly, sternly, thoughtfully, slightly, directly, kindly, anxiously, crossly, quickly, gloomily, cheerfully, gaily*). Milne has carefully selected these words to create the mood we have come to associate with the loveable "Edward Bear" stories.

Using the thesaurus, a vocabulary activity could be developed to help children understand the effect these special adverbs have on the story. Following story reading, the teacher might distribute worksheets containing sentences drawn from the text, such as:

1. "What I said was, 'Is anybody at home?'" called out Pooh very *loudly* (p. 210).
2. "No-no," said Pooh *carelessly* (p. 214).
3. "It all comes," said Pooh *crossly*, "of not having doors big enough" (p. 214).
4. "I was just beginning to think," said Bear, sniffing *slightly*, "that Rabbit might never be able to use his front door again" (p. 215).
5. "How long does getting thin take?" asked Pooh *anxiously* (p. 216).
6. "A week!" said Pooh *gloomily* (p. 217).
7. But Christopher Robin looked after him *lovingly*, and said to himself, "Silly old Bear!" (p. 219).
8. "It all comes," said Rabbit *sternly*, "of eating too much" (p. 214–15).

Children could use individual children's thesauruses to locate *-ly* synonyms for Milne's adverbs. As an in-class activity, each child might be responsible for the *-ly* adverb in one sample sentence. Once new adverbs are selected, children could reread key sentences orally and decide together which term is best — the one Milne used or their own. An alternative activity would be to locate antonyms and note how the story mood changes when antonyms are inserted into the sentences. A chart of synonyms and antonyms might be created to use later in creating more sentences regarding the storybook characters:

LOUDLY		CARELESSLY		CROSSLY	
S	A	S	A	S	A
noisily	faintly	thoughtlessly	cautiously	bitterly	gently
coarsely	softly	mindlessly	meticulously	scornfully	good-naturedly

SLIGHTLY		ANXIOUSLY		LOVINGLY	
S	A	S	A	S	A
scantily	robustly	fretfully	calmly	fondly	grudgingly
weakly	sturdily	apprehensively	peacefully	tenderly	hatefully

GLOOMILY		STERNLY	
S	A	S	A
moodily	joyfully	severely	vaguely
sullenly	lightly	rigidly	flexibly

ETYMOLOGY

Almost any lesson drawn from a middle- to upper-grade reading textbook will have a wealth of words that carry interesting "histories." Even simple, meaningless words have to come from somewhere! Words like *a, and, are,* and *to* are native Anglo-Saxon, whereas *call, both, take,* and *same* are Danish in origin. Of course, it is much more fun to discover things like the fact that *cantaloupe* was named after the town *Cantalupe* where it was first grown or that the eponym *sideburn* was derived from Ambrose E. Burnside's famous whiskers.

We suggest that you turn to etymology frequently as you plan vocabulary lessons, for two reasons: 1) etymology is a great way to expand children's vocabularies and knowledge in general; and, just as importantly, 2) children are bound to enjoy these activities so much they won't even realize they are studying vocabulary. Creating a positive attitude about words and the learning of word meanings is an important goal to strive toward.

Searches for word origins might precede story reading and serve as a means of developing background for the literature to be read. For example, in the Ginn Reading Program, Level 9, we find a brief biography of Laura Ingalls Wilder. What possible types of etymological studies might emerge?

1. Laura and her family lived in Wisconsin, Minnesota, South Dakota, and Missouri (among other places). Locate the origin of the names of each of these states.
2. Using an appropriate reference (see Chap. Five) research the meaning of the first names of each Ingalls/Wilder family member.
3. Figure 8.13 presents the first page of the biography. Note that several words

Young and daring Laura had quite an adventure at the footbridge. The life of the author, Laura Ingalls Wilder, was exciting, too.

Laura Ingalls Wilder, Storyteller

Peggy Warner

Think for a minute about where you now live. Now take away roads, telephones, cars, trains, and planes. Take away all your neighbors. Take away supermarkets. Take away zoos. You and your family are all by yourselves. You will build your own house. You will grow your own food.

It is hard to know what our country was like not too long ago. Laura Ingalls Wilder knew. She had crossed the plains with her family in a covered wagon. She knew what it was like to be a child in the 1800s. And she wrote it all down in books. She wrote these books to tell children about life in early

200

Figure 8.13. Etymological Studies: A Page from the Ginn Reading Program

are potentially good candidates for word studies even though they do not relate specifically to the biography: *telephone, supermarket, cars, trains,* and *planes* all entered our language rather recently. What is the origin of each word? How did *car* receive its name, etc?

A FINAL WORD

Developing a reading vocabulary is one major emphasis of basal reading programs. A broad meaning vocabulary is essential if children are to comprehend the stories found in their reading textbooks. Most basal series we have seen introduce and teach predetermined lists of words before text stories are read. Some series offer ideas for general vocabulary growth.

In this chapter, we have attempted to demonstrate how our vocabulary processes can be used to complement, supplement, enrich, reinforce, or review vocabulary in conjunction with basal readers. We do not wish to imply that one or even several of our vocabulary activities will transform students into masterful language users. *Occasional* attempts to improve vocabulary will have little effect. What we advocate is continuous, daily, teacher-directed work on vocabulary in settings that make sense to children. That is one reason we choose to include chapters on vocabulary instruction in textbook settings. We think children should be surrounded with words, should be encouraged to study and learn new words, and given an endless curiosity about language.

We realize that an entire book could be developed on how teachers might apply vocabulary processes to classroom textbook instruction; however, we chose to apply just one teaching suggestion representative of each vocabulary process defined in our book. Our hope is that you will view this as a chapter of sample ideas, or models, that will stimulate your own thinking when you plan lessons around the basal reader. Teacher's manuals for basal readers have many strong features; however, they were not designed to be followed religiously, page by page, nor were they created to replace sound, direct instruction by a good teacher. We encourage you to consider the numerous ideas we have offered for going beyond the basal. We think you will find our ideas will stimulate your children to broaden their mental horizons through vocabulary expansion. The more words a child *really* knows, the richer his/her thought processes will become.

REFERENCE

Clymer, Theodore, et al. The Ginn Reading Program. Lexington, Mass.: 1982.

9
Vocabulary Instruction in the Content Areas

In this chapter we will turn our attention to vocabulary instruction in the content areas. We know that students are expected to read most content materials independently and that knowledge of content vocabulary is crucial to gaining meaning from those materials (Kaplan and Tuchman 1980). Further, we are aware of the fact that students fare better in content reading when vocabulary-building programs are offered (Barrett and Graves 1981). Vocabulary lessons that draw on students' past experiences and build new experiences are the most valuable (Steiglitz and Steiglitz 1981). Hence, as in previous chapters, our focus will be on the importance of direct vocabulary instruction in total language settings. Our goal throughout the chapter will be to provide teaching strategies that will help teachers 1) introduce, review, and reinforce content-area vocabulary, and 2) lead students to apply vocabulary strategies independently when reading and studying.

We believe vocabulary knowledge and the acquisition of concepts go hand in hand. Other writers have referred to the vocabulary/concept phenomenon as the "chicken and egg" paradox (Estes and Vaughan 1978). Children need to understand basic concepts before words representing those concepts will make sense; yet, the vocabulary representing these concepts is essential for concept introduction and discussion. Our position remains true to the on-going theme of this entire book: vocabulary must be introduced in meaningful, experienced-based settings that encourage children to build bridges between new concepts and those already familiar to them.

Every content area has special words students must learn to read. The vast number of *technical vocabulary* items that permeate any content area can prohibit comprehension unless instruction is offered. Technical vocabulary refers to specific terms used to describe or discuss content-area concepts such as:

science	mathematics	social studies	English
reflection	integer	democracy	genre
refraction	cosign	feudalism	alliteration
gravity	geometry	treaty	clause
vector	angle	legislate	gerund

Students need to learn the concepts represented by key labels. *Multimeaning* words may also cause comprehension problems as readers move from one content area to another. *Casting a play* in English class is in no way related to *casting a ballot* in social studies class. The *organ* used in music class has no relationship to the *organ* studied in zoology. Teachers must be conscious of the number of potentially confusing multimeaning words children meet in content-area textbooks. *General vocabulary* is yet another cause of concern in content-area texts. These words are not content-specific but are used in all teaching areas (e.g., *resistance, guarantee,* and *accommodate*). Children must acquire a growing number of words in their sight vocabularies in order to process written information. Teachers should be cognizant of the fact that children may need assistance in learning words in each of these three (sometimes overlapping) categories (technical, multimeaning, and general) so that the reading of content-area assignments will not be an overwhelming, frustrating, and defeating task.

We have said that direct vocabulary instruction will benefit content-area reading. We believe that preteaching of words in meaningful settings is a sound addition to a lesson plan. If children don't learn the language of a subject, they simply cannot communicate with the teacher or understand the written materials. Once words have been identified, they should be defined in context with as many examples given as possible. When words are taught in context, students can draw on their prior knowledge of the language to assist them in determining word meaning. The position of a word in a sentence (syntax) as well as the meaningful language cues within the sentence (semantics) both assist a student in word-meaning exercises.

Preteaching content-area vocabulary to groups of children has greater potential for success than individual instruction (Readence et al. 1981). Time is used efficiently when words are introduced and taught to groups of children. However, an even greater benefit accrues during group instruction when students listen to one another discuss words and they practice using words in meaningful communication. Careful planning and direct instruction by the teacher plays an important role at this point. Demonstrations, models, examples, and films are often needed to help children acquire the meanings of important words. Teachers need to focus discussions and limit the time devoted to each vocabulary item. Follow-up reinforcement exercises should be assigned so that words presented to the entire group can be practiced by individual children. Review lessons might again be planned to incorporate whole-group discussion or sharing.

Teachers simply cannot teach all the new, difficult vocabulary children meet in their textbooks. Rather, essential words (technical, multimeaning, and general) must be taught regularly, using instructional strategies that will serve as models for children to follow when they independently approach unfamiliar words in printed material. Which words should be taught? Some books offer word lists, glossaries, notes along the margin, and words in dark or italicized print to aid vocabulary development. These textual aids relieve the teacher of the instructional obligation of having to isolate vocabulary items.

Herber (1970) has some good suggestions on narrowing the actual words to be taught in any subject area. First, he suggests that teachers sort out basic concepts that children must learn: "Technical vocabulary representing those concepts forms the basic list of words to be taught" (p. 155). The relative value of words within any unit is a second point of consideration. Not all words are critical to understanding major concepts within a unit. Finally, student competencies play a role in vocabulary instruction. Teachers must ask such questions as: How intelligent are my students? What level of reading ability have these children attained? Have the children had past experiences with this particular topic? We know that teachers cannot hope to teach each and every new word in content textbooks. Herber's guidelines offer sensible suggestions to selecting words for instruction.

Several years ago, Herber (1968) published basic vocabulary lists for each of the four major content-area subjects. Each list includes an abbreviated dictionary of definitions for these basic words. We think these fundamental lists will be valuable to you as you design lessons in the content areas. You may wish to update or adapt Herber's lists by incorporating any additional, essential words from your school's content-area textbooks. Some teachers might decide to organize Herber's lists in a different manner; for instance, the lists could be divided into grade, book, or unit levels.

Once you have decided on the set of words meriting direct instruction for any unit, additional decisions must be made; that is, techniques must be chosen to make vocabulary instruction as effective as possible for students. Remember, our goal is twofold — we want children to be able to read words with ease in order to comprehend specific lessons in the content areas, but we also hope we can teach vocabulary in such a way that children will acquire strategies that make independent word attack possible. First and foremost, we stress the meaningful presentation of whole words (see Chap. Six for our step-by-step teaching plans). We advocate direct, meaningful instruction preceding any games or activities that attempt to increase children's sight recognition of those words. Secondly, since we recognize the fact that students will continually come across words they cannot recall seeing before, we suggest that teachers occasionally introduce new content-area words using a combination of phonic, structural analysis, and context clues (see Chap. Seven for teaching hints).

Lessons designed to familiarize students with denotative word meaning are essential to success in content areas. We have selected the subject area of social studies to illustrate how our vocabulary procedure can be used to enhance instruction. Social studies materials are written in an exact, factual manner with a great deal of technical language. Students must learn word meanings and remember these technical terms as they progress through a unit of study.

Figure 9.1 shows the introductory page of a unit selected from a fourth-grade textbook. Note that the vocabulary items for this brief (four-page) lesson include *produce, products, grazing, pasture, silo, silage,* and *butterfat*. These terms, both technical and multimeaning, must be understood by the children if they are to thoroughly comprehend the lesson and then go on to the next several lessons on this same topic. Our sample lesson, based on the step-by-step plan we introduced in Chapter Three, might be used to teach the denotative meaning of the vocabulary items.

America's Dairyland

Wisconsin has many different kinds of farms. But the state is most famous for dairy farms and dairying. There are dairy farms on rolling green hills throughout much of the state. Large and small herds of black and white cows dot the farms. Wisconsin produces more milk than any other state. More cheese is made in Wisconsin than in any other state. Large amounts of butter, canned milk, and other dairy products are made here, too. These products make dairying one of Wisconsin's major businesses.

As you study about dairy farms in Wisconsin you will learn how milk comes to your home or store. And you will learn about a trip some fourth graders took to a dairy farm.

It Starts with a Cow

Just like you, the fourth graders in Mr. Hanson's class knew that milk comes from cows. But all of Mr. Hanson's students lived in the city. Most of them had never seen a real farm. They had never been inside a barn or petted a cow. The students wanted to learn how milk got from the cow to their homes. But first, they all wanted to see a farm and some cows.

David, one of the students, had an aunt who owned a dairy farm. The class wrote her a letter. They asked if they could come for a visit. She answered yes. At last the day came for the class to visit the farm.

A Visit to a Dairy Farm

As the class came to the farm they saw many cows out in the pasture. Some were lying in the shade. Some were grazing on grass. Other cows seemed to be just standing around. When the class reached the barn and the other farm buildings, they met David's aunt, Mrs. Riddle.

97

Figure 9.1. Denotative Word Meaning: A Page from a Fourth-Grade-Level Social Studies Text

Step 1: *Visualizing the Word.* Display each of the seven terms (*produce, products, grazing, pasture, silo, silage,* and *butterfat*) on the chalkboard. Point to ach term, read it to the children, calling attention to phonic elements or morphemic units that may aid students in pronouncing or understanding the new words (phonics: *sī́-lō; pro-dūće, sī́-lage, pród-ŭcts;* structural analysis: *graz ing; butter fat*).

Step 2: *Discussing the Word.* Hold a brief class discussion on each term, drawing on children's background or experiences. A picture, slide, or other visual aide can be used to extend word meanings.

Step 3: *Using the Word.* Display a picture of a farm setting. Ask children to select any word from the new vocabulary list and develop a sentence incorporating ideas displayed in the picture:

a. The farmer is putting *silage* into the tall, blue *silo.*
b. Many cattle are *grazing* in the *pasture.*

Step 4: *Defining the Word:* Put children into groups of two. Distribute key-word cards to each pair of children. Ask them to think of riddles to go along with each word. The riddles will be answered by key vocabulary items:

a. I'm thinking of a tall, narrow, cylindrical farm building that stores feed for animals. *(silo)*
b. I'm thinking of a word that names something dairy cows eat each day. *(silage)*

Step 5: *Writing and Reading the Word:* Following the reading of the four-page introductory text, ask students to write a paragraph telling anything they like about dairy farms. All seven key words should appear at least once in the story.

In the lesson above, key or technical vocabulary was introduced, defined, reviewed, and reinforced. Denotative word meanings must be taught directly if total reading comprehension is to be the result of the lesson. For students in need of extra help in recognizing or reviewing words, an anagram puzzle could be used. In the sample puzzle in Figure 9.2, other terms selected from the reading have been incorporated.

P	O	D	R	O	C	E	R	W	X	G
P	A	U	M	I	L	K	Y	T	N	F
Q	S	S	I	L	O	D	A	I	R	Y
R	T	V	T	Z	A	N	Z	B	C	S
R	E	D	D	U	K	A	D	E	I	E
P	A	S	T	U	R	E	F	L	G	C
H	S	I	J	G	K	E	A	L	M	U
N	O	D	P	Q	R	G	S	T	U	D
G	J	E	R	S	E	Y	X	V	W	O
B	U	T	T	E	R	F	A	T	D	R
Y	Z	A	B	C	H	E	E	S	E	P

KEY WORDS
produce
products
grazing
pasture
udder
silo
silage
butterfat
herds
record
Jersey
tank
milk
cheese
dairy

Figure 9.2. Word-Search Puzzle

In Chapter Eight we discussed how our vocabulary processes could be used to increase the effectiveness of teaching words in basal reading programs. Now, we would like to offer some ideas on how these same processes can be implemented as teachers introduce, reinforce, and review vocabulary in the content areas. In some instances, our ideas will lean toward vocabulary enrichment because we feel that each teacher has the responsibility to broaden and expand general vocabulary as well as content-specific vocabulary. As you will recall, our teaching processes promote the development of word meanings, not just the sight recognition of words. These processes adapt easily to content-area instruction, because as word meanings are established, the major concepts of any unit of study are also presented. Throughout the remainder of Chapter Nine we will introduce each process once again and demonstrate how it may be used to enhance instruction in one of the content areas taught at the elementary school level.

SYNONYMS

Perhaps work with synonyms is one of the most powerful tools for recognizing the precise meaning of words. Each word we have stored in our mental lexicon has a set of features attached to it. Since features accumulate through personal situations in which words are used, each of us will have a slightly different meaning for an individual word. For that reason, we believe that children benefit from group discussions that not only expand vocabulary as a whole but that also extend meanings of known words.

Music instruction provides an excellent setting for vocabulary expansion through use of synonyms. We recognize that music teachers must teach a specialized vocabulary and special music symbols as they prepare students to interpret, participate in, and enjoy vocal or instrumental music. In addition, music teachers naturally hope that their students will be motivated to read music-related books (biographies of famous musicians, books on the history of music, etc.) and magazines such as *Etude*. Thus, there are endless opportunities to teach vocabulary in the music classroom. For the purposes of this section, though, let us illustrate a lesson in which synonyms are used to clarify and expand a specific type of vocabulary common to music.

Skimming through a songbook, one finds vocabulary indicative of the suggested tempos for different selections (moderately, evenly, briskly, brightly, etc.). Print alone cannot teach tempo; a demonstration by the teacher is essential. However, a brief lesson on synonyms may clarify these terms, expand children's vocabulary, and prepare students to recognize synonymous terms song writers might use to indicate tempo. A teacher-guided lesson may result in lists of words such as the following:

moderately	evenly	briskly	brightly
calmly	smoothly	quickly	happily
gently	steadily	rapidly	joyfully
softly	uniformly	swiftly	merrily
mildly	peacefully	speedily	gaily
serenely	tranquilly	fleetingly	jubilantly

Once lists are generated children could locate a few of the terms in songbooks used in or out of the music classroom. Groups could prepare and demonstrate the slight differences in mood that can be portrayed by singing a song "softly," then "serenely." Children could show how a song intended to be sung "briskly" differs from one sung "peacefully." This lesson plan incorporates vocabulary expansion but relates the new vocabulary directly to music instruction.

ANTONYMS

Lessons on antonyms can be used quite effectively by content-area teachers as a means of teaching vocabulary. Naturally, not all words in any given lesson have antonymous counterparts. The teacher's task in any vocabulary lesson is to examine the vocabulary that must be taught and then determine the best strategy to use in teaching or reviewing specific words. For most units of study, a combination of techniques will be necessary.

During a perusal of a fourth-grade science text, a unit on *light* was found. For several of the major ideas included in the brief unit, opposite concepts were evident: *reflect/absorb; concave/convex; straight/curved; refracted light beam/ straight light beam*. In addition, a set of important terms such as *magnify, blurred, dimmer*, and *ancient* also seemed to be good candidates for inclusion in a lesson emphasizing antonyms. Once each of these concepts has been introduced, a review or reinforcement lesson might be based on the antonymous quality of the terms. For instance, given lead statements, the students might be asked to write or complete sentences that illustrate opposing ideas:

    a. A *convex lens* is thicker in the middle than at the edges.
    b. A *concave lens* is _____.
    c. The path of a light beam in the air is *straight*.
    d. When light is *refracted* the path is_____.

As a means of clarifying other important terms, students might be asked to identify or contribute simple lists of antonyms. For instance, an identification exercise might include problems such as:

Identify the opposite terms:

    a. *Magnify*   (diminish, decrease, reduce, increase)
    b. *Blurred*   (dimmed, clear, shaded, shadowy)

Students might also be asked to *list* opposite terms:

dimmer	**ancient**
brighter, clearer, glossy, brilliant	new, modern, recent, fresh, current

Exercises such as the ones given here clarify children's understanding of the key words. Word studies also raise children's awareness of words or call their attention to words that really are crucial to comprehending the unit. As an ancillary benefit, vocabulary skill is expanded.

HOMOPHONES

The following list of common homophones (Table 8) could be used by teachers as a reference when developing vocabulary exercises (Dechant 1973). Some terms clearly apply to specific content areas, other pairs or triplets lend themselves to general vocabulary study.

TABLE 8			
Common Homophones			
ail-ale	forth-fourth	pair-pare	steak-stake
ate-eight	foul-fowl	peace-piece	steal-steel
arc-ark	four-for	peek-peak	stile-style
awl-all	gail-gale	peel-peal	straight-strait
bail-bale	groan-grown	peer-pier	sun-son
base-bass	hair-hare	plane-plain	sweet-suite
be-bee	hale-hail	pore-pour	tail-tale
bear-bare	haul-hall	praise-prays	teem-team
beat-beet	heel-heal	principal-principle	their-there
bell-belle	here-hear	rain-rein-reign	through-threw
berth-birth	hew-hue	raise-raze	thrown-throne
blue-blew	horse-hoarse	rap-wrap	tide-tied
bored-board	hour-our	read-red	to-too-two
bow-bough	led-lead	read-reed	toe-tow
break-brake	leek-leak	reel-real	tolled-told
bread-bred	loan-lone	road-rode	vale-veil
buy-by	lye-lie	sail-sale	vane-vein-vain
cell-sell	made-maid	sea-see	wade-weighed
cellar-seller	mail-male	seem-seam	waist-waste
cent-sent-scent	mane-main	seen-scene	wait-weight
course-coarse	mantle-mantel	seer-sear	wave-waive
dear-deer	meet-meat-mete	sew-so-sow	way-weigh
do-dew-due	new-knew	sight-site-cite	week-weak
doe-dough	night-knight	slay-sleigh	whole-hole
fair-fare	no-know	sole-soul	wood-would
feet-feat	one-won	some-sum	wring-ring
fir-fur	or-ore	sore-soar	write-right
flee-flea	owe-oh	staid-stayed	wrote-rote
flew-flue	pain-pane	stare-stair	you-yew-ewe
flower-flour			

How could a lesson on homophones tie in with any specific content area? Let us suppose that a middle school class is engaged in a study of animals. One group of children chooses to research and report on their favorite animal, the horse. Books are read, articles skimmed, and films viewed. Following the group study and report, a teacher might distribute the following list of homophonic pairs:

horse/hoarse	sale/sail
weigh/way	pair/pare
fair/fare	hare/hair
gate/gait	load/lode
feat/feet	meat/meet
pail/pale	mane/main

Students could:

a. Write sentences that include both of the homophonic terms.

The *horse* was so *hoarse* that he could not even whinny.
My horse's *gait* was smooth and even as we approached the *gate*.

b. Select the term *most likely* to be associated with the topic of horses, and create a sentence.

There were seven other *entrants* in the derby.
Fran's *mane* shimmered in the sunlight.

A study of homophones not only builds content-specific vocabulary but builds general vocabulary knowledge as well.

MULTIMEANING WORDS

Multimeaning words abound in our language and cause endless frustration to the student. A child is likely to come across many words that look familiar and are, in fact, *sight words* (i.e., the child can pronounce the words with ease). Of course, the problem lies in assigning meaning. Words in specific content areas often act like chameleons as they take on features that coincide with their linguistic environment. Just one word will demonstrate the dilemma a reader faces:

ROOTS

English: The *roots* of these new words all contain short vowels.
Math: Find the square *roots* for each of these numbers.
Science: The plant *roots* well in vermiculite and water.
Social studies: The family *roots* lie in western Europe.

In each case, the reader must examine the context of the multimeaning word in order to determine its true meaning. Content-area textbooks will be full of words that exhibit multiple meanings. A teacher cannot possibly isolate and teach each individual word as it applies to the particular unit of study. We suggest that you select the major multimeaning words that appear in any unit and stress the context-appropriate meaning. A few examples include:

Mathematics: division, foot, mean, yard
Science: matter, cell, iron, mine

English: act, dash, draft, appendix
Social Studies: bill, trust, cabinet, race

These words are likely to be part of most students' oral vocabulary; however, the content-specific meaning may be unknown to them. The best way to teach these words is through demonstrations and discussions that take full advantage of context or meaningful settings. For instance, a *cabinet* to most students is a piece of furniture — they will need teacher guidance to learn the specifics of a "cabinet form" of government. Students know that a "mean" dog may harm them or that the teacher "means" what he says; however, *arithmetic mean* may "mean" very little without instructional guidance.

Figure 9.3 represents a social studies lesson designed to help students understand problems faced by immigrants in a particular section of our country. On just one page of this lesson, six multimeaning words have the potential for causing comprehension problems for some readers. The terms *character, settled, home* (countries), *run-down, flocked,* and *lower* may warrant explanation with some groups of children. We would suggest that the terms be incorporated into the lesson plan and used by the group in discussion and follow-up activities. For instance, you might create a series of sentences using different definitions for each key word. The students' task is to match each sentence with its proper definition:

      ___ 1. This old building has special   a. a unique quality or feature
            character, don't you agree?
      ___ 2. The leading *character* in our   b. a person
            play is talented.

SEMANTIC MAPPING

Semantic maps are excellent devices for building concepts and related vocabulary in content-area classrooms. As students actively participate in the creation of semantic maps, they are able to capitalize on prior knowledge and relate it to new concepts presented by the teacher and the instructional materials. Semantic maps are excellent tools for helping students to organize the multiple concepts that must be learned in any one unit. All academic subject areas can benefit from work with semantic maps as tools for the introduction, reinforcement, or review of concepts.

Content-area textbooks are full of terms that cause reading comprehension problems simply because students are unaware of which meaning an author intended. Direct instruction (using models, examples, demonstrations, and discussions) should precede any review/reinforcement activities in specific content-area vocabulary. The following teaching strategy (to be used in review/reinforcement) requires that students identify common meanings of words. Next, they are required to place the words into sentences designed to reflect specific content-area meanings.

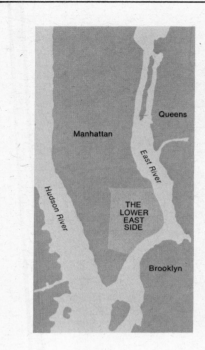

New York is a city of many neighborhoods. All of them are different. All of them have their own special character.

One of the oldest and most interesting New York neighborhoods is the Lower East Side.

AN IMMIGRANT NEIGHBORHOOD

In the nineteenth century, many Europeans immigrated to the United States. This means that they came to a new country to live. A large number of these immigrants were from Southern and Eastern Europe. Many of them settled on the Lower East Side of New York City. There they knew they could find other people from their home countries.

◆ get′ ō

◗ Most immigrants stayed in New York—the city where their ships docked. Can you explain why? What would they have needed to travel further that they probably did not have?

The making of a ghetto   By the time the immigrants arrived there, the Lower East Side was a slum. Most of the houses in the neighborhood were old and run-down. The streets were dark and narrow.

The immigrants who flocked to the neighborhood did little to improve it. Rents on the Lower East Side were already low. But immigrant families had very little money—not even enough to pay low rents. Often, several immigrant families had to share housing that was intended for only one family. This made the neighborhood more

246

Figure 9.3. Multimeaning Words: A Page from a Social Studies Lesson

Dick Kanter, Musician

This is Dick Kanter. He plays the oboe in the Chicago Symphony Orchestra. He earns his living by playing music. Musician is his earned identity.

Mr. Kanter began learning to play the oboe when he was 14 years old. He took lessons and played in his high-school band too. He learned to play well. Mr. Kanter says that his parents and teachers encouraged him to become a musician.

After high school, Mr. Kanter went to music school in Philadelphia, Pennsylvania. He studied music there for four years. Then Mr. Kanter joined the Navy. He played in the Navy band for four more years. Then Mr. Kanter got a job playing in the Chicago Symphony Orchestra.

During most weeks, the Orchestra meets eight times. About four of these meetings are practices. The other four are concerts. Often the concerts are at night. This means that many times Mr. Kanter is going to work when most other people are just coming home from work.

Figure 9.4. A Page from a Social Studies Textbook

Examples from Mathematics

A. *Word*   *Common Meaning illustrated*
   difference   It doesn't make any *difference* when we leave for the game.
   foot   Lavonne can hop on one *foot*.
   base   Ann did not get to first *base* on time.
   root   This part is the *root* of your plant.
B. *Sentence Completion Activity*
   1. Today we will learn to compute the square _____ of nine.
   2. Put a red mark under the _____ of the largest triangle.
   3. Find the ruler that is just one _____ long.
   4. The _____ between twelve and nine is three.
      (difference, foot, base, root)

A study of career opportunities is often featured in social science textbooks (see Fig. 9.4). Following the text lesson, students might find it interesting to learn more about the orchestra. A map could be developed to reflect the organization of instruments in an orchestra and be used as a means of review (see Fig. 9.5). We urge you to return to Chapter Four of this text and review the steps used in creation of semantic maps. This activity is invaluable in any content-area classroom.

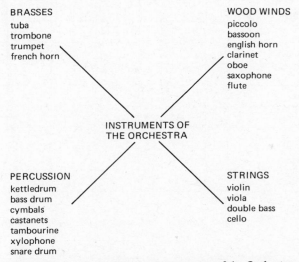

Figure 9.5. Semantic Map for *Instruments of the Orchestra*

SEMANTIC FEATURE ANALYSIS

Figure 9.6 represents a semantic feature grid (see Chap. Four) that summarizes the characteristics children noted following a study of clouds in their junior-high science class. Following a study on the class textbook, a selection of library books and a perusal of visual aids, the students created a semantic feature grid by listing all the cloud types studied, along with the features associated with the cloud types. In small groups the students' task will be to complete the grid by placing pluses or minuses in each box of the grid to associate types of clouds with their

	white and feathery	puffy	flat bottom	small and fleecy	thin white sheets	heavy and dark	rolls of blackish and bluish	sheets of gray or blue	wide blankets of gray	gray or whitish	low in sky	high in sky	mid-sky	storms
cirrus														
cumulus														
stratus														
cirrocumulus														
cirrostratus														
altostratus														
altocumulus														
nimbostratus														
stratocumulus														
cumulonimbus														

Figure 9.6. Semantic Feature Analysis: *Types of Clouds*

distinguishing features. At times they may need to return to reference materials to verify an answer. Once the grids have been completed, the entire group will meet to compare and contrast the different clouds that have been studied. In this case, the semantic feature analysis activity served as a review lesson, but it could have been an *initial* learning device for the less capable students who failed to learn on their own. Sharing information through discussion allows the more capable students to serve as tutors.

ANALOGIES

Analogies seem to be difficult for some students, but we feel that teachers can use analogical exercises with even the youngest children if care is taken to use words and concepts they clearly understand. Work with analogies requires that children think about the relationships between words and the concepts they represent.

Every content-area teacher will be able to make good use of this vocabulary-building strategy. A fourth-grade science quiz illustrates one way analogies might be used to review vocabulary:

    a. *Reflect* is to _____ as *refract* is to *bend.*
    b. _____ is to *reflect* as *black* is to *absorb.*
    c. *Meteorologist* is to *weather* as _____ is to *rocks.*
    d. *Cirrus* is to *feathery* as *cumulus* is to _____.

    (Answers: a = bounce; b = white; c = geologist; d = puffy)

In this quiz, students would be required to complete the analogies, using any words that made the statement correct. Then, a sentence or two explaining the relationship of one word to another must be given. For item c, for instance, a child might offer: "A meteorologist is a person who studies weather, and a geologist is a person who studies rocks." Thus, the child has reviewed vocabulary and, at the same time, has demonstrated an understanding of the important concepts being studied in class.

Other formats may also be used by content-area teachers as vocabulary is taught or reviewed. In the following examples, students supply appropriate titles for each list as they recall lessons read and discussed in social studies class.

Explorers	Rivers	Cities
La Salle	St. Croix	Prairie du Chien
Du Luth	Mississippi	Superior
Marquette	Fox	De Pere
Joliet	Wisconsin	Fond du Lac

A unit in beginning geometry subjects students to a substantial number of technical and multimeaning words *(sphere, cylinder, cube, box, pyramid, circle, square, triangle, rectangle, parallelogram, quadrilateral, line segments, endpoints, ray, line, parallel lines, parallel segments, vertex, angle).* Figure 9.7 (p. 192) shows a sample of an early-level lesson in geometry. Examine the third paragraph on the page shown in Figure 9.7. The child must read: "The *sides* of an *angle* are *rays.* The *vertex* of an *angle* is the *common endpoint* of its two *rays"* (italics our own). Each underlined word in those two sentences must be completely understood by the youngster if the total concept presented in this lesson is to be clear in the child's mind. We would anticipate that prior teaching would have included a step-by-step (see Chap. Six) introduction of each underlined term. However, most children need several exposures to words if retention is to take place. Analogies could be developed to help students think about and review concepts and vocabulary needed for this unit. Using the terms introduced in the first sentence of this paragraph, a teacher might create the following problems:

    a. *Pyramid* is to *flat face* as _____ is to *curved face*.
    b. *Cube* is to _____ as *sphere* is to *curved edge*.
    c. *Parallelogram* is to *four angles* as _____ is to *three angles*.
    d. *Circle* is to *sphere* as *square* is to _____.
       (Answers: a = cone; b = flat edge; c = triangle; d = cube)

Analogy is a superb device to use in helping students organize their thought patterns and think about how words and concepts are related to one another.

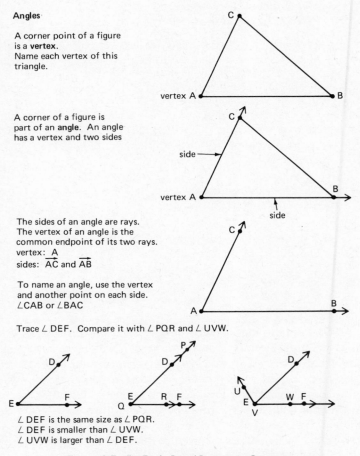

Angles

A corner point of a figure is a **vertex**.
Name each vertex of this triangle.

A corner of a figure is part of an **angle**. An angle has a vertex and two sides

The sides of an angle are rays.
The vertex of an angle is the common endpoint of its two rays.
vertex: A
sides: $\overrightarrow{AC}$ and $\overrightarrow{AB}$

To name an angle, use the vertex and another point on each side.
∠CAB or ∠BAC

Trace ∠ DEF. Compare it with ∠ PQR and ∠ UVW.

∠ DEF is the same size as ∠ PQR.
∠ DEF is smaller than ∠ UVW.
∠ UVW is larger than ∠ DEF.

Figure 9.7. An Early-Level Lesson in Geometry

DICTIONARY

The dictionary is a comprehensive reference tool that will be invaluable to the student as content-area materials are explored independently. Students are bound to come across words that have not been *taught* or have not been *learned* during class. An independent reference tool is a necessity when there is not one around to offer assistance on hard words. Teachers of all subject areas should be encouraging students to be word detectives, to search for word meaning rather than simply skip the word or guess at its meaning. Building a positive attitude toward dictionary usage is in a teacher's best interest. There is simply not enough time to teach all the technical, multimeaning, and general vocabulary students need to know in order to read their content textbooks.

Positive attitudes are created when school activities are challenging yet enjoyable for the students. So many times lessons using the dictionary are rather dull and routine. In Chapter Five we presented several sound alternatives for learning vocabulary through the use of the dictionary. Content-area teachers will be able to design exercises that teach vocabulary specifically related to units of study. We will provide one more lesson idea for you.

English teachers are often in search of ways to encourage students to use language in a creative manner. One way to help students gain proficiency is to offer samples of a particular style or technique and then ask students to create similar products. For example, a teacher might gather a set of epigrams or humorous witticisms to share with students (Bellafiore 1968, pp. 68–9).

1. *Home* is where you hang your hat.
2. *Time* is a paragraph; *life* is a short sentence and *death* is a period.
3. *Genius* is one percent inspiration and ninety-nine percent perspiration. (Thomas A. Edison)
4. *Heaven* is the Lord's window and *night* is his window shade.
5. *Shoes* are a man's best friend; they are continually being stepped on without a single complaint.
6. *Love* is a frame of mind and the girl is the picture.
7. *Work* is anything you have to do; *play* is anything you want to do, but don't have to do. (Mark Twain)
8. He is getting so *methodical* he eats alphabet soup from A to Z.

Ask students to look up the meaning of each italicized word just given. Then, as a group, discuss how the connotation of a word can be changed by linguistic ingenuity or craftiness. Next, offer a list of words *(anxious, able, beauty, character, good-natured, jury, love, movie, opera, price, quaint, sleep,* etc.). Have students use their imaginations to create a novel connotation for each term by writing epigrams or witty sayings.

THESAURUS

The thesaurus can be an invaluable tool for helping students expand and refine their vocabularies to include more vivid terms. Words from nearly every lesson taught in school have synonymous partners, and many terms list antonym counterparts as well. Comparing and contrasting word meanings through discussion is an excellent way to help students acquire preciseness in language.

An English teacher might distribute the following paragraph:

> It was a *nice* day, so Mary and Lorayne took a *nice* long walk through the *nice* countryside. The *nice* girls were thrilled to find *nice* flowers, *nice* birds, *nice* trees, and *nice* plants as they walked down the *nice*, *nice* country road. To their surprise, a *nice*, *nice* deer darted out from the *nice* woods. All too soon the girls had to end their *nice* walk and return to their *nice* homes in the *nice* city.

Students, individually or in pairs, could search through the thesaurus for more colorful or interesting words to replace the vague, overused word *nice*. Revised stories could be read aloud. Finally, groups could combine their alternative word lists and develop one or two model stories.

As a second step to the lesson described in the paragraph above, a teacher could examine one set of themes developed during a creative writing class. An asterisk might be inserted in four to five spots throughout the themes where modifiers could be added. Using the thesaurus, children can revise their themes to include appropriate adjectives or adverbs. Sharing the revised themes in a conference with the teacher offers an opportunity for children to share how they used words to convey a message or improve a description.

Practice exercises with the thesaurus will help students recognize the potential this reference tool has for improving the communicative quality of their language and help them develop the habit of searching for "just the right" word. We stress that lessons should always be meaningful and make full use of the rich context of language. Lists of words accompanied by a directive to "find synonyms for/antonyms for _____" do not hold much promise for lasting vocabulary improvement.

ETYMOLOGY

Every word we use had to come from somewhere! The study of word origins holds potential for teachers in every academic area. We suggest that you use this fascinating avenue of word study with your students often; we are certain you and your students will become more and more intrigued with words and their remarkable histories. Before you begin, be sure to gather a number of the appealing books that have been developed on etymology. We listed just a few in Chapter Five. Most standard dictionaries will give very brief etymological information. You and your students will want to have adequate references available.

As we mentioned, all words have a history; thus, etymology will be valuable to vocabulary enrichment in any field of study. Figures 9.8 and 9.9 were selected from a recently published social studies textbook. Note the attention given to the development of words in our language. As a follow-up or enrichment exercise, a teacher might choose one or several of the following two etymological studies:

1. Using a good dictionary or other reference resource, locate the original meanings for the name of each day of the week. From which branch of language did these names come?

Shows and games Life was very hard for poor people in ancient Rome. There were not enough jobs for all the people who lived there. At times, as many as 150,000 people were out of work. Food was given to the poor by the government and by rich people. But the government did not think that this was enough. They wanted to keep the poor people busy.

The emperors of Rome put on many shows and games for the Roman people. Citizens could spend as many as 150 days a year in theaters and arenas. Plays, most of them funny, were given in large open-air theaters. The most popular shows were dangerous chariot races and gladiator fights. The gladiators, armed with swords and other weapons, fought each other and wild animals.

▶ Can you think of a better way in which the government could have handled the problem of lack of jobs?

▶ glad′ē ā tər

History

WHAT REMAINS OF ANCIENT ROME?

Read the following Latin words:

Januarius	*Julius*
Februarius	*Augustus*
martius	*September*
Aprilis	*October*
maius	*November*
Junius	*December*

Say these words out loud. Even though they are Latin words, do they look familiar

Figure 9.8. Etymology: A Page from a Social Studies Textbook, 1

to you? Can you guess what they mean? Write these words in English on a piece of paper. Now compare the English words to the Latin words. Are they very different?

The ancient Romans had a great influence on our modern way of life. As you have just learned, there are English words that come from Latin, the language of the ancient Romans. In fact, at least 60 percent (six out of ten) of English words come from Latin. Other languages, including French, Spanish, and Italian, are also based on Latin.

Roads built by the Romans are still in use today. And many present-day European cities were first built by the Romans.

A sports arena built by the ancient Romans still stands in the modern city.

1. What is a city-state? Name the other city-state you have learned about.
2. How is modern Rome different from ancient Rome?
3. Name two things that helped Rome rule its empire.
4. How did Rome's geography affect its growth as a trading center?
5. In what ways has the civilization of ancient Rome influenced the life of people in the twentieth century?

Figure 9.9. Etymology: A Page from a Social Studies Textbook, 2

2. Using units in the textbook that your students have recently studied, select several words that are formed by combining unfamiliar roots (Greek roots: *demos* (people) + *kratia* (government) = *democracy*). Have students identify the origin of the words.

One good way to introduce connotation is to study *allusions* with a group of students. Following the reading of Greek myths in an English class, students could be assigned the task of researching several common words related to or drawn from mythology. The following questions represent those you might include on a student research guide:

a. Why do we say that a sleepy, sluggish person is *lethargic?* What was the *Lethe?*

b. How did the continent of *Europe* receive its name? Who was *Europa?*

c. How did the colored part of our eye, the *iris*, get its name? Who was *Iris?*

d. Where does *typhoon* come from? Who was *Typhon?*

The number of questions you decide to put onto the research guide will vary with the time available, the ability of your students, and access to references. The activity not only helps students develop an appreciation for connotative language but also deepens their understanding of words and their meanings. Be careful when assigning this activity . . . you may not get some of your avid readers out of the library! The stories behind some words are often too interesting to leave unread.

A FINAL WORD

The gift of language is a treasure each teacher can help students acquire. An adequate, appropriate vocabulary is of great importance to an individual's success both in and out of the classroom. Words symbolize ideas and help students clarify concepts and broaden their mental abilities. We believe that each content-area teacher not only can, but must, help students gain sufficient command of the language used to symbolize the subject matter being taught.

The purpose of this chapter was to provide examples of how our teaching processes can be applied in content-area subjects. We made an attempt to provide challenging activities that will arouse each student's interest in the English language. Our overall goal is to help individual students develop word study habits that will last a lifetime. We hope that you will return to earlier chapters in this book and reread the rationale and procedures outlined for using each vocabulary process in the classroom. As you read, remember that not all vocabulary-teaching procedures will apply to each unit of study; for example, not all lessons lend themselves to the creation of semantic feature grids nor do all words have antonyms. Examine the words you must teach in any one unit, then decide which teaching procedure will work best for you and the students you teach.

REFERENCES

Barrett, M. T., and Graves, M. F. "A Vocabulary Program for Junior High School Remedial Readers." *Journal of Reading* 25 (1981): 146–50.

Bellafiore, J. *Words at Work*, New York: Amsco School Publications, 1968.

Dechant, E. *Reading Improvement in the Secondary School*. Englewood Cliffs, N.J.: Prentice-Hall, 1973.

Estes, T. H., and Vaughan, J. L. *Reading and Learning in the Content Classroom: Diagnostic and Instructional Strategies*. Boston: Allyn and Bacon, 1978.

Herber, H. L. *Success with Words*. New York: Scholastic Book Services, 1968.

———— *Teaching Reading in Content Areas*, 2nd ed. Englewood Cliffs, N.J.: Prentice-Hall, 1970.

Kaplan, E. M., and Tuchman, A. "Vocabulary Strategies Belong in the Hands of Learners." *Journal of Reading* 24 (1980): 32–4.

Readence, J. E.; Bean, T. W.; and Baldwin, R. S. *Content Area Reading: An Integrated Approach*. Dubuque, Iowa: Kendall/Hunt, 1981.

Stieglitz, E. L., and Stieglitz, V. S. "SAVOR the Word to Reinforce Vocabulary in the Content Areas." *Journal of Reading* 25 (1981): 46–51.

10
Reflections on Vocabulary Development

Those who have acquired broad, extensive vocabularies are indeed fortunate. Words are powerful tools used to code, store, and retrieve knowledge about the world. A large, diverse vocabulary permits an individual to communicate ideas efficiently and effectively.

Vocabulary knowledge is especially critical to reading comprehension. One of the major tasks facing a teacher is to plan for direct instruction in vocabulary. Throughout this book we have presented strategies designed to help teachers work with children to expand their knowledge of words and word meanings. As each strategy was described, we stressed the importance of providing sound language experiences. We had two goals in mind as we made suggestions on vocabulary instruction: 1) that each child will increase his/her repertoire of words and use those words in all areas of the language arts (listening, speaking, writing, and reading), and 2) that the actual strategies we have outlined will become useful vocabulary building tools as children read independently.

Our living language grows and changes continuously as new words are added to the already vast lexicon and old words become vested with new meanings. How can teachers of reading make sound instructional decisions as to which words are worth teaching? In Chapter One, we made the suggestion that three broad categories of basic words merit instructional time: 1) high-frequency sight words; 2) selection/critical words, and 3) old words/new meanings. Knowledge of these basic words is essential to a successful reading experience. *High-frequency sight words* are words that appear so often in print that even beginning readers must learn to read them quickly and accurately. *Selection/critical words* are terms that are topic-specific. For instance, a story about hockey might include words such as *goal, fans, puck, hockey stick, skates, shoulder pads, jersey, uniform, shin guards, elbowing, icing, roughing, misconduct, penalty box, referee, fans,* and *net.* Knowledge of selection/critical words is imperative to a successful reading experience. *Old words* take on *new meanings* as context changes and often cause significant problems in comprehension. Using the topic of hockey once again, we find numerous words that have very special meanings: *period, stick, fans, sieve, icing.* Direct instruction of basic words in all three categories is highly important for reading development.

Children will enjoy learning new words if challenging, meaningful lessons emerge from the teacher's plan book. Our instructional vocabulary components, as defined in Chapter Two, have been tested time and again in classrooms and have proven to be effective stimulators of vocabulary growth. The twelve components grouped into three basic categories include:

VOCABULARY-BUILDING COMPONENTS

1. CLASSIFICATION
   a. Synonyms
   b. Denotation/Connotation
   c. Antonyms
   d. Semantic Mapping
   e. Semantic Feature Analysis
   f. Analogies
   g. Homophones
2. MULTIMEANING
   a. Polysemous Words
   b. Homographs
3. RESOURCES
   a. Dictionary
   b. Thesaurus
   c. Etymology

Teachers will find that activities based on these processes will help students extend and sharpen their language ability.

Teaching Reading Vocabulary has focused on direct instruction in *meaningful* vocabulary development. Chapters Three, Four, and Five explicitly defined each of our twelve vocabulary-building processes; in each case several teaching strategies were suggested. A step-by-step teaching plan was offered as a guide for vocabulary lessons. We hope that you will study each process in detail and skim through our classroom-based activity plans. Next, consider the actual words you must teach in your own classroom. We know that most words on your list will fall into one of our three basic categories (*high-frequency sight words, selection/critical words*, or *multimeaning words*). Then, with our processes and sample activities coupled with your specific word lists, begin to make wise instructional decisions. Which processes will work best with the words you must teach? Which activities can you use or adapt to teach the essential words on your lists? Remember, words are unique entities. You will not be able to select one vocabulary process and use it to teach all of the words on any one list. For example, not all words have antonyms nor do all lessons lend themselves to the development of a semantic feature grid. Be selective as you design lessons for children's vocabulary development.

Success in reading requires a continuous increase in *sight vocabulary*. Every reader needs to build a storehouse of whole words that can be recognized and pronounced instantly, without any mediated decoding. Before reading instruction can be initiated, however, children must discover some of the essential relationships between oral and written language. In Chapter Six, we have dealt with the topic of print awareness. We then moved on to an identification of three categories of words teachers must help children commit to visual memory: 1) high-frequency sight words, 2) self-selected/key vocabulary; and, 3) selection/critical words. *High-frequency sight words* are words that appear so often in printed material that mastery is absolutely essential for readers of any age. *Self-selected/key vocabulary* items are the meaningful content words drawn from an individual's oral vocabulary. *Selection/critical* words are topic-specific words that appear in a passage and carry the meaning. Chapter Six offered a five-step teaching plan designed to introduce and teach sight words in total language settings.

Reading instruction would be a dull, tedious procedure if all words had to be taught via the sight method. Readers need strategies for unlocking the pronunciation and meaning of unfamiliar words they meet in print. Chapter Seven was devoted to a discussion of the three major word-identification skills; numerous teaching suggestions were offered. The chapter began with a look at the word-identification skill that provides children with a means of *pronouncing* an unfamiliar printed word. *Phonics* skill enables children to pronounce a word in the anticipation that, once pronounced, the word will be recognized as part of oral vocabulary. The section on *structural analysis* focused on learning word meanings through an examination of meaningful parts of words: roots and attached affixes. Finally, a section on context analysis looked at ways a reader could estimate an unfamiliar word's meaning by examining syntactic and semantic cues surrounding the word. We believe that these three word-identification processes are essential skills that must be mastered in order to allow children to freely and successfully pursue independent reading. Most good readers use these skills simultaneously and automatically when they read. Obviously, each skill and related subskill must be isolated for instruction initially. However, we have proposed that all lessons include practice or application of skills in *real* reading situations (sentences, passages, or stories). We hope that teachers will provide numerous practice opportunities in which children must use a combination of the three major word-identification skills (phonics, structural analysis, and context) to solve word problems.

We consider Chapters Eight and Nine to be rather unique features of this book. In these two chapters we have given numerous examples of how teachers can apply our eleven processes to extend vocabulary instruction in basal readers and textbooks in the content areas. Why have we included these chapters? Most schools use basal readers and some form of content-area textbooks as the basis of classroom instruction. Teaching vocabulary is *central* to lesson development in both categories of instruction. It is our belief that vocabulary instruction, in and of itself, will fall to the wayside unless words are used by children in meaningful settings. Hence, we have demonstrated sound techniques for teaching words drawn from these widely used classroom materials. We know children must learn these words and the concepts represented by the words. Total language experiences are stressed in the anticipation that words heard, spoken, written, and read will be retained by the children.

A FINAL WORD

By the time most children complete their formal educations, their vocabularies have expanded from those first initial words that made their parents beam with pride to perhaps more than 100,000 words that they can understand, read, and use. Certainly this massive vocabulary growth was not accomplished simply, automatically, or through one method of instruction. In this short book we have tried to define, elaborate upon, and make recommendations for vocabulary instruction.

We feel it important that you always remember that you will have children in your classes with a wide range of reading ability, interests, and experiential backgrounds. Some of the activities we presented in the preceding chapters are full group activities while other activities were intended for individuals. School children are individuals and each is different. Some activities will work with and be of interest to some children, but not work with others. We assume that you will use only those activities that are appropriate for your students and will make whatever modifications you deem necessary to account for the wide range in ability, interest, and experience that surely exist within your class.

We maintain two very strong beliefs about all aspects of reading acquisition and thus about vocabulary development. The first is simply the importance of reading. We hold to the old adage that we "learn to read by reading." Certainly skill instruction is important, for one will not read if one is not able to read. But once children have acquired some basic proficiency in reading, that proficiency develops with practice, practice in reading, not in doing work sheets. If the only time we golfed was during our weekly golf lesson, we would never become very good golfers. "Practice makes (more nearly) perfect!" The same is true of reading and of vocabulary expansion. The more we read the more new words we learn and the more skillful we become. As we said earlier, research has clearly shown that the key element to reading comprehension is word knowledge. So we urge you to encourage, promote, provide time for, and reward wide and frequent reading by your students. As they read more and learn of reading's many pleasures, reading will become the reward itself.

Our second belief centers on the importance of you, the teacher. Both research and common sense tell us that the key to learning anything is a skillful, inspirational teacher who possesses both enthusiasm and clarity. We view the school and your classroom as a "sheltered environment." All teachers know that it is much easier to teach reading to children who come from homes in which their parents and brothers and sisters read to them, homes in which there are books and magazines and newspapers, homes in which every member of the family has a library card: in short, homes in which reading is valued. All teachers also know that many children do not come from such homes. Many come from homes in which everyone is too busy or too absent, or in which parents and siblings cannot or do not read, homes in which the children are never read to. It is especially for these children that the school need be a sheltered environment.

Teachers carry such enormous influence with their pupils; this is especially true in the elementary school. So we urge you to be a model to your students. Read to them daily, no matter how rigid the schedule or how old the child. Let them see you reading daily and not just teacher's manuals and lesson plans. Provide time each day for them to read freely — with your encouragement, guidance, and praise. Inasmuch as possible, avoid skill-drill drudgery and in its place select activities that have the potential of being fun and even exciting, as well as being instructive. We hope we have provided you with some ideas that will be of help in stimulating an enthusiasm for words and for reading. You, the teacher, are the key. The burden is heavy, the pay is light, and the days are long, but the rewards can be so great. Watching children learn and develop and knowing that you have had a hand in it is thrilling.

As you pursue the tremendously important tasks of developing and expanding vocabulary and comprehension, we ask you to remember these words of Samuel Johnson:

> He that thinks with more extent than another will want words of larger meaning; he that thinks with more subtlety will seek for terms of more nice discrimination . . . Yet vanity inclines us to find faults anywhere rather than in ourselves. He that reads and grows no wiser seldom suspects his own deficiency but complains of hard words and obscure sentences and asks why books are written which cannot be understood? (*The Idler*, No. 20)

REFERENCE

Johnson, S. *The Idler and the Adventurer*. The Works of Samuel Johnson, vol. 2. New Haven, Conn.: Yale University Press, 1963.

Bibliography

Agnew, A. T., "Using Children's Dictated Stories to Assess Code Consciousness," *The Reading Teacher*, Vol. 35, (January 1982) 450–454.

Allington, R., and Strange, M., *Learning Through Reading in the Content Areas* (Lexington, Mass.: D. C. Heath, 1980).

Anderson, R., Stevens, K., Shifrin, Z., and Osborn, J., "Instantiation of Word Meanings in Children," *Journal of Reading Behavior*, Vol. 10, (1978) 149–157.

Aukerman, M. D., "Acquisition and Transfer Value of Initial Training with Multiple Grapheme-Phoneme Correspondences," *Journal of Educational Psychology*, Vol. 65, (August 1973) 28–34.

Balch, M. C., *A Problem with Sight Vocabulary Lists: Multi-Meaning Words* (Unpublished master's thesis, The University of Wisconsin, Madison, 1976) 1–81.

Barrett, M. T., and Graves, M. F., "A Vocabulary Program for Junior High School Remedial Readers," *Journal of Reading*, Vol. 25, (November 1981) 146–150.

Barrett, T. C., "Taxonomy of Cognitive and Affective Dimensions of Reading Comprehension," *What is "Reading?": Some Current Concepts*, T. Clymer, ed., (Chicago: University of Chicago Press, 1968).

Becker, W. C., "Teaching Reading and Language to the Disadvantaged—What We Have Learned From Field Research," *Harvard Educational Review*, Vol. 47, (1977) 518–543.

Becker, W. C., Engelmann, S., Carnine, D. W., and Rhine, W. R., "Direct Instruction Model," *Making Schools More Effective*, W. R. Rhine, ed., (New York: Academic Press, 1981).

Blachowicz, C. Z., "Metalinguistic Awareness and the Beginning Reader," *The Reading Teacher*, Vol. 31, (May 1978) 875–882.

Block, K. K., *Vocabulary Development: A Problem in Learning and Instruction* (Unpublished manuscript, Pittsburgh: Learning Research and Development Center, 1976) 43–44.

Bloomfield, L., and Barnhart, C., *Let's Read: A Linguistic Approach* (Detroit: Wayne State University Press, 1961).

Bourque, M. L., "Specification and Validation of Reading Skills Hierarchies," *Reading Research Quarterly*, 15(2), (1980) 237–267.

Calfee, R., Venezky, R., and Chapman, R., "How A Child Needs to Think to Learn to Read," *Cognition in Learning and Memory*, L. Gregg, ed., (New York: John Wiley and Sons, 1972).

Chall, J., *Learning to Read: The Great Debate* (New York: McGraw-Hill Book Company, 1967).

Chomsky, C., "Approaching Reading Through Invented Spelling," *Theory and Practice of Early Reading, Vol. 2*, L. B. Resnick and P. A. Weaver, eds., (Hillsdale, New Jersey: Lawrence Erlbaum, 1979) 43–65.

Clay, M., *Reading: The Patterning of Complex Behaviour* (Auckland, New Zealand: Heineman Educational Books, 1979).

Collins, A. M., and Quillian, M. R., "Retrieval Time from Semantic Memory," *Journal of Verbal Learning and Verbal Behavior*, Vol. 8, (1969) 240–247.

Culyer, R. C., III, "Guidelines for Skill Development: Word Attack," *The Reading Teacher*, Vol. 32, (January 1979) 425–433.

Cunningham, J. W., "An Automatic Pilot for Decoding," *The Reading Teacher*, Vol. 32, (January 1979) 420–424.

Cunningham, P. M., "Investigating A Synthesized Theory of Mediated Word Identification," *Reading Research Quarterly*, 11(2), (1975–1976) 127–143.

Cunningham, P. M., "Teaching Were, With, What, and Other Four-Letter Words," *The Reading Teacher*, Vol. 34, (November 1980) 160–163.

Dale, E., *Bibliography of Vocabulary Studies*, 5th ed. (Columbus: Ohio State University, 1975).

Dale, E., *Audiovisual Methods in Teaching* (New York: Holt, Rinehart and Winston, 1969).

Dale, E., "Readings That Made A Difference: Serendipities for All," *Journal of Reading*, Vol. 23, (April 1980) 586–588.

Davis, F. B., "Two New Measures of Reading Ability," *Journal of Educational Psychology*, Vol. 33, (1942) 365–372.

Davis, F. B., "Fundamental Factors of Comprehension in Reading," *Psychometrika*, 9(3), (1944) 185–197.

Davis, F. B., "Research in Comprehension in Reading," *Reading Research Quarterly*, 3(4), (1968) 499–544.

Davis, F. B., "Psychometric Research on Comprehension in Reading," *Reading Research Quarterly*, 7(4), (1972) 628–678.

Dechant, E., *Reading Improvement in the Secondary School* (Englewood Cliffs, New Jersey: Prentice-Hall, 1973).

Deighton, L. C., *Vocabulary Development in the Classroom* (New York: Columbia University Press, 1959).

Dickerson, D. P., "A Study of Use of Games to Reinforce Sight Vocabulary," *The Reading Teacher*, Vol. 36, (October 1982) 46–49.

Dolch, E. W. "A Basic Sight Vocabulary," *Elementary School Journal*, Vol. 36, (1936) 456–460.

Downing, J., *Reading and Reasoning* (New York: Springer-Verlag, 1979).

Downing, J., "Reading—Skill or Skills?", *The Reading Teacher*, Vol. 35, (February 1982) 534–537.

Downing, J., and Oliver, P., "The Child's Conception of a Word," *Reading Research Quarterly*, Vol. 9, (1973–1974) 568–582.

Duffelmeyer, F. A., "The Influence of Experience-Based Vocabulary Instruction on Learning Word Meanings," *Journal of Reading*, 24(1), (October 1980) 35–40.

Durkin, D., *Teaching Them to Read* (Boston: Allyn and Bacon, 1978).

Durkin, D., "Reading Comprehension Instruction in Five Basal Series," *Reading Research Quarterly*, 16(4), (1981) 519–544.

Durr, W. K., "Computer Study of High Frequency Words in Popular Trade Juveniles," *The Reading Teacher*, Vol. 27, (October 1973) 37–42.

Ehri, L. C., "Word Consciousness in Readers and Pre-readers," *Journal of Educational Psychology*, Vol. 67, (1975) 204–212.

Ehri, L. C., "Linguistic Insight: Threshold of Reading Acquisition," *Reading Research: Advances in Theory and Practice*, Vol. 1, T. G. Waller, and G. E. Mackinnon, eds., (New York: Academic Press, 1979).

Ehri, L. C., and Wilce, L. S., "Do Beginners Learn to Read Function Words Better in Sentences or in Lists?", *Reading Research Quarterly*, 15(4), (1980) 451–476.

Estes, T. H., and Vaughan, J. L., *Reading and Learning in the Content Classroom: Diagnostic and Instructional Strategies* (Boston: Allyn and Bacon, 1978).

Farr, R., and Roser, N., *Teaching A Child to Read* (New York: Harcourt Brace Jovanovich, 1979).

Frank, M., "10-4 for Teachers, Are Your Ears On?", *The Good Apple News*, (Carthage, Illinois: Good Apple, 1976).

Fry, E., "The New Instant Word List," *The Reading Teacher*, Vol. 34, (December 1980) 281–289.

Geoffrion, L. D., "Reading and the Nonvocal Child," *The Reading Teacher*, Vol. 35, (March 1982) 662–669.

Gipe, J. P., "Investigating Techniques for Teaching Word Meanings," *Reading Research Quarterly*, 14(4), (1978–1979) 624–644.

Gipe, J. P., "Use of a Relevant Context Helps Kids Learn New Word Meanings," *The Reading Teacher*, Vol. 33, (January 1980) 398–402.

Guralnik, D. B., and Friend, J. H., eds., *Webster's New World Dictionary of the American Language*, 5th ed. (Cleveland, Ohio: World Publishing, 1966).

Harris, A. J., and Jacobsen, M. C., *Basic Elementary Reading Vocabularies*, (New York: Macmillan, 1972).

Hayden, B. J., Jr., "Teaching Basic Function Words," *The Reading Teacher*, Vol. 35, (November 1981) 136–140.

Hayes, D. A., and Tierney, R. J., "Developing Readers' Knowledge Through Analogy," *Reading Research Quarterly*, 17(2), (1982) 256–280.

Herber, H. L., *Success with Words* (New York: Scholastic Book Services, 1968).

Herber, H. L., *Teaching Reading in Content Areas*, 2nd ed. (Englewood Cliffs, New Jersey: Prentice-Hall, 1970).

Hiebert, E. H., "Developmental Patterns and Interrelationships of Preschool Children's Print Awareness," *Reading Research Quarterly*, Vol. 16, (1981), 236–260.

Huey, E. B., *The Psychology and Pedagogy of Reading* (New York: Macmillan, 1908).

Hunt, C. L., Jr., "Can We Measure Specific Factors Associated with Reading Comprehension?", *Journal of Educational Research*, Vol. 51, (1957) 161–171.

Hunter, D. L., "Spoken and Written Word Lists: A Comparison," *The Reading Teacher*, 29(3), (1975) 250–253.

Ignoffo, M. F., "Thread of Thought: Analogies as a Vocabulary Building Method," *Journal of Reading*, Vol. 23, (March 1980) 519–521.

Jenkins, B. L., Longmaid, W. H., O'Brien, S. F., and Sheldon, C. N., "Children's Use of Hypothesis Testing When Decoding Words," *The Reading Teacher*, Vol. 33, (March 1980) 664–667.

Johnson, D. D., *Factors Related to the Pronunciation of Vowel Clusters*, Technical Report #149 (Madison: Wisconsin Research and Development Center, University of Wisconsin, 1970).

Johnson, D. D., "A Basic Vocabulary for Beginning Reading," *Elementary School Journal*, 72(1), (October 1979), 29–34.

Johnson, D. D., "Word Lists That Make Sense — And Those That Don't," *Learning Magazine*, Vol. 4, (November 1974) 60–61.

Johnson, D. D., "Expanding Vocabulary Through Classification," *Reading Instruction and the Beginning Teacher: A Practical Guide*, J. F. Baumann and D. D. Johnson, eds., (Minneapolis: Burgess Publishing Company, 1983).

Johnson, D. D., Moe, A., and Baumann, J., *The Ginn Wordbook for Teachers: A Basic Lexicon* (Lexington, Mass.: Ginn and Company, 1983).

Johnson, D. D., Toms-Bronowski, S., and Buss, R. R., "Fundamental Factors in Reading Comprehension Revisited," *Reading Research Revisited*, L. Gentile, and M. Kamil, eds., (Columbus, Ohio: Charles Merrill, 1983).

Johnson, D. D., Toms-Bronowski, S., and Pittelman, S. D., *An Investigation of the Effectiveness of Semantic Mapping and Semantic Feature Analysis With Intermediate Grade Level Children*, Program Report 83-3 (Madison, Wisconsin: Wisconsin Center for Education Research, University of Wisconsin, 1982).

Johnson, S., *The Idler and the Adventurer, Works of Samuel Johnson, Vol. 2.* (New Haven, Conn.: Yale University Press, 1963).

Kaplan, E. M., and Tuchman, A., "Vocabulary Strategies Belong in the Hands of Learners," *Journal of Reading*, Vol. 24, (October 1980) 32–34.

Kean, J. M., and Personke, C., *The Language Arts: Teaching and Learning in the Elementary School* (New York: St. Martin's Press, 1976).

Kepper, L., *Creative Approaches to Vocabulary Development within an Individualized Reading Program* (Unpublished master's thesis, The University of Wisconsin, Madison, 1977).

Kessel, F., "The Role of Syntax in Children's Comprehension from Ages Six to Twelve," *Monographs of the Society for Research in Child Development*, 35(6), (1970).

Kibby, M. W., "Passage Readability Affects the Oral Reading Strategies of Disabled Readers," *The Reading Teacher*, Vol. 32, (January 1979) 390–396.

Kurth, R. J., "Building A Conceptual Base for Vocabulary," *Reading Psychology*, Vol. 1, (Summer 1980) 115–120.

LaBerge, D., and Samuels, S. J., "Toward a Theory of Automatic Information Processing in Reading," *Cognitive Psychology*, Vol. 6, (1974) 293–323.

Labov, W., "The Boundaries of Words and Their Meanings," *New Ways of Analyzing Variation in English*, C. Bailey and R. Shuy, eds., (Washington, D.C.: Georgetown University Press, 1973).

Lancaster, W., Nelson, L., and Morris, D., "Invented Spellings in Room 112: A Writing Program for Low-Reading Second Graders," *The Reading Teacher*, Vol. 35, (May 1982) 906–911.

Lansky, B., and Lansky, V., *The Best Baby Name Book in the Whole Wide World* (Newton, Mass.: Meadowbrook Press, 1979).

Lapp, D., Flood, J., and Gleckman, G., "Classroom Practices Can Make Use of What Researchers Learn," *The Reading Teacher*, Vol. 35, (February 1982) 572–585.

Lindsay, P., and Norman, D., *Human Information Processing* (New York: Academic Press, 1972).

Mason, J. M., "When Do Children Begin to Read: An Exploration of Four Year Old Children's Letter and Word Reading Competencies," *Reading Research Quarterly*, Vol. 15, (1980) 203–227.

Mass, L. N., "Developing Concepts of Literacy in Young Children," *The Reading Teacher*, Vol. 35, (March 1982) 670–675.

McKee, P., "Vocabulary Development," *The Teaching of Reading: A Second Report*, The Thirty-Sixth Yearbook of the National Society for the Study of Education, Part I., G. M. Whipple, ed., (Bloomington, Illinois: Public School Publishing Company, 1937) 277–302.

Meltzer, N., and Herse, R., "The Boundaries of Written Words as Seen by First Graders," *Journal of Reading Behavior*, Vol. 1, (Summer 1969) 3–14.

Moe, A. J., "Word Lists for Beginning Readers," *Reading Improvement*, 10(2), (1973) 11–15.

Morris, W., *American Heritage Dictionary* (Boston: Houghton Mifflin, 1979).

Murray, J. A., ed., *Oxford Dictionary*, 13 vols. (London: Oxford University Press, 1923).

Otto, W., and Askov, E., *Rationale and Guidelines: The Wisconsin Design for Reading Skill Development* (Minneapolis: National Computer Systems, 1974).

Otto, W., and Chester, R., "Sight Words for Beginning Readers," *The Journal of Educational Research*, 65(10), (1972) 435–443.

Pearson, P. D., "A Psycholinguistic Model of Reading," *Language Arts*, Vol. 53, 3 (March 1976) 309–314.

Pearson, P. D., and Johnson, D. D., *Teaching Reading Comprehension* (New York: Holt, Rinehart and Winston, 1978).

Platts, M. E., *A Handbook of Games, Activities, and Ideas for Vocabulary Enrichment* (Stevensville, Michigan: Anchor, 1970).

Read, C., "Preschool Children's Knowledge of English Phonology," *Harvard Educational Review*, Vol. 41, (1971) 1–34.

Readence, J. E., Bean, T. W., and Baldwin, R. S., *Content Area Reading: An Integrated Approach* (Dubuque, Iowa: Kendall/Hunt Publishing Company, 1981).

Richeck, M., "Readiness Skills that Predict Initial Word Learning Using Two Different Methods of Instruction," *Reading Research Quarterly*, Vol. 13, (1977) 201–222.

Roget, P., *St. Martin's Edition of the Original Thesaurus* (New York: St. Martin's Press, 1965).

Rosenshine, B., "Skill Hierarchies in Reading Comprehension," *Theoretical Issues in Reading Comprehension*, R. J. Spiro, B. C. Bruce and W. F. Brewer, eds., (Hillsdale, New Jersey: Lawrence Erlbaum Associates, 1980).

Rubin, D. C., "The Effectiveness of Context, Before, After, and Around a Missing Word," *Perception and Psychophysics*, Vol. 19, (1976) 214–216.

Rumelhart, D. E., and Ortony, A., "The Representation of Knowledge in Memory," *Schooling and the Acquisition of Knowledge*, R. C. Anderson and R. J. Spiro, eds., (Hillsdale, New Jersey: Lawrence Erlbaum Associates, 1977).

Rumelhart, D. E., "Schemata: The Building Blocks of Cognition," *Theoretical Issues in Reading Comprehension*, R. J. Spiro, B. C. Bruce, and W. F. Brewer, eds., (Hillsdale, New Jersey: Lawrence Erlbaum Associates, 1980).

Samuels, S. J., "Automatic Decoding and Reading Comprehension," *Language Arts*, 53(3), (March 1976) 323–325.

Schell, L. M., "Teaching Decoding To Remedial Readers," *The Reading Teacher*, Vol. 31, (May 1978) 877–882.

Shuy, R. W., "What Should the Language Strand in a Reading Program Contain?", *The Reading Teacher*, Vol. 35, (April 1982) 806–812.

Sloop, C. B., and Garrison, H. E., *Phonetic Keys to Reading*, 2nd ed. (Oklahoma City: Economy Publishing Company, 1972).

Smith, F., *Understanding Reading: A Psycholinguistic Analysis of Reading and Learning To Read* (New York: Holt, Rinehart and Winston, 1971).

Smith, R. J., and Johnson, D. D., *Teaching Children to Read*, 2nd ed. (Boston: Addison-Wesley, 1980).

Spearritt, D., "Identification of Subskills of Reading Comprehension by Maximum Likelihood Factor Analysis," *Reading Research Quarterly*, Vol. 8, (1972–73) 92–111.

Sternberg, R. J., Powell, J. S., and Kaye, D. B., "Teaching Vocabulary-Building Skills: A Contextual Approach," *Classroom Computers and Cognitive Science*, A. C. Wilkinson, ed., (New York: Academic Press, in press).

Stieglitz, E. L., and Stieglitz, V. S., "SAVOR the Word to Reinforce Vocabulary in the Content Areas," *Journal of Reading*, Vol. 25, (October 1981) 46–51.

Taylor, W. L., "Cloze Procedures: A New Tool for Measuring Readability," *Journalism Quarterly*, 30 (Fall 1953) 360–368.

Templeton, S., "Young Children Invent Words: Developing Concepts of 'Wordness,'" *The Reading Teacher*, Vol. 33, (January 1980) 454–459.

Thomas, E. L., and Robinson, H. A., *Improving Reading in Every Class—A Sourcebook for Teachers*, 2nd ed. (Boston: Allyn and Bacon, 1977).

Children's Bibliography

Bellafiore, J., *Words at Work* (New York: Amsco School Publications, Inc., 1968).

Carroll, L., *Through the Looking Glass—Illustrations*, rev. ed., G. Ovenden, ed., (New York: St. Martin's Press, 1979).

Clymer, T., Venezky, R., et al., *Ginn Reading Program, Inside My Hat (Level 4), Mystery Sneaker (Level 9), Flights of Color (Level 13)* (Lexington, Mass.: Ginn and Company, 1982).

Drysdale, P., *Words To Use, A Junior Thesaurus* (New York: William H. Sadlier, 1971).

Durrell, D. D., and Murphy, H. A., *Speech-to-Print Phonics* (New York: Harcourt Brace Jovanovich, 1964, 1972).

Gwynne, F., *The King Who Rained* (New York: Windmill Books and E. P. Dutton, 1970).

Gwynne, F., *A Chocolate Moose for Dinner* (New York: Windmill Books and E. P. Dutton, 1976).

Holt School Dictionary of American English (New York: Holt, Rinehart and Winston, 1981).

Keller, H., *The Story of My Life* (New York: Doubleday, 1954).

Monroe, M., *My Little Dictionary* (Chicago: Scott, Foresman, 1964).

Parramore, B., and D'Amelio, D., *Scott, Foresman Social Studies* (Chicago: Scott, Foresman, 1979).

Romano, L. G., and Georgiady, N. P., *Exploring Our State*, Social Studies Series (Chicago: Follett Publishing Company, 1977).

Scarry, R., *Storybook Dictionary* (Racine, Wisconsin: Golden Press, 1966).

Schomburg, C. E., *Cities and Suburbs*, Economy Social Studies (Oklahoma City: The Economy Company, 1982).

Thoburn, T., Forbes, J. E., Bechtel, R. D., and Nelson, L. D., *Macmillan Mathematics*, Grade 4 (New York: Macmillan, 1976).

Thorndike, E. L., ed., *Thorndike Dictionary* (Chicago: Scott, Foresman, 1935, 1942).

Thorndike, E. L., and Barnhart, C. L., eds., *Scott Foresman Beginning Dictionary* (Garden City, New York: Doubleday, 1976).

Wagner, R. F., and Wagner, M. H., *Stories about Family Names* (Portland, Maine: J. Weston Walch, 1961).

Index

A

Acronyms, 67, 83
Affixes, 128, 129–132, 142
    activities involving, 137–139
    See also Prefixes; Suffixes
Alphabet, as a guide to the dictionary, 53, 57
American Heritage Dictionary, 52, 57, 83
Analogies, 5, 6, 10, 14–15, 19, 37, 46–49, 198
    categories of, 47
    use of, in teaching, 47–49, 166–168, 188–190
Analytic phonics, 119
Antonyms, 5, 6, 10, 11–12, 19, 20, 25–27, 47, 52, 198
    activities involving, 26–27, 153, 154, 157–158, 181
    categories of, 25–26
    complementary, 25–26
    contradictory, 25, 26
    contrary, 25, 26
    contrasted, 26
    definition of, 25
    relative-pair, 25, 26
    in thesaurus, 58, 62, 87
    vocabulary instruction and, 181
Auditory perception, 126

B

Balch, M. C., 96
Basal reading program, vocabulary instruction in, 151–173, 199
    analogies and, 166–168
    antonyms and, 153, 154, 157–158
    connotation and, 155, 157
    denotation and, 155
    dictionary and, 169–170
    enriching vocabulary component of basal readers, 151, 153
    etymology and, 171–173
    homophones and, 159–160
    multimeaning words, 161
    semantic feature analysis and, 163–165
    semantic mapping and, 162–163
    synonyms and, 153–155, 157, 158
    thesaurus and, 170–171
    See also Ginn Reading Program
Basic sight vocabulary (*see* Sight vocabulary, basic)
Baumunn, J., 96

Best Baby Name Book in the Whole Wide World, The, 84
Blends, 118
Block, K. K., 33
Bloomfield, L., 7

C

Chall, J., 119–120
Chester, R., 96
Class relations, 34
Classification, 5–6, 7, 10–15
    activities in, and vocabulary development, 37–49
    analogical thinking, 5, 6, 10, 14–15, 19, 37, 46–49
    categories of, 5, 10–15
    semantic feature analysis, 5, 6, 10, 19, 37, 41–46
    semantic mapping, 5, 6, 10, 12–13, 19, 37–41
Cloze procedure, 14, 92
    in contextual analysis, 144–146
Code-consciousness (*see* Print awareness)
Collins, A. M., 35
Communication process, listening, 19, 35
    reading, 19
    speaking, 19, 35
    vocabulary and the, 1, 19–20
    writing, 19
Compound words, 127
    activities involving, 134–136
    definition of, 132
    structural breakdown, 132–134, 135
    underlining, 134
    word building, 134
    word puzzles, 135
Concepts, 33–37
    definition of, 33–34, 35
    semantic networks, 35–41
    vocabulary knowledge and, 175
Configuration, 112, 113
Connotation, 5, 6, 10, 19, 20, 23–25, 198
    activities involving, 24–25, 155–157
    definition of, 12, 23
Consonants, 117, 118, 119
    double, 117
Content areas, vocabulary instruction in, 175–196, 199
    analogies and, 188–190
    antonyms and, 181